Building a Successful Business

Proven steps to grow your business & develop you leadership skills.

MARK DYBLE

WHAT PEOPLE ARE SAYING ABOUT
Your Guide to Building a Successful Business

'If you're thinking about starting a business or aiming for the top of the ladder as an employee, you almost certainly have a strong belief in yourself. If you don't have that inner self belief – then save yourself a lot of aggravation and take an easier road in life. But if you do have that belief, **Your Guide to Building a Successful Business** will help you to apply it, and your abilities, to create and drive a successful business. It will help to fill the gaps in your knowledge and experience and, crucially, will help to show you where they are.'

Frank Martin DL, Chief Executive Officer,
Hornby plc

'Mark has taken his "catalyst" techniques and put them on paper, which has resulted in an holistic approach to business. This is a treasure trove of ideas to motivate and stimulate, presented in an accessible way across different levels, so that you will not get bogged down. It reframes, it's practical, it's a great refresher and I can see it being the catalyst for many new and reborn ventures to come. With an eclectic mix of quotes to hang the ideas on and carry thoughts with you, all you need is that commitment Mark asks for to just give it a go. I can't wait to read this book again and discover another gem to try for myself.'

Diane Earles, Regional Director,
The Chartered Institute of Marketing

'The journey to starting, developing and growing a successful business can be both challenging and rewarding. Business Leaders and decision makers will benefit greatly from the content of **Your Guide to Building a Successful Business** as it provides a valuable insight into every step of that journey. It captures the years of knowledge and experience that Mark Dyble has and is a fantastic guide to overcoming challenges by implementing a methodology and approach that is sustainable and will assist as you start, develop and, most importantly, grow your business.'

Colin Brew, Director of Relationships & Place,
GC Business Growth Hub

'Business success doesn't happen by chance. It takes meticulous planning, analysis and action to get results. **Your Guide to Building a Successful Business** gives you the know-how to make your business a success. It's full of shrewd ideas – and real-world examples to show you how to implement them. I recommend you read it and commit to putting those ideas into practice.'

Matthew Benham, Owner,
Brentford FC and Matchbook

'*Your Guide to Building a Successful Business* draws on Mark's varied career across management and, more recently, as coach and MD-whisperer. This is a big book but one full of insights, hints, and tips. For me, the stand-out feature is the emphasis on action which, for the lonely, often isolated owner-managers I work with, is often the missing element to making progress as well as leading a more fulfilling and healthier life in the round. I see this as a book to dip into for inspiration. Even if the individual suggestions do not chime with your situation, they will have done their job by provoking you to take your own, most appropriate first step into action. What more would you want? I will also be recommending this book to entrepreneurship students so that they can get inside the mind of the hands-on general manager.'

Magnus George, Professor of Entrepreneurship,
Lancaster University Management School

'I really enjoyed reading *Your Guide to Building a Successful Business*. I have read a lot of management books over my career and usually found just a couple of points in each that helped me improve my performance. This book however has breadth and real depth that suits an entrepreneur. More importantly, it is easy to read. It not only makes an enlightening read (no matter where you are in your business lifecycle) but would also serve as a great reference book that can be studied in a more specific way as problems/opportunities crop up. The book brings structure, order and understanding to the chaos of running your own business. It can allow you to step back and analyse yourself and your performance as a leader of your business, that should lead to both personal and business improvements. If there is one book you can buy when running or planning your own business, this would be it.'

Kirk Robertson, Owner & CEO,
Sportswear International

'Having been a business owner for many years, transitioning out of the corporate world to the challenges of the owner-managed arena, I wish someone had been able to give me a copy of *Your Guide to Building a Successful Business* back in 2001 when I started my journey and that I'd taken the time to read it! Fortunately for me, I was introduced to Mark as a business coach and became familiar with many of his invaluable insights and advice which helped me to lead my business to a successful trade exit in 2017. I guess like many before me, I thought I had a good understanding of what I was heading into, but the harsh reality is that everything starts and finishes with yourself at the head of your organisation so A) you'd better have a good plan and B) you'd better have the systems and processes to implement and deliver it. I think the book is a fabulous business aid and reference book for all budding entrepreneurs who can benefit from the years of experience of a seasoned business professional who will at the very least give you sound advice, solid guidance, and food for thought, but hopefully instil some sound basic business principles that will serve you well from the very beginning of your journey until hopefully a very successful end.'

Conrad Broadbent, Owner and Chief Executive Office,
First Capital Cashflow and Patient Plan Direct

'I have known Mark several years now and he has coached a significant percentage of our Franchise Owners around numerous areas he covers in *Your Guide to Building a Successful Business*, with highly impressive results both for the individual owners and Right at Home UK as a Group. Reading the book is like reading a bible on "Building a Successful Business", full of practical, well explained, easy-to-follow tips and ideas that if followed can generate a difference to your business. The book really is a common-sense guide for beginners and the experienced alike on the key steps needed to manage and build your business and indeed yourself as a leader.'

Ken Deary FCCA QFP, Chief Executive Officer,
Right at Home UK

'Starting and then running a business can be a hugely fulfilling endeavour, but it can also be a very lonely and tiring journey. What you need is a travelling companion who has scouted out the route ahead and who'll give you common sense, no frills advice to keep you on track, and that is what Mark does for you in this book. *Your Guide to Building a Successful Business* isn't a book about business. It's a book for business leaders who need fast and sure-footed advice from someone who gets straight to the point. I wish I'd had this book in my pocket when I was setting out on my journey.'

Anthony Preston CBE, Founder & former Chairman,
Pets at Home

'Mark has great insightfulness regarding the challenges of running a business. He can work closely with an owner or leader to ensure they don't get swallowed up with the day-to-day issues but rise above them to work on the bigger matters that will make a real difference to how a business can grow. In addition, his empathic nature and care for the people he works with is second to none. *Your Guide to Building a Successful Business* reflects that personality and brings together a wide range of practical ideas and insights in a very readable format that will help you develop your business and yourself.'

Jackie Hyde, Managing Director,
Dot2Dot & Stanmore Insurance Brokers

'*Your Guide to Building a Successful Business* does exactly what the title suggests. Staying away from unnecessary theory and jargon, the book offers a comprehensive compendium of practical business and management ideas and advice for business owners, entrepreneurs and aspiring leaders. Ranging from the intricacies of managing cash to managing effective meetings, from the tactical to the strategic, it has something for everyone. The direct and concise style makes it ideal as a reference guide that can be picked up at any time. Whether you read it fully or choose one section at a time, you and your business will benefit greatly from the insight and experience in this guide to building a successful business.'

Xavier Duran, MBA Programme Director,
Manchester Business School

Building a Successful Business
By Mark Dyble
ISBN: 978-1-8384513-0-1
Copyright © 2021 Mark Dyble

Copyeditor and proofreader: Siân-Elin Flint-Freel
Book design by Tanya Back, www.tanyabackdesigns.com

All information, methods, techniques and advice contained within this publication reflect the views and experiences of the author, whose intent is to provide readers with various choices and options. We are all individuals with different beliefs and viewpoints, therefore it is recommended that readers carry out their own research prior to making any such choices. While all attempts have been made to verify the information contained within this book, neither the author nor the publisher assume responsibility for any errors or omissions, or for any actions taken or results experienced by any reader.

For my father, Michael.
A generous man who truly lived his life to the full.
1936 – 2021

Contents

Foreword

Running a business is a helter-skelter experience. It can be fun, exciting, challenging, full of opportunity, lifegiving and rich in meaning and purpose; it can also be frustrating, painful, exhausting and draining. Businesses face common opportunities and problems: the appointment of a star performer, great customer feedback, a new customer, a new product opportunity or systems improvement, these things give life and energy. The loss of a key customer, a complaint from a customer, a breakdown in the supply chain, an unexpected change in government regulations, and a global pandemic are just some of the things that can leave you gasping for breath almost as if you have had an encounter with a Harry Potter 'Dementor'.

These are just some of the common joys and pains that business leaders come across and must be fit to face. In *Your Guide to Building a Successful Business*, Mark has taken the key issues common to all business leaders to provide an 'on demand, all purpose' tool you can access easily to support you to be 'fit to lead', to have 'time to lead', and to be leading a business which is 'fit to be led'.

I have known Mark for many years and this book, now your book, has 'Mark Dyble' running through it like lettering runs through seaside rock. It is at once deep and reflective, actionable and practical, conceptual and accessible, addressing everyday problems and common bad practice with an approach that is strengths and best practice based.

Your Guide to Building a Successful Business combines a depth of thought about the deeper purpose of business and life (which we all need to wrestle with) with practical day to day (not so common) common-sense ideas and solutions. Mark offers us an amazing tool as we journey through the pleasures and the pains of business leadership, so that we come through our journey in good shape.

Use and enjoy!

Jill Garrett
Leadership Consultant & former European Managing Director,
The Gallup Organization Europe.

Introduction

I KEEP six honest serving-men
(They taught me all I knew);
Their names are What and Why and When
And How and Where and Who.

RUDYARD KIPLING

What's in this book

Your Guide to Building a Successful Business will share simple, practical, proven strategies and tactics that you can deploy to grow and improve your business. The benefits will come in the areas of:

- **Mindset** — how you approach your task of building your business.
- **Time** — having more of it to invest in higher-value and more interesting activities.
- **Team** — engaging and trusting your workforce to work collaboratively and constructively in building the business.
- **Money** — increasing the profits and cash in your business.

A business model

Imagine your business as a classical building. It needs secure Foundations on which to build, robust columns which together support the growth of your business (Business Development), which in turn underpin opportunities for Multiplication or expansion. Finally, as a completed, stand-alone business, its apex represents Results.

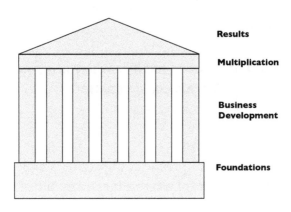

Results

Multiplication

Business
Development

Foundations

A warning about ideas

Ideas by themselves don't change anything. You have to act. The ideas in this book will only work if you implement them. No action, no results. Big action, big results.

Action is the foundational key to all success.

PABLO PICASSO

Who will benefit from this book?

Those brave souls who've thrown caution to the wind and have embarked on the challenging journey of creating and growing a business. The people who've stepped away from the relative security of a regular, monthly salary, and who know that running your own business is a tough gig. In the early days, you may even be earning less than the minimum wage, spend most of your waking hours working, and the rest of them tossing and turning in bed worrying about how you're going to make payroll on Friday. Succeed or fail, you are the women and men in the arena, daring greatly. This is a book for you. The ideas shared will enable you to make business life a little easier and a little better – perhaps even speeding you along on a steeper trajectory to greater things.

There are many important things that impact your businesses. However, the most important thing is you — the person building it. The better you become, the better your business becomes — books (and audios, seminars, webinars, courses, mentors, coaches) are vital in shaping you into the competent business leader you need to become.

As well as independent business owners, the book will benefit ambitious individuals in any business, big or small, who have or aspire to a position of leadership. It will be of particular value to anyone thinking of setting up their own business.

Perhaps it's time to sacrifice who you are for
who you could become.

JORDAN PETERSON

Why this book will be helpful

It will give you plenty of practical, impactful, simple-to-implement ideas for developing all aspects of your business. Any one of those ideas has the potential to improve your business, and therefore improve your life.

That may seem a big statement, one that you would dismiss outright as being too far-fetched. However, I would say that whilst you can learn from your mistakes, you can learn far more from other people's mistakes. You can learn over a few weeks what others have learnt over a lifetime.

When you should read this book

Ideally before you start your business building journey. Failing that, start now. Literally.

If you believe you're too busy to read, but still want things to be better, here are a few ideas for getting value out of the book:

- Leave the book in plain view where you can't miss it (your desk or worktop – perhaps leave it on the shelf in the loo). You're more likely to pick it up and dip into it if it's in plain sight.
- Schedule a coffee break in your diary and commit to read it for just ten minutes. This is enough time to find an idea you're excited about implementing.
- Find a buddy who also wants to read the book. You can agree to meet or call to swap notes and tell each other about the ideas you're running with. Being accountable to someone increases the likelihood of you keeping a commitment.
- Commit to sharing something from the book with one of your colleagues or your partner or one of your children. Again, any mechanism that invokes commitment and accountability increases the likelihood of you taking action.

If you really are too busy to read it, you definitely need to read it! Skip straight to the time-management section within the Leadership chapter. Life's too short and important to be constantly busy.

*A person who won't read has no advantage
over one who can't read.*

MARK TWAIN

How you could read this book

The book is designed so you can flick through it and quickly find an idea that appeals to you. It's more a guide than a book that you read cover to cover – although you can do that if you wish. As soon as you find an idea you like, stop, and make a commitment to give the idea a go. A successfully implemented idea will fuel your motivation to pick the book up again and find a second, and then a third idea.

Have a specific aim when you read, an idea that sparks your imagination, an idea that you can quickly put into practice. For example, "I want a simple idea to improve my productivity that I can implement today."

Read for a short period of time. Little and often works better than reading cover to cover.

This book has margins. They're for scribbling notes. Even better, it's helpful to have a blank notebook alongside you as you read so as to capture your thoughts, ideas, insights and actions. Over time, that notebook will become the most valuable book in your possession.

The aim of the exercises is to stimulate your thinking and give you the opportunity to capture ideas that will be helpful to you and your business. Thoughts and ideas have a short life (about 40 seconds) unless they're captured in some way. At the end of each chapter is a summary checklist exercise that allows you to identify and then prioritise the ideas you want to implement.

Read every day. That's how knowledge works.
It builds up, like compound interest. All of you can do
it, but I guarantee not many of you will do it.
WARREN BUFFETT

The business model

It's useful to have a visual representation of what a built business looks like. The following series of diagrams shows how a business builds up from the foundations to its apex – your completed business. The model used throughout this book is represented by a classical building with four main stages:

- Foundations
- Business Development
- Multiplication
- Results

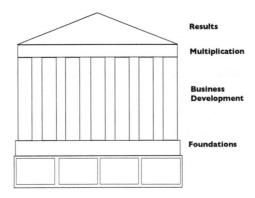

This business model gives you a simple view of all the elements that need to be put in place as you build your sustainable and profitable business.

Start with the end in mind.

STEPHEN R. COVEY

Results

You and your business are two separate entities, even though it often feels like the two of you are inseparable. Keep in mind that a successful business is one that's profitable, sustainable, thriving and can operate without you. It's like raising a child. You know that one day your child will leave home and find their own way in the world. Your job as a parent is to do your best to equip them to survive and thrive in that

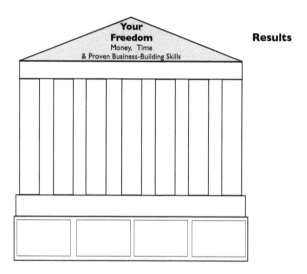

world. Think of your business as something you'll let go of to survive and thrive in the world. At that point you will receive three things:

- Money – you've sold your business or you're taking a passive income from it.
- Time – you no longer have to work in that business.
- Skills – you've learnt how to build a business. The second one will be easier.

Results are the aim of the game.

Foundations

Ironically, it's possible to construct and live in a building that doesn't have foundations. The problems come when you start to expand that building. Without foundations, it starts to subside and break apart. At that point, one of two things happen. You either contract, downsize and go back to what you were before, or you put foundations in place.

Anyone who listens to my teaching and follows it is wise,
like a person who builds a house on solid rock.
Though the rain comes in torrents and the floodwaters
rise and the winds beat against that house, it won't
collapse because it is built on bedrock.
MATTHEW 7:24-25

Those foundations are:
- Leadership
- Planning
- Finance
- Team
- Systems

Leadership

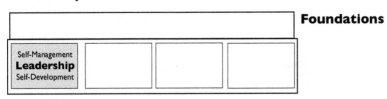

Your development as a leader will have a greater impact on the success of your business than anything else. This foundational block will help you create a practical and meaningful leadership development plan that you'll be able to incorporate into your schedule. And recognising that you are already busy, this block will help you carve out that time by firstly focusing on time management.

It's important to start working on yourself before you start working on developing your team. Integrity is a key aspect of strong leadership. If you want your team to be better at what they do and to take their personal growth and development seriously, you must be a credible role model. They will typically copy what you do and how you act. You are the heart of your business's culture.

The better you get, the better your business gets.

Planning

Quite simply, a plan is your step-by-step guide to achieving your business aims. This book will introduce a simple, practical planning system which can be delivered in manageable, quarterly chunks.

An average person with a plan will outdistance
a superhero without one.

The book will also guide you through a process for establishing a vision for your business, clarifying the purpose of your business, and determining its core values.

Finance

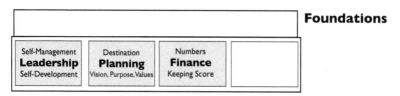

This foundation block introduces you to money, finance and the basic numbers you need as a business owner. You need to know that your business is profitable; that there's more cash coming in than going out; that you have sufficient funds to invest for growth; and that the value of your business is increasing.

Love them or hate them, if you're playing the game of
business, keep score and know your numbers.

Team

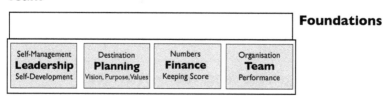

The commercial world is a tough place. And building a business is even harder. If you're on this journey, you want committed and competent people with you; people who are good at what they do – but still want to get better; people who are willing and able to collaborate with each other; people who believe what you believe and who share your values. Perhaps you feel that's idealist – but why not? This section looks at how to find and pick good people, how to deploy and develop them, and how to get them working well together.

People are not your greatest asset. The right people, with the right attitude, in the right places, are your greatest asset.

Systems

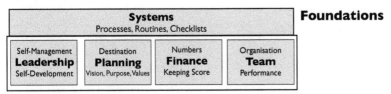

A system is simply a series of steps that produce a desired outcome. If followed, systems give you better and more consistent results with less effort. It's far easier to train people to follow a system than it is to allow each individual to work out their own particular way of producing the desired outcome. Good systems free your people to invest more of their time in higher value activities, such as developing customer relationships or working on improvement initiatives. You'll be able to systemise around 80% of everything your business does. Systems are the tool that enables you to build a business that works without you. They are the lever that allows you to lift far more than you thought possible.

Give me a lever and a place to stand and I will move the world.

ARCHIMEDES

Business Development

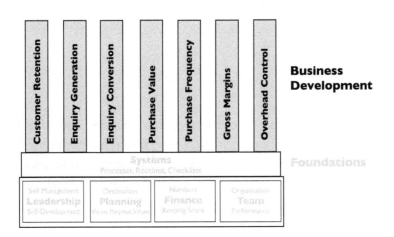

The business development 'columns' contain seven elements, all of which will grow your profits. When combined, incremental improvements in each can have a transformational impact on your overall profits.

Those seven elements are:
1. Customer retention
2. Enquiry generation
3. Enquiry conversion
4. Customer purchase value
5. Customer purchase frequency
6. Gross margins
7. Overhead control

This section contains many practical and proven initiatives for improving these seven business development elements.

Multiplication

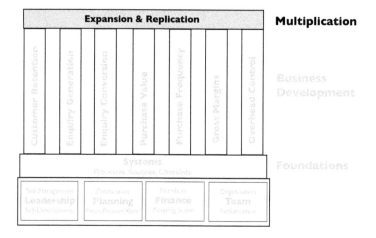

It's helpful to view the foundational blocks and the business development pillars as a prototype. Once those elements are in place, you're in a sound position to expand or replicate your business. A useful mindset to have at the outset is that you're building something that you can then franchise – in essence, you're creating a business in a box.

Results

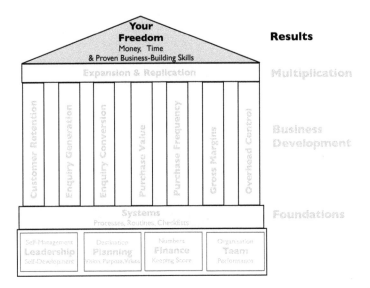

Which brings us back to results. The end you're aiming for is a sustainable, profitable business that can survive and thrive without your involvement. At this point you may have a general manager running it. Or you may be speaking to a corporate finance specialist about selling it. Most importantly, you will have a host of options.

CHAPTER 1

Leadership

*Of all the important things in a business,
you are the most important.*

Yet, you are probably the most neglected. It's exceptional if the financial projections for a new or small business show any budget for enhancing the leadership or management skills of the person running it. Most business owners' diaries have no entries for personal development.

"When we're successful, when I can afford it, when I have the time, then I'll do something about my own development."

Worse still, there's an unhelpful belief that running a business, like being a parent or a spouse, is something that should come naturally. Any suggestion that learning or training might be beneficial is an indication of weakness and failure. Something to be avoided.

Nothing could be further from the truth. Wherever you're starting from, the skills to run and grow a business can be enhanced with guidance and effort. Time and money spent on your personal development is an investment – it returns better financial performance and a stronger and more resilient business.

The better you get, the better the business gets.

In addition to having a vision for your business, it's equally important to have a vision for yourself, both personally and professionally.

This chapter will lay out the characteristics of a strong leader and the tasks of a managing director. Most people running businesses, especially in the early days, have multiple roles and the thought of 'just' being a managing director is perhaps a dream. But it's good to know what you're aiming for – and it's critical to understand your responsibilities.

How can you invest more time on your own leadership development when you're running at a hundred miles an hour and life is crammed full? Time – the resource everybody wants more of. Whilst creating more hours in the day is impossible, using the hours you have more wisely is possible. This chapter will show you how you can gain better control of your time and start allocating more of it to the things that matter most. Time can't be managed; it just keeps flowing. Even though it may not feel like it, you do have choices. You can choose what you'll work on and when.

What is commonly called time management is really self-management.

In addition to dedicating more time to important tasks, equally critical is the energy, focus and concentration you're able to bring to those tasks. You will learn how to manage and restore your energy and how to become more focussed.

When you've enhanced your time and energy management skills and have started to redress the balance between low value and high value tasks, you can then create a personal development plan.

Your personal development is one area of your business where you have total control. You're free to choose what you work on, when you work on it, and how you work on it. Whilst it's all about you, and only you can make the necessary changes, you don't have to do it alone – you can engage mentors, coaches or others to guide and support. Your responsibility is to realise your full potential in creating a thriving business, to equip yourself with the commercial and leadership skills necessary to give your organisation the best chance of success. Your job is to become the very best leader you can be.

Committing to a personal development journey means letting go of an old version of yourself and working on a better, upgraded version. It's a change programme. The success of that programme will depend on your thoughts and beliefs, how you perceive change and how you believe the world works. In fact, your thoughts and beliefs may be the most critical element of your development programme. For that reason, this chapter starts by looking at your mindset – how your mind has been set in relation to personal change and growth.

More specifically, this chapter covers:

- **Mindset:** Choosing fertile ground for your thoughts, the starting point of your decisions, actions and results.
- **Your role:** Being clear on your responsibilities and deliverables.
- **Activity management:** Spending more of your time on the things that matter most.
- **Energy management:** Bringing your focus and energy to the things that matter most.
- **Leadership development:** Your primary role and a life-long journey of discovery and growth.
- **Habits:** Replacing the unhelpful ones with helpful ones.
- **Resilience:** Building on your natural resilience to see you through the inevitable hard times that life will present you with.
- **Gratitude:** Learning to be both ambitious and content.
- **Rest:** The paradoxical strategy that delivers better results.

Choosing the right mindset

Your mind is unbelievably powerful. It is the fertile seedbed of the things that appear and grow in your life. How you set your mind is the foundation of the business leader you become, and in turn, how successful your business becomes.

Think and grow rich

When he was ten years old, my son Jake wandered into my home office and pulled Napoleon Hill's classic text *Think and Grow Rich* off the bookshelf.

Jake: Is that all I have to do?

Me: Sorry?

Jake: To become rich. Is that all I have to do?

Me: What?

Jake: To become rich. Do I just have to think? And I'll become rich?

What an excellent question! I'd never read it like that. Think. And grow rich. Just think. And he'll grow rich. Really? There's plenty that needs to happen between thinking and riches, but thinking the right thoughts was a differentiator based on the extensive success research that Napoleon Hill carried out. (He studied in detail the business lives of over 500 millionaires.)

> *Whatever the mind can conceive and believe, it can achieve.*
>
> NAPOLEON HILL

Changing your mind

A belief is an engrained way of thinking that you hold to be true. The way you act reveals what you believe. And it's your actions that determine your results. You may not be aware of your beliefs directly. And you may not have arrived at those beliefs through your own considered investigation – they may have been adopted unconsciously from your parents, your peers, your teachers and your environment.

The question of whether beliefs are true or not is arbitrary. A better question is whether they're generating the actions and results you want in your life. Are they helpful or unhelpful? If you're wanting improved results, track back and check out what your mind is telling you. It is possible to change your mind. In fact, changing your mind is probably the most powerful thing you can do to precipitate the improvements you want to see.

The number one attitude requirement to becoming a better business leader is a willingness to change your mind. To admit that you may have got something wrong. To accept that you may not know something. To assume that there's likely to be a better way. In effect, to have an open mind.

> *Progress without change is impossible. And the person*
> *who can't change their mind can't change anything.*
> GEORGE BERNARD SHAW

The second most important attitudinal requirement is courage – a willingness to have a go. Not just to think about acting differently; not just to make different decisions; but to actually have a go and do something different, not knowing what the outcome will be.

This book contains plenty of proven ideas that when implemented will improve your business. However, changing yourself has the potential to not only improve your business, but to transform it.

A business or a job?

Here's a thought. Are you building a business that will be completed one day (in the same way that you might build a house and hand over the keys to the new owners when it's completed)? Or are you keeping yourself busy and paying the bills and going on a few holidays until the day you retire?

You'd probably say that you're building a business. However, based on your decisions, actions and results, how would an independent observer (perhaps an investor) answer that question? Do they see someone building a business with a focus on completing it and handing over the keys? Or do they see someone with a job?

If you're building a business, at some point that business will be able to operate without your involvement. When will that be? Perhaps you want to get your first business completed as soon as possible, so you can move onto your second, incorporating all the learnings you've gained from building the first one.

Exercise: The game of business

- For you, what's the aim of this business?
- What will your business look like when it's finished?
- How long will you be involved?
- What are your key measures when it comes to valuing the business?
- What are the handful of key things you'll focus on?
- How will you make sure you enjoy the process and have some fun along the way?
- What will you do when you've 'finished' the business? What will you do with your money, your time and your business-building experience and skills?

Who do you think you are?

Are you an accountant, an engineer, an optician? Or are you a business owner who's building an accounting practice, an engineering business or a chain of opticians? Your identity – how you see yourself – will have a profound impact on your decisions, actions and results. Is it time to sacrifice who you are for who you could become? Is it time to stop being a technician and start becoming a business owner?

Take responsibility for everything that happens in your life

Life can be like a game of snakes and ladders. You roll the dice. Sometimes fate throws you a one, sometimes she rolls you a six. Sometimes you find yourself at the bottom of a ladder – an opportunity. You can pass right on by if you wish. Or you can take advantage of the opportunity and climb the ladder – but that's hard work. Sometimes you land on the head of a snake. Down you go, dumped in the dirt, battered and bruised. You then have two choices. You can sit there, feeling sorry for yourself, complaining about how life is unfair. Or you can get up, dust yourself down, and go again. What will you do?

Much of what happens to you in life is down to chance. Right from day one: where you're born; how able and healthy you are; who your parents are; where you go to school. Succeed or fail, you're not totally responsible for the outcome of your life.

However, when things go wrong, many people have become good at playing the helpless victim. Or making excuses, blaming circumstances or other people. Perhaps there's some truth in what they say. Perhaps it was someone else's fault. Whatever the rights and wrongs of the situation, when you hold circumstance or someone else responsible, you become impotent in terms of improving the situation. You give away your power. If circumstance or other people are responsible, only they can do something to change and improve the situation. But perhaps they're only 95% responsible and you're 5% responsible. So, there is an element you can work on. There is something you can do.

When things do go wrong, track back to discover what the real cause was. Rarely is it the major catastrophe you imagine. More often than not, it's the daily accumulation of little things. Things you did or things you didn't do. Take responsibility.

You can choose to hold yourself responsible for everything that happens in your life. That opens up the powerful possibility of being able to do something positive and practical about your future.

By accepting responsibility, you take back control. You start thinking about things that you could have done to get a better result. Once this channel is open, your spirits lift, your imagination kicks in, and you see the situation in a more positive light.

For example, perhaps a team member hasn't followed a basic instruction and this has caused a customer to be let down. You can't believe they could be so stupid. You clearly told them what to do – several times. It's their fault – it's certainly not yours. However, if you put your "I'm responsible" hat on, how might you look at that situation? Could you have checked their understanding of the instruction? Could you have followed up the instruction by putting it in writing? What could you do differently next time to get a better result? If you take some responsibility for the poor outcome and think about what you'd do differently next time, perhaps your colleague might feel encouraged to look at what they can do differently next time too.

Perhaps you're late for a customer meeting. You make your excuses and blame the traffic. You're stressed and flustered at the start of your meeting. Who's responsible, you or the traffic? Could you have left earlier to get to the meeting, anticipating there might be bad traffic? If there wasn't bad traffic and you arrived early, perhaps you could use the extra time to make a couple of calls or read a book.

Perhaps someone in the office didn't tell you that your partner telephoned whilst you were in a meeting and you didn't know you were meant to pick up your child from nursery. And now the nursery is phoning to see where you are. Could you have taken the initiative and asked if there were any messages for you when you came out of your meeting?

Taking responsibility opens your mind to doing things differently in the future. Always ask:

- Could I have done something different?
- What have I learnt?
- What will I do next time?

Blame and excuses put you in the passenger seat. Taking responsibility puts you in the driving seat.

> *I must tell you that I should really like to think there's something wrong with me. Because, if there isn't, then there's something wrong with the world itself. And that's much more frightening! That would be terrible. So, I'd rather believe there is something wrong with me, that could be put right.*
>
> T. S. ELIOT, THE COCKTAIL PARTY

Take Aim. Fire

Humans are goal-seeking beings. It's hardwired. Humans also have the unique ability to see the future. And to create the future. A picture in the mind becomes an aim; there's action, and a new reality emerges – something that didn't exist before. What power you have.

To have any value, an aim must be accompanied by action. An aim without action is pointless. However, action without an aim can be worse if it takes you in a direction you don't want to travel. The more specific your aim, the better the chance you'll hit your target.

For example, "At the end of today's management meeting we also need to discuss what we're going to do about ABC's demands for lower prices." Compared to, "The aim of this dedicated meeting is to find a workable solution to keeping ABC Ltd. as a customer, rewarding them for their loyalty and the amount of business they place with us, without compromising the published tariffs we have with other customers." Both meetings may result in a good solution. However, the second meeting with its more specific aim is more likely to produce a better result.

You may prefer to use other words than aim – goal, objective, intention, target, ambition, aspiration. The key is to recognise that having an aim works. It's a vital skill and a helpful habit to cultivate.

If you're new to 'taking aim' or setting goals, you'll need to build up your goal-setting muscles. You don't need to pick anything major to start with. The intention when you start is to prove to yourself that goal-setting works.

- Pick something small.
- Write down your goal.
- Make it specific so that your aim is precise. You need to recognise it when you achieve it, so it needs to be measurable. As a test, without you explaining it, give your written goal to someone else and ask if they know what they have to achieve.
- Note down why you're aiming for this goal. What will be the benefits?
- Make it something you feel excited about. In this instance, you might just be excited to see if goal setting works.

Excitement is critical. A goal should motivate you to take an action immediately. If it doesn't, the chances are you won't follow through.

Once you complete this short, simple goal-setting process, your goal will be embedded in your subconscious. As you start working towards it, the resources you need to achieve it will come into view.

With a bigger goal, you'll want to develop an action plan of the steps you need to take to achieve it. Given that you're starting with small goals, it's not vital that you have an action plan. But it is vital that you take action.

Traditional goal-setting guidelines insist on a deadline. Whilst deadlines can be helpful, the real value of a goal is that it sets a specific direction of travel and motivates you to take immediate action. Achieving the goal by an arbitrary and non-critical date is of secondary importance. Not meeting a particular date can induce a feeling of failure and be counterproductive.

For example, if you set a goal of 24 new customers by year-end and you only get to 20, it's likely you'll achieve your goal by February – and 20 is probably acceptable progress. By contrast, if you must have a tender submitted by 11:59am on Friday, then that's a critical deadline. Be careful how you use deadlines.

Whatever you do, have a deliberate and conscious aim. One that excites you. One that propels you to take action now. Ingrain the habit of always asking, "What's my aim?"

Accepting failure

A willingness to have a go necessitates an acceptance of making mistakes and failing. Even looking stupid. Even people saying you're mad and you should have taken the easy, safe option. Having a go is the only way to achieve anything of significance; the only way to fulfil your potential; the only way to learn and grow.

It's important to become aware of your attitude to failure – which can be subtle. Do you tend to do things you know you can do? Do most of the things you do work out? Is maintaining an appearance of competence important to you? If you're not failing sometimes, then perhaps you need to push a bit harder. It's like learning to ski or ride a bike. If you're not falling over, perhaps you're not trying hard enough.

Procrastination can be a sign of a fear of failure. Putting something off because you don't know whether it'll work or not. And something not working out is something that might reflect poorly on you. If the marketing campaign is a flop, you must be a flop. Somehow what you do becomes wrapped up with who you are – your identity. Get used to separating what you do and who you are. Ironically, if your marketing campaign isn't going to work, you want to know as fast as possible.

If you're going to give yourself permission to fail, extend the same privilege to your team. There are many business owners who talk about (boast even) the many mistakes they've made, but who don't tolerate mistakes from their team. People learn quickly to play it safe in cultures that don't tolerate failure. If a colleague gets their head taken off when they put it above the parapet, they learn to keep low, keep quiet and play it safe. You want your team looking for ways of doing things better. Within their areas of responsibility, encourage them in that pursuit. And expect and accept failure along the way. Even celebrate failure.

Exercise: Practise new things that might fail

- List some small things that carry a degree of risk – you feel slightly nervous about them and you don't know what the outcome might be.
- Pick one of them and do it.
- Note down how you felt beforehand, what happened, and how you felt afterwards.
- Run another 'experiment' tomorrow. Build the habit of taking personal risks. But start small.

Think of these experiments as a strength training programme. You're going to start off with light weights and a few reps. You're going to train for a short period every day. You're going to gradually increase the weights. You'll keep a log of your daily activity. Perhaps you'll find an accountability partner or a coach. Over time you'll get better at having a go and accepting mistakes and failings as a healthy and vital part of your personal development.

Over and above the positive impact it'll have on your personal growth, you'll become a role model to the people around you. You want to attract and encourage people who'll look for ways to do things better – and make mistakes in the process.

Have a go! And be willing to fail.

I know!

These are probably the two most powerful words when it comes to stifling your learning and growth. You say these words because there's a part of you that wants to hurry on to the next, more important activity. Pondering and thinking just aren't action-orientated enough for you. Your brain is telling you that you know that already – move on.

The other reason is that your ego wants to look important and clever – and certainly doesn't want to appear ignorant. Many business owners feel they should know everything about growing a business – which is an impossibility.

In the same way that accepting responsibility for everything that happens to you can be a helpful attitude, so too is accepting that there's a great deal you don't know. Having a 'don't know' attitude changes every situation and interaction into a learning opportunity.

Ironically, the most knowledgeable people also tend to be the ones who admit to knowing least. "The more I know, the more I know I don't know." With an open mind, every person you meet can teach you something. Every situation and experience can teach you something. Every book can teach you something. A second and third reading will usually teach you things you missed the first time.

> *Curiosity didn't kill the cat. And what you don't know, will hurt you.*
> JIM ROHN

A willingness to question everything, a willingness to learn, a willingness to be open-minded will get you further and faster than protecting your ego and believing you've got it all sorted.

How you do anything is how you do everything

The most that can be asked of you is that you do your best. Whatever you do, succeed or fail, big or small, seen or unseen, give it your best shot. That's a virtuous but tough creed to live by.

And giving your best might not be good enough. You might not win a contract, or you may lose a client. A team member may leave, or a marketing promotion may bomb. However, if things don't work out, let it not be because you didn't give it 100%. Don't let your report say "could have tried harder".

Whether you're contemplating personal or business improvements, start with the small things. Adopt the mantra that how you do anything is how you do everything. Aim for excellence in the small things. Learn how to bring your best efforts to small things. And train your team to adopt the same attitude. Over and above the pride in doing small things well, people will notice. "Wow! If they take such care and attention over their office gardens, I know they'll look after me well. They can have my business."

Commit to doing your best in all situations, however small and seemingly unimportant.

Ask for help

Only you can do your press ups, but you don't have to do them alone. Consider working with a business coach – someone whose primary role is to draw out your potential and accelerate your growth as a leader. It can take someone else to help you become aware of who you are today and who you could become tomorrow.

Other benefits of working with a coach:

- **Accountability**: When you decide to do something, it's good to have someone help you distil exactly what you're going to do, and why, and when, and to turn that into a commitment. Knowing that person is going to come back to check on you is sufficient impetus to ensure you honour your commitment.

- **Sounding board**: Having someone to probe your thoughts and ideas with searching and challenging questions improves your thinking, improves your decisions and generates better actions and outcomes.

- **Business knowledge**: Working with someone with broad commercial and leadership experience will expand your knowledge and bring practical ideas from other businesses and other sectors.

- **Introductions**: An experienced coach will introduce you to other people who'll be able to help you and your business. They'll introduce you to appropriate books, articles, courses, etc. that will help you with the challenges and opportunities that lie in front of you.

- **Systems**: They will have a system for developing you and your business.

- **Results**: You'll see measurable improvements. And you will start to enjoy your business more. A coach should be a catalyst to better outcomes.

- **Inspiration**: You should feel a greater sense of enthusiasm and higher levels of energy when you're working with a coach. Yes, it should feel challenging, but it should feel invigorating.

Another option is to find an accountability partner or to establish a mastermind group of fellow business owners.

Beware of nice people – the people who always say you're marvellous and you can achieve anything. You're not and you can't. Also avoid the people who will happily and willingly drag you down to their level of mediocrity. It's said that you become the average of the five people you spend most time hanging around with. Become aware of who you spend most time with and what impact they have on you.

Exercise: Your people environment

- With who do you spend most of your time?
- To what degree are they building you up? Or holding you back?
- Do you need to start moving in different circles?
- Who do you aspire to be like? Who could your role models be?
- Who wants the best for you? Who challenges you?
- Who could you spend more time with? (It's even possible to 'spend time' with people who we can't meet face to face via audio and video recordings.)

Seek out sincere, competent people who care about you – and ask for their help.

Seeing yourself in different mirrors

Self-awareness is a key attribute to develop if you're serious about improving as a business leader. Once you become self-aware, you can start to manage and improve yourself – you can see what needs fixing and fix it. Other people who truly care about you can help with developing your self-awareness and your self-management.

You can also become self-aware by looking in mirrors. If you want to gain awareness about your physical well-being, you might stand in front of a glass mirror in your underwear and jump up and down. That will say something about your physical health.

Exercise: Everyday mirrors

- What does your dressing room mirror say about you?
- What do your clothes say?
- What do the state of your desk drawers say?
- What do your bookshelves tell you?
- What do the television programmes you watch say?
- What does the state of your car tell you?
- What do the people you hang around with say about you?
- What do the standards of your team say about you?
- What does the state of your bank balance tell you?
- What do the state of your business accounts tell you?

If you want to become aware of where you're at, look in the mirrors that are all around you.

Scarcity or abundance?

In any transaction, does one person win and one person lose? If you get more, does that result in someone else getting less? A scarcity mentality can result in people holding onto what they've got; to becoming risk averse; to feeling guilty that their ambitions will cause suffering for others. Economic history shows that fears of scarcity and resources running out are unfounded. Technology and innovation have increased the abundance of an already abundant world. There is more than enough for everyone.

Think of money. Perhaps you were told by a parent that money doesn't grow on trees. Therefore, perhaps you think money is a scarce commodity. That it's difficult to get. That it might run out. Perhaps money not growing on trees is just an unhelpful belief. Perhaps it does grow on trees. Money is absolutely everywhere. Your customers' pockets are stuffed with it. The pressure of all that money is building, desperate to flow somewhere. Why not to your business and your pockets?

Your role

To perform well in a role, the first and most important ingredient is clear expectations – a succinct, well-defined, clearly written, understood, and agreed set of expected outcomes that are to be delivered in a certain amount of time (in exchange for taking home a certain salary at the end of the month). You are no different, even if you're the boss.

You may have several roles, especially in a young business – salesperson, HR manager, IT help desk, and managing director.

Simply recognising that you have several roles with separate deliverables can be an eye opener and give you a degree of clarity and calm – and explain why you're so busy! Becoming clear on the key deliverables of each role allows you to be more deliberate about how you organise your week. You can then use your calendar to ensure you're scheduling dedicated time, energy and focus to each role. Here's how one business owner carried out the exercise and produced three distinct roles.

Example: The multiple role business owner

Managing Director
- Establish sufficient team capacity and capability to handle the next 12 months' forecasted growth.
- Coordinate functions in the business to ensure that service quality and delivery exceeds client expectations.
- Deliver net profits in excess of £100,000 and generate sufficient unallocated cash to reduce business loan by £50,000 over the next 12 months.

Sales & Marketing Manager
- Generate at least eight qualified enquiries each month.
- Convert at least five enquiries into client projects each month.
- Obtain at least one new project referral from existing clients every six months.

Financial Controller
- Ensure invoices are correct and issued within 24 hours of job completion.
- Ensure clients pay in full, and on time or early.
- Monthly, update the six-month cash flow forecast, detailing the next two months by week.

'Responsible for' does not necessarily mean that you have to complete the task personally. You may delegate or outsource the task – but you're responsible for it being done to the required standard and on time.

The role descriptions tell you what has to be produced. They don't tell you how it has to be done. That's down to the individual. (Although as general practice, you'll want people to create processes for doing repeating tasks. See Systems chapter.)

As the business changes and grows, priorities and responsibilities will change. Role responsibilities are not set in stone and should be reviewed and updated periodically. You should look at them at least once a year to see if they're still relevant.

It may be that you look at those key deliverables and think that, despite being incredibly busy, you're not fully delivering on them. Maybe you're wondering what you're doing with your time. That's common for many people. Accept the current situation. It's neither good nor bad, it's just how it is at the moment. The coming pages will share strategies for moving forward from that point.

If you've started your own business, you may not think of yourself as a managing director. And you probably don't have a job description. However, even though no one is going to force you to have one, you will benefit from doing so.

Exercise: Appointing an interim managing director

- Imagine a health issue means you're not going to be around for 12 months. (But you'll be coming back fighting fit.) You need to employ someone to run things whilst you're having treatment. You also need to clarify what they're responsible for and what outcomes you expect in return for that large salary. You're going to get exactly what you specify.
- Write the interim managing director's job description.
- Now put your name under the job title.
- And crack on with delivering those outcomes.

This exercise will help you craft a meaningful job description for yourself. (And, on the basis that your aim is to create a business that is independent of you, you are in effect an interim managing director.)

The role of a managing director

This is a role that many people misunderstand. In large part, a managing director is focused on the future, cultivating a thriving business for tomorrow. Yes, you need to ensure that today is being looked after, and executed according to plan, but day-to-day operational matters should be someone else's responsibility. Should be. In reality, in a small, young, growing business you will be involved in day-to-day matters.

Wherever you and your business are today, you want to gradually spend less time on urgent daily tasks and more time on activities that will impact the future. And you want to learn to appropriately delegate more and more tasks to the team around you. The first aim is to reduce your number of roles until you become a full-time managing director.

The key deliverables and responsibilities of a managing director:

- **Business Strategy:** Developing, communicating and implementing a credible business strategy and sound business model.
- **Vision:** Creating and communicating a vision that inspires and draws the organisation forwards.
- **Innovation:** Innovating to ensure relevance, distinction and progress in the marketplace.
- **Planning:** Developing, communicating and implementing 12-month and 90-day plans.
- **Financial Planning:** Annual financial budgeting including investment planning.
- **Profit & Cash:** Overseeing the achievement of the annual profit and cash goals.
- **Reporting:** Monthly reporting of financial, operational and business development performance (perhaps to a non-executive director, a chairman, the business owner, or a business coach).
- **Culture:** Creating a culture and working environment that allows all staff to flourish and perform at their best.
- **Communication:** Creating meeting structures and schedules that facilitate a healthy two-way flow of information throughout the organisation.
- **Team:** Performance management of direct reports.
- **Recruitment:** Attracting, selecting, retaining and developing team members with the right attitudes and skills to perform well in their roles.

- **Clients:** Retaining and developing profitable clients.
- **Business Development:** Identifying potential clients and securing them as clients.
- **Compliance:** Ensuring that everything the organisation does is legal, honest, decent and truthful. Identify a set of values that drive sound decision-making and desirable behaviours and actions.

It's unlikely that you can currently tick off all these responsibilities. However, it's good to know what you're aiming for. As mentioned previously, responsible for doesn't mean you have to do everything on the list. You'll want to establish a team of competent and committed people around you – ideally people who are better than you!

> *Rome wasn't built in a day –*
> *but they were laying bricks every hour.*
> JOHN HEYWOOD

You will also want to write a specific annual commercial target for your managing director (you). There should be an aim for each of the responsibilities outlined in the previous list. Reorganise the list with what you believe are the most important elements at the top. Yes, it's all important. But at this time, some elements will be more important than others and you want to focus on those first.

Activity management (a.k.a. time management)

If you're like most people in business, life is full on and hectic – even chaotic at times. Perhaps you've become addicted to the adrenaline rush of being permanently busy and constantly in demand. Being busy is something that society promotes and values, equating someone's importance to how busy they are. Avoid that trap – being busy has nothing to do with the importance of what you're doing.

Perhaps you're frustrated and fed up with running at a hundred miles an hour, never seeming to get around to the important stuff, and never able to have any downtime.

Wherever you're at, it's a racing certainty that you're not totally happy with your time management. You know you could be doing better. Everybody does. And the truth is, managing your time well is a never-ending improvement journey. So, cut yourself a little bit of slack. You're probably doing better than you give yourself credit for.

To make any sort of improvement, you need to carve out a protected slither of thinking and planning time. You need to assess what's happening at the moment in your business life, what's good and what's not so good, and create a mini improvement plan. You want to build on the good stuff and let go of the not so good stuff.

The aim of time management isn't so much about cleverly cramming more in; it's about pruning things out and cultivating a more impactful performance. It's about clearing the way for the important things in business and in life to flourish.

Simple things to stop

Before you adopt any new time management techniques, you already know some of the unhelpful things that you should stop doing. The difficulty is that you're probably operating on automatic pilot. Many of your activities have become engrained, subconscious habits which therefore may take effort to undo. So, start with something easy.

Exercise: Stop it

- Jot down the activities that produce little real benefit and are a waste of your time.
- Which one will be easy to stop doing?
- What will be the benefits of stopping?
- Will anyone else be affected if you stop? Will they really care? How will you manage that if they do care?
- What's involved in stopping?
- If you commit to stopping, what might weaken your resolve as the days go by?
- How will you overcome this?
- What will you do if you stumble and fall back into old ways?
- When and how will you reward yourself for cutting out this waste-of-time activity?
- You've thought through your 'stop one thing' plan. So, stop it. Just for today. You can decide tomorrow if you want to 'stop it' again.

Stopping one little thing isn't going to change your life. But it will prove that you can do it. When you've done one thing, move on to the next thing to stop. Put your list somewhere visible and cross out your time wasters one at a time as you banish them to history. At a business planning workshop, this is the list that one delegate generated.

Example: A list of low-value or waste-of-time activities:

- A 60-minute team meeting that lasts the best part of three hours every week.
- Replying to every new email each time it pings across the screen.
- Answering the same questions from the team every day.
- Spending 16 hours driving every week. (Wow. Really? That's a lot of driving.)
- Calling the team several times a day to see how the job is going (and probably slowing them down and irritating them).
- Writing a blog – that no one asked for and probably no one reads. Never had a comment back about one!
- Making tea & coffee for everyone in the office every day – two or three times a day!
- Commenting on friends' Facebook posts.
- Reading the newspaper cover to cover.
- Checking how much cash is in the bank every day – sometimes twice a day.

This is how he then used the questions in the previous exercise and applied it to his list:

- *Which one would be easy to stop doing today?* Instantly replying to email.
- *What will be the impact of stopping?* Will anyone else be affected? Will they care? Probably not. People (clients in particular) have got used to me replying instantly. But they never say anything on the occasions when I can't reply instantly.
- *What's involved in stopping?* Not being prompted to reply. Not seeing that I've received an email. I'll just turn off the notifications feature.

CONTINUED

- *If you commit to stopping, what might weaken your resolve as the days go by?* I might be tempted to check my inbox to see if I've received any emails.
- *How will you overcome this?* I'll close down the email application. I could even take it off the menu bar. I'll have certain times of the day when I'll check email. Initially I'm going to check it every two hours for fifteen minutes and see how that works.
- *What will you do if you stumble?* By turning off email notifications, I don't think I will. But I might get carried away and spend more than fifteen minutes answering emails. I'll use my phone timer to limit myself to fifteen minutes.
- *How will you reward yourself?* Not sure I need a reward for such a small thing. I'll let Marie know what I'm doing and tell her I'll take her for coffee on Friday if I get through the whole week. She'll probably remind me she's been telling me I'm a slave to email for ages – but she'll be an encouraging supporter.

You can review how this exercise has gone at the end of the week and decide if you want to carry on the following week.

As soon as you've eradicated the first thing on your 'stop it' list, you can credit yourself with a certain amount of free time each week. It might be just 30 minutes initially. However, that 30 minutes of free time is like a vacuum, and unless you're disciplined, all sorts of other low-value things will rush in and fill it. So, with confidence, schedule a 30-minute 'time management improvement' session in your calendar. You can use your first 30-minute session to think through how you'll tackle the next thing on your list. Committing to and honouring this mini planning appointment with yourself is far more important than you imagine. It's dedicated time focused on making a better future – a better performing you and, in turn, a better preforming business. You're sending an important message to yourself about what your job is – creating a better tomorrow.

Exercise: Scheduled improvement planning sessions

- Open your calendar and block out 30 minutes early one morning this week.

- Label it 'Improvement Planning' and put a 24-hour reminder notification on it.

- Put an improvement planning 30-minute block in each of the next four weeks. As you move forward, you will be able to increase this to 60 and then 90 minutes.

When it comes to having this critically important, non-negotiable meeting with yourself, you may want to hold it off-site, or at least somewhere where you won't be interrupted or distracted. It's not essential that it's first thing in the day, but it's preferable. Your energy levels will be higher, you'll have sharper focus, and the urgencies of your day won't have crowded in – hopefully. The purpose of starting with four weeks is to give you a decent opportunity to make progress, but not to make you feel you're committing to this for the rest of your life. You can review the process and your progress after the fourth session. If it's not working for you, you can try something else. If it is working, you can carry on – perhaps with some refinements. However, I am confident it will work.

Track your activities

Once you've eradicated one or two of your worthless activities and are making progress, the next step is to start understanding what you actually do with your time. Note down what you do during your working day for the next five days. This can be as simple as keeping a notepad with you and writing down each new activity and the time you start it. Alternatively, there are plenty of free activity monitoring apps available that digitise the process. (Toggl works well.) You may feel that this is another activity to add to an already overflowing 'To Do' list. However, the time and effort you invest in this exercise will quickly save you more time in the future by helping you to re-prioritise what you do, make you more productive and reduce the number of activities you do.

You can use one of your diarised 30-minute Improvement Planning sessions to set up your activity tracking. In the following session, you can analyse your results. However, in reality you'll want to do this for more than five days. It takes a little while to get into the routine of tracking – and to remember to turn on the timer. Time tracking apps alert you if you haven't started your timer and allow you to manually input activities, which is useful if you're out and about or walking around a workshop or a warehouse.

The first two benefits of embarking on an activity tracking exercise aren't obvious. Firstly, subconsciously, you tend not to do things that you know you shouldn't be doing. The thought of writing down that you spent 30 minutes sorting all your files by colour or 10 minutes watching TikTok videos is an effective deterrent. Secondly, if you're used to multi-tasking – writing a proposal but also dealing with incoming emails, answering people's questions and checking WhatsApp messages – you tend to reduce those interruptions because it becomes difficult to keep an accurate activity log. Once you start your activity log, your helpful inbuilt desire to make it accurate will work to your advantage.

When you have a full week's data, you can spend one of your improvement planning sessions analysing it, looking for patterns and seeing where you can make changes.

Exercise: Analysing and valuing your activity data

- Go through your list with a red and green pen. Highlight in green the activities you consider to be high value. Highlight in red the activities you consider to be low value and that you'd like someone else to do. Just looking at the relative amounts of red and green on the paper will give you a high-level pattern.

- Go through your data and add up the time spent on different activities. (If you're using an app, you'll get a summarised report automatically.) How does this compare to what you thought?

- Another useful exercise is to estimate how you're currently valuing your time. Look through your list of tracked activities and write next to each activity the estimated cost of outsourcing it.

It's illuminating – sometimes frightening – to complete the outsource costing exercise. Having given each activity an hourly rate, you can calculate how much your whole week would have cost to outsource and determine an effective hourly rate.

For example, if you spent time carrying out accounting updates, you might value this at £25 per hour on the basis that you could have outsourced it to a bookkeeper for that cost. If you spent time clearing up the office kitchen before going home, you might value your time at £10 per hour on the basis that you could have outsourced this to a cleaner. One business owner calculated that writing a proposal for a prospective new client equated to £165 per hour (based on how long the survey and proposal took them, how many proposals turned into projects, and how profitable their average project was). Does it make sense for them to spend their time washing coffee cups or carrying out surveys and writing proposals?

The most powerful impact of this costing exercise is that you have £10 per hour and £165 per hour jobs on the same piece of paper (using the previous example). If one of your team showed you this, the answer's obvious without either of you saying anything. The question is how you reduce the low value jobs to be able to focus on the higher value ones. There may be a few easy, obvious wins but it's likely you're going to have to change things over time.

Having carried out your activity tracker exercise, a useful tool for categorising your activities is the Eisenhower matrix (named after the highly effective, productive and two-time American president, Dwight D. Eisenhower).

When you understand the value of time,
the resource and the wealth of time, you will be
running away from the crowd, you will be
running away from distractions.

SUNDAY ADELAJA

The Eisenhower Matrix

The Eisenhower matrix is a two-by-two matrix that classifies activities or tasks based on their importance and their urgency. A task's importance can be thought of in terms of the size and significance of the benefits of doing it or the consequences of not doing it. Urgency can be thought of as the criticality of when the task is done. Importance is a subjective measure that depends on your long-term business goals and your values. The more something moves you in the direction of those goals, the more important it is. It's therefore crucial to have long-term goals and objectives. You don't want to head off with energy and enthusiasm chasing the wrong goals – or no goals. Direction first, speed second.

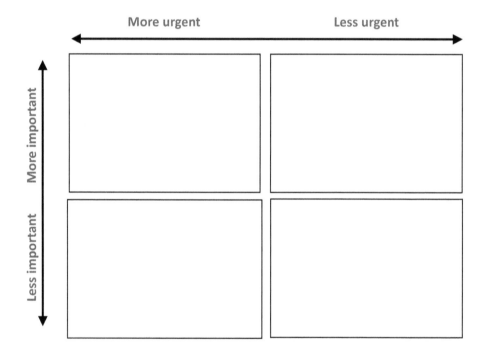

Exercise: Categorising your activities

- Take the activities from your activity tracker and put them in one of the four quadrants in the Eisenhower matrix.
- Take a different coloured pen and add in the things that you'd like to do but you're currently not finding the time to do. (You may wish to refer to the managing director responsibilities exercise earlier in this chapter.) These additional activities are all likely to appear in the important but less urgent quadrant (top right).

This is the output generated by one company director. It took two sessions to complete the exercise, principally to make sure the items in the 'Important & Not Urgent' quadrant were the items she believed were most important to the future of the business.

More urgent ← → **Less urgent**

More important

Important & Urgent
- Completing customer quotes
- Returning customer phone calls
- Submitting tenders
- Answering important emails
- Speaking with walk-in prospects
- Resolving office disputes
- Calling Dad on his birthday
- Catching train to London

Important & Not Urgent
- Quarterly Planning
- Monthly management meeting
- Negotiating with suppliers
- Leadership training
- 121 with direct reports
- Creating customer case studies
- Developing processes for lads
- Getting fit

Less important

Urgent but Not Important
- Submitting the VAT return
- Renewing the insurance
- Completing technician schedule
- Checking email
- Writing social media posts
- Delivering supplies to site
- Checking time sheets
- Ordering supplies for lads

Not Important & Not Urgent
- Constant interruptions - all day!
- Checking social media
- Criticising the lads - & everyone!
- Complaining about government
- Reading news alerts all the time
- Constantly grazing & making cups of coffee every 5 minutes
- Box sets (into the early hours)

Your aim is to spend all your time in the top two important quadrants, and ideally most of your time in the top right quadrant – important but not urgent. Top right activities are all to do with the future and creating a better tomorrow. However, being realistic, urgent things do happen and you'll have to respond to those. You'll also find – especially in the early days of building your business – that you have to spend time on things that you consider less important but still have to be done by someone. And if you don't have anyone available, it's you who will have to get them done. Whilst we might think that bottom right is a no-go quadrant, the reality is that you will find yourself in there periodically – you're only human! The key is to recognise you've been subtly sucked in and get out again as quickly as possible.

Having categorised your activities, the next step is to do something with them. For the activities in each quadrant, here is the recommended action:

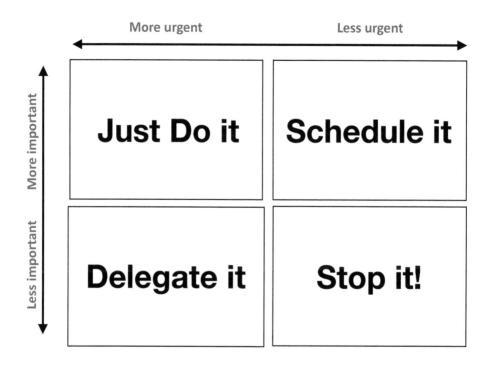

The following exercises will help you create an action plan to get better control of what you're doing and increase the time you can invest in high value tasks. The aim of your plan is to move yourself towards spending more time on activities with long-term benefit.

Cutting out unimportant, non-urgent tasks

Examples might be producing reports that you've always produced, but on reflection, no longer add any value; or writing and sending out a newsletter because every other company sends out a newsletter – but it doesn't bring in any business and no one seems to read it apart from you and your mum; or downloading your bank statements into a spreadsheet and reconciling them even though your new digital accounting software does the same job in 20% of the time.

Exercise: Stop it revisited

- Firstly, for every activity that you currently do, ask if it really needs to be done at all.
- If it doesn't, can you just stop doing it?
- If not, what needs to happen to make it disappear?
- Who needs to do what and when?

Delegating less important tasks

These will typically be the tasks that you costed in the activity analysis exercise as relatively low value. The challenge with these tasks is that they take upfront time and effort to prepare for delegation. Often, you'll think that it's easier to do it yourself than find someone else to do it, explain what needs doing, get frustrated when they spend twice as long doing it as you would, and then have to correct it when they get it wrong. If it was a one-off activity, it would be easier to do it yourself. However, this is likely to be a recurring task that you do every day or every week. If it takes you two hours to train someone to do a 15-minute weekly task, you breakeven on that training time after eight weeks (2 hours training / 15 minutes saved per week = 8 weeks). After that, you save 15 minutes every week for the rest of your life. That's a decent return on your investment.

Before delegating it, you'll have to document the process for doing it. This is also a good opportunity to understand if the task can be automated in some way. An internet search often returns new, inexpensive software that simplifies and automates many business processes. The next step is to train the person you're delegating it to. You'll have to monitor their progress and help them gain competence and confidence. Once they've got it, let go and trust them get on with it. Delegation could be to a colleague, a new part-time employee, a contractor or a freelancer, or it could be outsourced to a third party.

There's a big difference between delegation and abdication. Don't just dump stuff on other people and look the other way – unless you want to have a bigger workload in a month's time. Another important consideration is the person's capacity. Are they able to absorb this additional task? Do they need to stop doing something themselves? Do they need to adjust their priorities? Do they need to do something more efficiently? Or delegate something?

Creating processes and training people are important, high value, and non-urgent tasks. They appear in the top right quadrant of your Eisenhower matrix.

It can be difficult delegating tasks that you do better than anyone else. It may be emotionally hard letting go. Remember, you're only considering lower value tasks – not mission critical ones. Even though you may do them better than anyone else, other people will be able to do them adequately. Your objective is to free up your time so that you can reinvest it in higher value tasks.

Exercise: Delegate it

- If the activity has to be done, do you personally have to do it?
- If not, who else could do it?
- How and when could you delegate it to them?
- Do you need to create a process for doing it?
- What training is required?
- How will you monitor that it's being done correctly?

Getting on with urgent, important tasks

For the moment, you'll have to deal with all these tasks. However, you and your team can add those urgent and important must-do-today tasks to an issues list and gradually resolve each of them, thus reducing your important and urgent tasks to only those that are beyond your control.

Exercise: Just do it

- Which are the imperative must-do-today tasks that suddenly appear?
- Of those tasks, which have become urgent because they've been left to the last minute?
- Which ones have a root cause that has never been determined and resolved?
- Which are the ones that are unforeseen and have popped up as a result of outside forces?

Prioritising and focusing on high value activities

Most of the important things in business and in life aren't urgent. You want to work diligently and thoughtfully on those important activities, but your urgent tasks loom large and always seem to take priority. It seems as if for every urgent task you slay, two more appear in its place, and those important, non-urgent tasks forever recede into the distance. There's one distinct difference between urgent tasks and non-urgent ones – urgent tasks have a deadline. This may be a real deadline (the tender has to be in by 11.59pm tonight) or an imposed deadline (a client has just called with an urgent problem). You're wired to react to deadlines. Strategic planning, building customer relationships or nurturing team members don't have deadlines, so they constantly find themselves bumped down the list.

Exercise: Scheduling tasks

- Prioritise the activities you've identified as important but not urgent. (The ones you currently do and the ones you currently don't do but would like to be doing.)
- Note the benefits of carrying out each those activities.
- Next to each activity, determine how frequently and for how long you'd like to spend on each. e.g. two hours on finances each week; or four hours doing one-to-ones every month; or a day planning every quarter.
- Being realistic about how busy your life is at the moment, determine how many of those activities you can do. If you can only do one, that's fine. Better to be realistic and achieve a small step than overreach and take a fall. And remember that freeing up more of your time is key so 'freeing up time' might be right at the top of your list.
- The critical step is to schedule those activities in your calendar, with a start time, finish time, a location, and a notification reminder. Ideally schedule the activity first thing in the day.

There are two ways to help get important non-urgent tasks done. One is to use the power of deadlines. Introduce a time factor into your thinking and schedule these tasks in your calendar. It's not a guarantee that you'll honour the appointment, but it significantly increases the likelihood that you will. The other technique is to identify the benefits of doing the task. Investing a couple of minutes articulating how the task will progress you and the business helps in redressing the balance between urgent and non-urgent tasks.

You might also want to think of a scheduled business planning day like attending a friend's wedding – whatever business emergency came up or whoever asked for an urgent meeting, you'd put them off and attend your friend's wedding. Or you might think of a scheduled one-to-one meeting with a direct report like an appointment for life saving treatment at the hospital – come what may, you'd make that appointment; nothing would stop you being there. It's amazing that when you get back from the wedding or the hospital, the world's still spinning and somehow your team have coped. The same is true of planning days and one-to-ones. Often your team have coped better than you expected. Perhaps they're better than you thought. Hmm? Perhaps you might deliberately leave them to cope more often.

Another technique for investing more time working on your important, non-urgent tasks (let's call them your significant tasks) is to rearrange your day. It's likely that you operate some kind of daily to-do list system (discussed shortly) that you've (ideally) created at close-of-play the previous day. Certain things on that list can only happen at specific times (meeting over lunch with Rob at 1pm). Everything else should be put in priority order, based on its importance (benefits of doing it or consequences of not doing it). Make sure that there's one significant task on your list – perhaps it's creating a better process for making presentations to potential clients. By definition, this should be at the top of your list. You'd like to spend an hour each morning working on your new presenting process. Tomorrow's going to be a busy day, so you decide to only schedule half an hour – but you still commit to it and schedule the time. You even decided to get up 30 minutes earlier. The routine of doing significant work every day, even for just 30 minutes, is a powerful and impactful habit to develop – and will significantly impact your business over time.

In addition to these self-management tools, here are other practical, proven techniques that will improve your effectiveness and efficiency, particularly when it comes to working on significant tasks.

Close your door

Don't have an open-door policy and don't be available to help your team. It may sound progressive to have an open-door policy and to be constantly available to solve every problem and answer every question – but it's not. It may bolster your ego, but it will decimate your productivity and distract you from doing what you're paid to do.

Close your door and get on with your work. Answer questions and queries at designated times of the day. And let your team solve their own problems – that's what you pay them to do and that's how they learn and grow. If you must have a problem-solving surgery, ask people to pop back at 5:30pm. It's amazing how many problems get solved by 5 o'clock.

Hang a 'Do Not Disturb' sign on the door. Turn your desk around so your back is facing the door – seriously. Tell the office that when your door's closed, you're only to be disturbed if the building's on fire.

If you're unfortunate enough to have to sit in an open plan office, get yourself some noise-cancelling headphones and a baseball cap. Open plan is okay for the cross fertilisation of ideas, but its hideous when it comes to being able to concentrate on important and challenging work.

Clear your desk

If you're going to work on something important, clear everything else off your desk. Don't spend time organising it and tidying it, simply bundle it up and put it in a drawer. Unplug the landline. Critically, put your mobile on silent. Or better still, put it in a drawer in another room so you're less tempted to look at it. Or give it to someone else to field your calls. If this important piece of work involves a computer, close down all the applications you don't need. In particular, close down your email and all social media.

Turn off notifications.

Turn off all the notifications on your phone and your computer when you need to concentrate. And never turn them on again. Probably the only notification you ever need is for upcoming calendar appointments. Recognise that there's a war on to grab your attention. Get back in control.

Create a distraction-free environment

Remove all the potential distractions from your working environment. You may even want a designated place where you work on the important tasks, deliberately designed to be distraction free – no books, no windows, no pictures, and definitely no phones. Perhaps somewhere that's away from the office. You'll do better work and for longer in a distraction-free environment.

Your mobile phone – a blessing and a curse

Time isn't your most precious resource – your focused attention is. Your phone – particularly when it pings, rings, flashes, or vibrates – has become the most effective weapon in destroying your focused attention.

Looking at phones has become habitual. Seeing it, feeling it, hearing it, triggers your hand to reach for it.

Exercise: Phone trigger awareness

- Simply notice what causes you to look at your phone.
- Where are you?
- What are you doing?
- What is it that grabs your attention just before you look at it?
- For the moment, raising your awareness is enough to start breaking the habit.

Not only are phones a source of debilitating distractions, they also effectively serve to undermine relationships. If someone's having an important face-to-face conversation with you and their phone pings, even if they don't look at it, it suggests there's something else more important than your discussion. Even a phone lying on someone's desk is enough to signal they're waiting for something important to interrupt your conversation. It's subtle. But relationship building is one of your significant tasks. Give people your full attention.

There's a school of thought that says that subconsciously you feel more important the more notifications you receive. Current culture intimates that busy equals important and reacting to and responding to notifications, subconsciously, boosts feelings of importance.

The point isn't to dispense with your phone – they're a communication marvel and a vital asset in the modern world. The point is to prove that you control your phone, not the other way around. Your phone is a tool you choose to use when it's appropriate.

Exercise: Your phone is a useful tool that you control – not the other way around

- Give your phone to someone else for an hour.
- Go out for lunch and leave your phone in the office.
- Go to a meeting and leave your phone in your desk drawer.
- Go for a walk or a cycle and leave your phone at home. No, you won't know how many steps you've done or what your average speed was.
- At night, leave your phone downstairs. If you need an alarm, buy one.
- One day, deliberately leave your phone at home and see what happens.

Major on the major

Before you tackle your important projects and tasks, you may be tempted to deal with all the little stuff first. The theory goes that if you get all the small stuff out of the way, you'll be able to focus fully on the important stuff. The small stuff always takes longer than you think. And also has this magical property of self-propagating. Invariably, important stuff becomes the first think you'll do tomorrow – after you've checked and responded to those pesky emails. Groundhog day.

Besides, even if you do manage to get all the small stuff done, your energy levels will be depleted by the time you get around to your important project.

Don't major on minor things. Major on the major.

Email

Keep your email application turned off and out of sight. Turn off email notifications. Schedule specific times in the day when you'll check and action your emails. It's far more efficient to batch the same kinds of tasks together and deal with them in one go. You can even use the out of office email feature to let people know when you reply to emails. This might be at lunchtime and close of play. Or it might be on the hour, every hour. It doesn't really matter, just be deliberate about it.

At the beginning of the relationship with new clients, discuss and agree how you'll communicate, including email communication. Your new client wants you fully focused on doing your best work for them – they certainly wouldn't want you distracted by responding to emails suddenly pinging across your screen.

Like your phone, email is your tool. You control it – don't let it control you.

If you do reply immediately to email, you're communicating to the sender, perhaps a client, that you're sitting waiting, prepared, ready to respond immediately to whatever request they have. You're creating an expectation that will precipitate even more email queries. Before you know it, there's been a dozen emails zipped across the ether. And you've probably copied in a couple of colleagues too, jamming up their inbox with lots of reading.

Occasionally, after an email has been left for a couple of hours, another email appears saying, "Ignore last email – all sorted".

If you have a backlog of thousands of emails – literally, in some cases – delete or achieve all of them apart from those from the last two weeks. If someone has sent something important that you haven't replied to and have now archived, they'll send it again. Before the days of being able to access emails on holiday, it's amazing how fast you could work through two weeks' worth of emails when you returned. Many of them could be deleted immediately as they weren't relevant any longer. The same is true of your current backlog – most if it isn't any longer relevant. You could just delete it. How good would that feel?

Before you work through your (reduced) backlog, focus first on developing a system for coping with what lands in your inbox today. Once you have a new system in place, you can then go back – if you really need to. This two-step approach works for any backlog: Firstly, develop a process that works going forward; secondly, tackle the backlog if there's value in doing so.

Example: Reducing email

- Send fewer emails. The more you send, the more you'll receive. Determine if the communication is required. If it is, determine if email is the best communication tool. Sometimes a conversation, a phone call or a WhatsApp recorded message is better.
- Educate your colleagues as to what they should email to you. Many communications you don't need to know about. Stop people c.c.ing you in – you either need to know or you don't. What they're tacitly (and possibly unknowingly) doing is passing responsibility for what they've said to you. Copying you in on emails should be the exception, not the rule. Also, educate your team to write succinct, short emails.
- Unsubscribe to newsletters, etc. that are of no value to you.
- Hit the junk button for things you consider to be junk (rather than just deleting them). Your email will learn to divert these things to junk in the future.
- Don't look at or respond to emails out of hours. Often, it's that immediate response that precipitates more email. And you have other priorities outside of work.

Example: An email system

- Deal with emails in batches. Ideally only one or two batches a day. Have a designated and scheduled time(s) when you deal with your emails. Batching will result in you processing more emails in less time.
- As you go through your day, make a note of emails you have to send. Resist the temptation of sending emails sporadically during the day. Once you open up your email, your natural inclination is to start working through your inbox. Stick to your schedule.
- Have an automated message that lets people know when you action your emails. If something is urgent, ask them to call you.
- Read through emails in order and do something specific with each one. Your something specific might be:
  » Delete it after reading it. Get out of the habit to replying

to every email. There's no need to reply 'thanks' – you're just cluttering up someone else's inbox.

» Action it if it takes less than five minutes to deal with. And get into the habit of writing short replies. A 20 second WhatsApp voice message is often the clearest and fastest response.

» Schedule it for another time. You could set up a flag or folder system. Have 'Today' and 'This Week' folders. If something goes into Today, it's important, will take longer than five minutes, and you'll complete it at a scheduled time during the day. The aim is for your Today folder to be empty at the end of the day. As part of your end-of-day routine, you scan through the emails that are in your This Week folder and select which ones you'll work on tomorrow and move them to your Today folder.

» Delegate it. Forward it on to a colleague who's in a better position to deal with it. Clarify your expectations of when it needs to be dealt with.

• Just say no. If you can't do something or don't want to do something, just say no.

• Measure and record how long you spend processing emails each day. If you want to improve something, measure it. Over time, you'll see that you're spending less time on emails – and probably improving your effectiveness at dealing with them at the same time.

One manager decided that they'd use the coloured flags that were a feature of their email system to help them organise their emails. It took a little trial and error, but this is the system they created that worked for them. Something similar will work for you.

Example: Coloured flags

- Red – urgent, important and requires time and thought. Must be done before the end of the day. Reschedule other tasks. Check all red flag emails at 4pm.
- Blue – reply expected. Go through sent emails and highlight the ones where a reply is essential. Check blue-flagged emails on a Friday afternoon.
- Yellow – need to refer to this email at some point in the future. e.g. Zoom call access codes, train details, insurance cover details, etc.
- Green – recurring emails that get sent to groups of people on a regular basis. Will use this for regular monthly invoices.
- Purple – action emails for clients that need referring to next time there's a meeting.
- Orange – interesting but not urgent stuff (blogs etc.) Read these if there's time – or waiting for planes, trains and automobiles. Review every so often and unflag and delete redundant ones.

Email is not evil. It's an effective means of communication if it's managed well. If *you* manage it well. You can adopt this system or you can use your own. The key is to have a system. Monitor how it goes. See what works for you and adapt it to suit your needs. Any system always beats no system.

Is there a need to have emails on your phone? Don't have emails on there as a matter of course. Determine if you really need to access them. If you do, tuck the icon away on a distant screen so you have to make an effort to access it. As mentioned previously, avoid distracting temptations by removing them or making them difficult to access.

Similarly, is there any reason to check your emails before you go to bed, or as soon as you wake up? For most people, there isn't. It's just a bad habit. Put your phone away after a certain time in the evening and retrieve it when you start work the following day.

Batching

As talked about earlier, grouping the same tasks together and tackling them at the same time is more efficient than tackling them randomly throughout the day.

Phone calls are more efficient when batched. As with emails, you could answer your phone whenever it rings, regardless of what you might be working on. Or you might decide that you make all your calls twice a day, perhaps at 10.30am and 2:30pm.

If you've had your mobile on silent (whilst you've been working on an important task or project), you can return all your missed calls at your scheduled phone calling time. Or if you have the efficient luxury of someone else answering the phone, they can let the caller know that you'll call them back between 10:30am and 11:00am or 2:30pm and 3:00pm, asking the caller which time would be most convenient.

If you're the go-to person for answering your colleagues' queries, perhaps you hold a couple of question-answering surgeries each day rather than being constantly interrupted.

Social media can also silently and stealthily erode your effectiveness. Whether it's personal or professional, batching social media activity together at predetermined scheduled times will reduce the amount of time required to achieve the same impact. Company culture and disciplines around social media merit a section – a book! – of their own. Suffice to say, it's best to keep notifications turned off, and the apps themselves hidden away out of sight. If posting and replying to posts is an important aspect of your job, schedule a number of times a day, for fixed durations, when you'll complete that activity.

As well as batching things together on a daily basis, you can batch together weekly and monthly tasks too. Perhaps the first Tuesday of every month is the day when you have all your formal one-to-ones with your direct reports. Perhaps on a Monday all invoicing is sent to clients. And on a Thursday, all remittances are sent to suppliers.

Answering colleagues' queries

Having a scheduled time when you answer people's questions is a good start. Also, insist that staff come along with what they think the answer is. If you think they can find the answer for themselves (even if you could give them the answer), it's better to point them in the right direction and let them do their own research. It's not as efficient for them in the short term but making them more self-reliant will benefit you, them and the business in the long term.

There are two things at play when someone asks for help.

Getting an answer from you is the fastest and easiest thing to do. We might call this laziness, but from their point of view it's the most effective and efficient thing to do. And we've trained them well. We've probably told them to come to us if they have a question, and we always answer their question.

The more subtle thing at play is that answering questions and solving problems is what you're good at. It tells you you're indispensable and gives you a feeling of importance. If no one ever needed you, how might you feel? Recognising the psychology at play here is important. You need to manage your ego's desire to feel important in the eyes of those around you. Better to have an increasingly competent and resourceful team.

Energy management

Energy management is as important as activity management. You come into each day with a certain amount of energy that gradually depletes. Different activities and different people will absorb different amounts of your energy. Certain things will restore or boost your energy. Becoming aware of your energy flow will help improve your effectiveness and efficiency.

You want to start your day with a full tank of energy and be on virtually empty by the end of the day. You don't want to run dry before the end of the day – but equally you want to use the energy you've got. Anything less would be a waste.

Here are a few strategies and tactics that will help increase and restore your energy, and help you get more miles per gallon.

Take regular breaks

Intuitively you'd think that the longer you work, the more you produce. However, countless studies in all walks of life show that both quality and quantity of output reduces when you keep on working without stopping. This is true for both physical and mental activities.

Even if you're bursting with energy and enthusiasm, taking a short break every couple of hours will improve your productivity and, more importantly, the quality of what you're producing. Experiment and see what works best for you: five minutes every hour; a walk around the block every 90 minutes; 15 minutes every two hours. Stretching your legs and getting five minutes' fresh air will restore some energy.

Taking breaks does not come naturally to driven individuals and you may find it hard. Stopping can be harder than keeping going. Cramming more into every unforgiving minute seems like the way to go – and it's served you well so far. But if you're truly interested in producing more and better work, experiment with introducing breaks into your working day for a few weeks and see what happens. If you decide that you'll take a five minute walk every couple of hours, you'll also discover that your best solutions, thoughts and ideas magically pop into your head whilst walking.

> *Only ideas won by walking have any value.*
> FRIEDRICH NIETZSCHE

Exercise

Short periods of modest exercise will reduce tiredness and increase energy. Whilst cardiovascular health is important, in terms of increasing energy levels, there isn't the need to engage in medium or high intensity workouts. A brisk walk or cycle ride will suffice.

Whilst it's true that you'll benefit more if you do more exercise, those benefits tail off significantly as you increase the amount of exercise you do. The difference to your health (all other things being equal) between doing no exercise and walking briskly for half an hour (two miles) every day is huge. Pick a point one mile away and simply walk there and back. Or start with half a mile. Arranging to walk with someone else is helpful as it raises your commitment level – you don't want to let the other person down. If you do walk with someone else, bear in mind that walking briskly is a pace at which you probably don't feel like talking.

Hydration

Most people are dehydrated to some degree. Simply drinking a little more water throughout the day will increase your energy levels and make you sharper and more alert. Have a glass first thing in the day. You will have become dehydrated overnight. Have a glass or bottle of water in clear sight on your desk. When you notice it, have a drink. Every time you go for a cup of coffee or tea, also have a glass of water. Think of things that you do every day and use them as a trigger for having a drink of water.

Being well hydrated will naturally reduce your food intake. People often mistake thirst for hunger and eat rather than drink.

Energy vampires

Some people suck the life out of you. Avoid them as much as possible – even if they're family members. Become aware of who gives you energy (energy zappers), and who drains you of energy (energy sappers). With this increased awareness, make different choices about who you spend time with.

You may not be able to totally avoid your energy sappers, but you can manage the situation to limit their negative impact. Commit to doing something about it. Perhaps emails are better than phone calls, or phone calls better than face-to-face meetings. Perhaps save those interactions for the end of the day so they don't impact on all the other good things you want to do. Perhaps you have to confront some of their energy-sapping behaviour (in a constructive, non-confrontational way). Sometimes you may just have to tell them straight.

Consider the situation as a learning or training experience. If you want to be calmer or more tolerant, you might relish spending time with someone who complains about everything. They may have been deliberately sent to build up your tolerance muscles. Or even turn it into a game. Every time they criticise a colleague, you'll find something positive to say about that colleague. Perhaps the person who always thinks of why something won't work is the person who is secretly challenging you to make your plan more robust. Be imaginative and find an angle to manage energy sappers.

In some instances, you may even eradicate them from your life.

Flow

As with people, some tasks will give you energy, some will drain you of energy. Do more of the things that give you energy, and dump the rest – well, start to do something about them.

You may think that all tasks would drain you of energy. However, that doesn't seem to be the case. Think of occasions when an hour doing a task you dislike feels like eight hours; and conversely, you do something you love for 40 minutes – and then look at the clock and discover you've been doing it for two hours.

Generally, tasks that we like and that we're good at (usually we're good at things we like) give us energy – we feel alert, engaged, excited and focused.

There will be tasks you enjoy and tasks you don't. If you're in the right role, there will be far more tasks you enjoy. 'Enjoy' doesn't necessarily mean those tasks are easy or even that you're competent at them. 'Enjoy' means you're fully immersed and energised by the challenge of getting better and achieving a great result. You look forward to them; time seems to stand still when you do them; you make good progress; you keep getting better.

If you discover an imbalance in favour of tasks you don't like and aren't particularly good at, you need to change roles. Seriously. Even if it's a well-paid, high status role. At the end of your days, you don't want to check out with a healthy bank account, having got through life; you want to know that you've lived life to the full, that you've been fully alive. Besides, doing something that makes you feel fully alive might also increase your chances of having a healthy bank account.

If you feel that you're doing something that matters, it will also give you energy. If you're doing something that feels like a waste of time and has no significance, it drains you of energy.

Do what you love doing. It will give you energy and make you feel alive. Dump or minimise the rest – or transform how you view them.

A good night's sleep

The most important aspect of good health and high energy levels is a good night's sleep – seven to eight hours every night, seven nights a week. Five hours' sleep during the week and twelve hours at the weekend isn't as good.

Getting a good night's sleep may take time to cultivate. There are both physical and psychological factors that affect it, and to a large degree, your sleep pattern is habitual. If your sleep isn't as good as it could be, it will take deliberate effort and a little time to establish a better routine.

Anecdotally, people who are 'early to bed, early to rise' seem to be happier and achieve more. However, they've probably developed other good habits too.

These things will help improve your sleep:

- Go to bed at the same time every night and get up at the same time every morning – ideally seven days a week.

- If you spend most of your day engaged in mental activity, it's good to build in exercise and fresh air so that your body is physically tired too.

- Preparation is important for good quality sleep. In the same way that having a close down routine for work (shutting off email, creating a plan for tomorrow, etc.) is helpful, so too is a close down routine for your day. Do things that relax your mind and body. (Reading a novel, taking the dog for a walk, having a bath, etc.) Avoid activities and substances that make it difficult to fall asleep, such as television (especially the news – don't fill your head with negative, disturbing stories just before bed), your phone, other screens, food and caffeine. Alcohol may send you to sleep but it doesn't promote good sleep and is best avoided.

- Avoid eating late at night so your stomach gets a rest. Ideally, structure your eating so that you have a 14 hour overnight fast. Whilst it's important to keep hydrated during the day, avoid drinks in the evening, so there's less likelihood of having to visit the loo during the night.

- When you go to bed, go to bed – don't watch television, listen to the radio or read books. Do those activities elsewhere. Make your bed a trigger for going to sleep.

- Keeping your bedroom cool (18°C) will help you sleep better.

- If you're lying awake thinking, get up and do something until you feel tired and then go back to bed.

Adopt these practices, and over time your ability to sleep well and fully restore your energy levels will improve.

Maintaining a healthy weight

Through personal experience, I know that when I'm closer to 80kgs, I have more energy, more alertness, more vitality; I'm sharper, more imaginative and more enthusiastic. When I'm carrying extra weight, and heading towards 90kgs, it saps my energy and dulls my imagination and alertness. Ironically, I don't notice the slight, subtle dullness as the weight creeps on. What I do notice is the increase in vitality as it drops off (which gets harder and harder as the years pass). My sad realisation is that I just don't need to consume the number of calories I used to. My current aim is to replace a lifetime's habit of eating what I want with becoming a more modest eater – because that spring in my step and that increased vivacity for life is worth it. But I find it hard.

Perhaps clients should weigh me before every business coaching session to ensure they're getting the high-octane version of me!

Eating energy-giving foods

Large meals have the effect of diverting energy to digesting food rather than dealing with life's challenges. As mentioned previously, good hydration is more important than satiating your hunger. Two or three meals a day is sufficient, without the need to snack. For many people, eating is habitual rather than a biological necessity. There's also so much temptation around, it can be difficult to avoid snacking and over-eating.

In the same way that placing a glass of water on your desk increases the likelihood that you'll drink it, the opposite is also true. Hiding away – or not buying – biscuits, snacks, chocolate and sweets increases the likelihood that you won't eat them.

There's plenty of information available on which foods to eat and which to avoid. So much so, that all that information might be confusing and potentially paralysing. In terms of maintaining good energy levels, here's a summary:

- Drink water throughout your day.

- Aim to give your stomach a 12 to 15-hour break. (Dinner at 7pm and breakfast at 7am is 12 hours. Dinner at 7pm and breakfast at 11am is 16 hours.)

- Eat two or three meals a day. Avoid snacks if possible – even Milky Ways.

- Consume a modest amount of protein. Eat nuts, pulses, beans, oily fish, white fish and limited amounts of animal proteins.

- Eat raw things (salads, etc.), lightly cooked things and lots of naturally colourful things (peppers, tomatoes, cauliflowers, apples, plums, bananas, etc.). Avoid processed foods.

- Consume lots of green things (peas, spinach, courgettes, broccoli, kale, asparagus, etc.). But not Crème de Menthe!

- Avoid sugar and things that contain high levels of sugar (fizzy drinks, confectionary, etc.). Sugar will give you a short-term energy high, but you'll then plunge into a sugar low. You want blood sugar stability, not highs and lows.

- Limit consumption of things that are white or beige in colour (pastry, pies, bread, pasta, rice, potatoes).

If you were responsible for the performance of a Formula One racing car, you'd be very particular about what you put in it. No crap or cheap stuff; you'd want the best fuel, the best engine oil, the best lubricants. The truth is that you are responsible for the performance of a highly complex, high potential machine. Put in the right amounts, of the right stuff (the best you can afford), at the right time, and you'll be on your way to maxing your energy levels and your performance.

Exercise: Energy tracking

- Track how you're feeling energy-wise throughout your day. Each hour, give yourself an energy score out of 10 and relate it to when you last ate and what you ate. (Again, the first step in self-improvement is self-awareness.) Experiment and see what works best for you.

Leadership Development

All of us will periodically find ourselves in a leadership role, whether by design or circumstance. If you're a business owner, a director, a manager, a supervisor, or even self-employed, you are a leader – more correctly, you're in a position of leadership. (If you're self-employed or a freelancer, you're leading your one and only team member, you.)

If you're the boss and your team are following you, you're a leader.

If they're going through the motions and not really following you, you're not a leader, even if your business card and ego tell you that you are.

You're a good leader if people follow you of their own free will. Forcing people to do things is tiring and doesn't build a self-sustaining business. Take away the force, and things soon start to crumble. You look behind you and there's no one there. Before getting into the detail of developing your leadership skills, it'll be useful to understand where you think you are today.

Measuring your effectiveness as a leader

You're not a good or bad leader. Such subjective and binary judgements are unhelpful. You are where you are. It doesn't really matter if you're a two out of ten or an eight out of ten. (Ironically, a two gives you huge scope for improvement.) The key question is what value you see in developing your leaderships skills. The instinctive, rhetorical answer is of course you want to improve. But are you willing to pay the price; to make the sacrifices; to change what has served you so far?

Exercise: Leadership improvement benefits

- What are the benefits of being a better leader?
- How would they impact your business?
- How might they translate into a better financial performance?
- What benefits would accrue to you personally?
- To what degree do you believe what you've just written?
- Is there a compelling case to investing time and effort in becoming a better leader?

If you're a business owner or go-getting individual, you're probably someone who doesn't stop moving and doing. You've got where you are because you're driven, you're hard working, you're tenacious, you don't take no for an answer, you keep pushing – and perhaps there are enthusiastic folk who get pulled along in your slipstream. However, your organisation will get to a point where there's a need for strategic leadership – doing everything yourself can only get you so far. You have to slow down to speed up. It's like transitioning from being a two-finger typist to a ten-digit typist. Beyond a certain point, the name of the game becomes finding the right people to join your bigger-than-you cause and harnessing their collective talents and industry to make an impact on the world.

Your biggest roadblock to on-going growth might just be you.

By the way, no one is interested in making you a rich person. You may become one, but that's a by-product of serving the world in some way. People don't follow you because they want to make you rich, they follow you because they feel inspired and want to be part of something significant and meaningful.

And neither is anyone interested in profits per se. Profits are an essential ingredient to fuel the growth of a business and to reward risk-taking investors. They're also a reflection of delivered value – how much you're positively impacting the world. Not to be profitable is a sin. However, profits aren't why people follow you.

If you're convinced that developing your leadership skills is a worthwhile commitment, how do you go about it? A good place to start is to assess where you are today. You could also get feedback from those around you, but in the first instance it's sufficient to simply carry out a self-assessment and create a simple improvement plan.

To carry out your self-assessment, it's helpful to breakdown leadership into different characteristics or skills. There are many definitions and lists of leadership qualities. On the following pages are leadership characteristics defined by two renowned experts, Napoleon Hill and John Maxwell.

Napoleon Hill's list of leadership qualities:

- **Courageous:** Courage to overcome our doubts and faith to overcome our fears.

- **Self-Controlled:** Drive our dark side into a corner and let our positive side flourish.

- **Justice:** Having and exercising a keen sense of justice.

- **Decisive:** Definiteness of decision. Indecision is the thief of opportunity. Make early decisions.

- **Planning:** Having definite plans.
- **Exceeding Expectations:** Doing more than you get paid for. Sowing seeds. Making an investment. Rendering the service with the vision of the future.
- **Pleasant:** Pleasing personality. Be attractive. The best gift you can give someone is your attention.
- **Sympathetic:** Having sympathy & understanding for others and their situations.
- **Detailed:** Having mastery of the details.
- **Responsible:** Willingness to accept full responsibility. What happened to me might not be my responsibility, but I am responsible for my reaction.
- **Cooperative:** If two or three agree then nothing is impossible. Position of honour, respect, influence.
- **Visionary:** That we can look further into the future than everyone else – the people will look to us for that.

John Maxwell's list of leadership qualities:

- **Character:** Choose based on values, even if the consequences are negative; walk your talk; don't compromise or cut corners; face the music and apologise sincerely for wrongs; do the right thing, even if no one is looking.
- **Charisma:** Embrace life with passion; appreciate others; help others; give others hope; share your wisdom, resources, time; focus on others; help others grow personally & professionally.
- **Commitment:** The measure of commitment is action; set goals, commit & pay the price until they're achieved; avoid blaming others, making excuses, criticising or condemning.
- **Communication:** Take the complex and make it simple; connect with people; be convicted; be direct and to the point; meet people where they're at; walk in their shoes.
- **Competence:** Be responsible; always be learning & improving; consistently perform at a high level; focus; be demanding of yourself; go the extra mile; inspire others to excellence.

- **Courage:** Face your fears and do it anyway; stand up for what you believe is right; take risks; feel uncomfortable; courage is contagious

- **Discernment:** Find the root cause of the issue or problem; listen to your gut (bodily intelligence); analyse successes and failures to discover the essential ingredients; discover the essence of things.

- **Focus:** Learn to concentrate; learn mastery; focus on strengths; focus on learning & improvement; focus on major things; focus on priorities; identify & eliminate distractions & weaknesses.

- **Generosity:** Recognise what you have; be thankful for what you have; put people before tasks & things; share; give; treat money as a resource; invest in something that will outlive you; mentor someone.

- **Initiative:** Know what you aspire to; take action; take risks; make mistakes; change your mindset; find opportunities; make opportunities; keep trying; go again.

- **Listening:** Connect with people; learn from every interaction; listen to your people, your suppliers, your clients; meet people on their turf; find common ground; be perceptive & listen to what's not said.

- **Passion:** Find what makes you feel alive, where you don't notice time passing; cultivate a strong desire for your cause or purpose; love life.

- **Positive Attitude:** Choose to see opportunity in everything; cultivate a 'can do' outlook; be cheerful and pragmatically optimistic; expect good outcomes; be wholehearted in thought and action.

- **Problem Solving:** Be tenacious; learn to be creative; anticipate; accept the situation; see the bigger picture; see the opportunity; be methodical; focus on your goal; focus on the solution; listen to others; keep positive.

- **Relationships:** Learn to understand people; love people; be accepting of the person (but not necessarily their behaviour or actions); help people; take the first step; be honest & sincere; meet people where they're at.

- **Responsibility:** Work hard; go the extra mile; look in the mirror when things go wrong; avoid blaming, criticising, condemning; don't make excuses; own up; hang in there; get better; respond positively .

- **Security:** Be comfortable in your own skin; develop confidence in your ability to survive & prosper; keep things in proportion; be honest and straight forward; be genuine with everyone you meet; be authentic.

- **Self-Discipline:** Lead yourself; set & follow priorities; major on major things; be consistent; do what you have to do even when you don't want to; focus on outcomes; do what it takes, however long it takes.

- **Servanthood:** Serve others, whoever they are; be humble; enhance the lives of others; cultivate a service mentality and attitude; help other people; take the time to see & understand the needs of others.

- **Teachability:** Keep moving, keep learning, keep growing; read & listen; aim to become an expert; admit & learn from mistakes; identify excellence in others & learn from them; focus on your strengths; love learning.

- **Vision:** See further ahead than others; take time out to create the bigger picture; speak clearly & passionately about a better future; paint a vivid picture with clear, strong words; be insightful; see what others don't.

Exercise: Leadership development

- Pick one of these two lists (or create your own by picking the characteristics you think are important from both lists).
- Give yourself a score out of ten for how you believe you're performing against each characteristic.
- Pick one or two characteristics – no more – that you'd like to improve. Pick one with a relatively high score and one with a low score. If you only want to work on one characteristic, pick the one with the high score. You'll make more progress by developing a strength. Go with your gut and pick ones that you're excited about improving. Excitement is an important ingredient when you're creating a personal improvement plan.
- Think about improving your score out of ten by just one point. You may want to get to a ten, but if you're currently at four, ten is a long way off. But five is doable.
- Note the benefits of improving in the area(s) you've picked.

CONTINUED

- What will people see, notice or experience as a result of your improvement (the evidence)?
- To increase by one point, think about what you might do more of or start doing? And what you might do less of or stop doing?
- How can you implement these ideas? Keep initial actions small and easy.
- What might go wrong or get in the way of making the improvements? How can you reduce the likelihood of these things getting in the way? And what will you do if they do go wrong?

Use this style of template to capture your scores and planned actions:

Leadership Qualities		Score	Start Doing/Stop Doing/ More of/Less of
1	Courageous		
	Courage to overcome our doubts and faith to overcome our fears.		
2	Self-Controlled		
	Drive our dark side into a corner and let our positive side flourish.		
3	Justice		
	Having and exercising a keen sense of justice.		
4	Decisive		
	Definiteness of decision. Indecision is the thief of opportunity. Make early decisions. They're vitally important. New decision to correct bad decisions.		
5	Planning		
	Having definite plans.		

6	Exceeding Expectations		
	Doing more than you get paid for. Sowing seeds. Making an investment. Rendering the service with the vision of the future.		
7	Pleasant		
	Pleasing personality. Be attractive. The best gift you can give someone is your attention.		
8	Sympathetic		
	Having sympathy & understanding for others and their situations.		
9	Detailed		
	Having mastery of the details.		
10	Responsible		
	Willingness to accept full responsibility. What happened to me might not be my responsibility, but I am responsible for my reaction.		
11	Cooperative		
	If 2 or 3 agree then nothing is impossible. Position of honour, respect, influence.		
12	Visionary		
	That we can look further into the future than everyone else – the people will look to us for that.		

This process of:
- breaking a skill into its constituent parts;
- self-scoring;
- aiming for small improvements in only one or two areas;
- committing to daily actions;
- and thinking through what might hinder progress and how to deal with hindrances if they happen;

is a process that can be applied to many areas of your personal development and business development. Consider using this tool and technique with your team or in other areas of your business.

Humility as a leader

One characteristic that is surprisingly missing from these lists of leadership characteristics is humility. Being willing to accept you do not know it all; far, far from it. Being self-assured; but not proud. Not seeking the limelight; but shining a light for others. To know that silence can be more powerful than a torrent of words. That willingness to put others first. To service above self. Being comfortable in your own skin. True humility is powerful and attractive. From humility comes leadership. Do you want to add *humility* to your list of leadership characteristics?

> *With the greatest leader above them,*
> *People barely know one exists.*
> *Next comes one they love and praise.*
> *Next comes one whom they fear.*
> *Next comes one whom they despise and defy.*
> *When a leader trusts no one, no one trusts them.*
> *The great leader speaks little.*
> *They never speak carelessly.*
> *They work without self-interest and leave no trace.*
> *When all is finished, the people say,*
> *"We did it ourselves."*

17TH VERSE OF THE TAO TE CHING BY LAO TSU. (WAYNE DYER. CHANGE YOUR THOUGHTS, CHANGE YOUR LIFE.)

From the whirlwind that created and grew your business, you will transition progressively into the servant-leader who will facilitate, enable, grow and encourage others to work collaboratively to do far more than you could ever do alone. Emotional intelligence, coaching, relationship building, identifying potential, and developing talent will become increasingly valuable skills.

Servant leadership isn't soft, fluffy and nice. You're still fully responsible. You still have to make tough decisions. You still have to let people go when they're not up to the job or transgress the company's values.

Servant leadership isn't popular. The world loves and encourages glitz, glamour and popularity. It seems to encourage and reward competing and comparison, winning and being number one. And then, for some bizarre reason, tearing those people down – which isn't too hard if those accolades and accomplishments are built on sand.

> **Compare yourself to who you were yesterday,**
> **not to who someone else is today.**
> JORDAN PETERSON. (RULE FOUR FROM HIS 'TWELVE RULES FOR LIFE' BOOK.)

Focusing on strengths and managing weaknesses

Within your role, there will be things you're good at and things you're not so good at. You may be tempted to think that your priority is to fix the things you're not so good at. That can be important and merits some attention. However, what's more important is developing what you're good at. Disciplined and well directed effort invested in your talents will produce high skill levels in that area – and you'll enjoy the development process. By contrast, the same time and effort invested in what you're not so good at might just get you to okay or average – and the process will be a grind.

Often parents, teachers and managers encourage us to fix what we're not so good at. You come home from school with a report that shows three As, two Bs, and an E. Which subject gets most attention? Your E. Or you have an appraisal and the six aspects of your role get scores of three nines, two eights and a three. Which area does the conversation revolve around? Your three. It is important to talk about your three, and how it might become a four or a five. But it's more important to invest time talking about developing your eights and nines. That will impact you and the organisation far more.

Always put your energy and attention where you'll get the greatest return and work on what you're good at. As a by-product, your weaknesses will become less and less relevant.

Bear in mind that a weakness is only a weakness if it adversely affects how you carry out your role. You may not be good at spreadsheets and feel you should be better because everyone else in the office are real whizzes. If you rarely need to create a spreadsheet, why bother? And if you did need to create one it sounds like there's someone in the office who'd love to help. Finding someone who loves doing what you're not so good at is one good way of managing your weaknesses.

When it comes to your weaknesses, it's unlikely that you'll ever turn them into strengths. So, don't try. Aim to manage your weaknesses. That might mean getting good enough to be average or passable. Or it might mean delegating or outsourcing that element of your role. As you build your team, think about how people's strengths (including yours) blend together and make individual weaknesses irrelevant.

Put some effort into managing your weaknesses but put most of your energy and effort into developing your strengths.

Developing helpful habits

Life tends to become a series of routines. What you do becomes habitual. And for good reason. Routines and habits are efficient. You don't have to expend energy thinking. You can operate on autopilot.

What negatively impacts our performance usually isn't something which needs a transformational change, it's small, ingrained and unhelpful ways of working. And behind those ways of working, ingrained and unhelpful ways of thinking. These sometimes go back to your childhood and the influence of parents, teachers and peers. You don't have to psychoanalyse where they come from – although that might be interesting and helpful – you just have to recognise that if they've been around for that long, they may take some time to undo and replace. To improve, you have to change, and to change you have to break out of those old habits and routines and establish new ways of working.

The process steps of a habit

A habit is an unconscious, automatic, repeating behaviour or action. It's a process with these elements:

- Trigger
- Desire
- Action
- Reward

For example, you see a glass of water on your desk (trigger). You immediately feel a little thirsty (desire). You take a drink (action). You swallow the water and feel refreshed, and realise you were thirsty (reward).

The habits you label as good tend to have a longer-term benefit but involve some pain in the short-term. Bad habits have a short-term benefit but often have long-term negative consequences. A classic example is cigarette smoking.

What you do daily compounds over time.

Creating a picture of your ideal future self

Whilst you may be accepting of who you are today, everyone has a picture of a better self tomorrow. It's a natural human desire to keep growing into a better version. If you want to improve and grow, the first step is to become more observant and more self-aware. To start noticing your habitual thoughts and actions. However, that's hard – you have blind spots. Ask someone else to study your habits – those repeating daily actions – and determine if they're moving you towards or away from your better future self. In fact, you could invite your future self to walk alongside you and judge what you do – and what you're about to do!

Exercise: Creating an image of your future better self

- List your relationships and roles (leader, father, sister, son, colleague, friend, trustee, etc.). You can pick just your work role if you wish, although the habits that impact one area of your life tend to affect every area of your life.
- Imagine it's 12 months' time (or five years' time – you choose the time frame). Describe the better version of you in each of your roles.
- What are you doing?
- Who are you with?
- What's your health like?
- What are your energy levels like?
- What's your attitude like?
- What contribution are you making?
- How are you helping people?
- What disposable income have you got?
- How are you feeling?

Exercise: Critique your current activities and routines

- Invite your future self to look at what you're doing on a regular basis each day.
- List the habits that are moving you towards the vision of your future self.
- List the habits that are hindering your improvement and progress.
- Perhaps keep your future-self alongside you as you move through your day. Be aware that they're watching what you're about to do. Will they approve or not!?
- Notice your thoughts and behaviours. Become more observant. Become self-aware.

Everything you do is either moving you towards or moving you away from – there isn't any neutral.

Exercise: Breaking your habits into their constituent parts

- For each good and bad habit, observe and understand the process.
- What's the trigger? What's the environment like? Are you with someone in particular? What are you doing? How are you feeling?
- What desire does the trigger precipitate? (This can happen very fast and can be subtle.)
- What do you do?
- What's the benefit?

Once you observe your bad habits and break them down into process steps, they lose a great deal of their power. You can remove or avoid their triggers. You can also articulate their long-term consequences, another tactic for breaking their hold. If the trigger does occur, you can create and plan a different process. Often what's required is just a second or two to arrest that automatic response and replace it with a better alternative. Typically, it's best to replace bad habits with good ones, rather than trying to eradicate them in isolation.

You may believe that willpower and motivation would be key ingredients in creating your ideal future self. Ironically, they're overrated and can't be relied upon. Sometimes you feel like performing at your best – and other times you don't. The beauty of habits is that they happen automatically. You create your own playbook to ensure you do those small, daily helpful actions without thinking about it.

Starting small

By making the new habit simple, small and easy to do you are more likely to stay motivated. Initially, you don't have to be concerned about your results, just about repeating the action. More reps and bigger weights can come later. Start small, so small it's easy to succeed. Have a big dream for yourself – but start small.

The small seed of a new habit needs decent soil if it's to grow. Environment is probably the most powerful factor in establishing a new habit and replacing an unhelpful one. Your aim is to create a fertile environment that gives your new behaviours the best chance of germinating and flourishing. The opposite is true for bad habits. You want to adapt your environment to reduce the temptation of bad habits reoccurring.

If you want to eat more healthily, put a bowl of apples on your desk. If you want to eat less chocolate, take it out of your drawer and put it in the bin. If you must have chocolate somewhere, perhaps keep it on top of the cupboards in the staff kitchen. These tactics don't guarantee that you'll eat apples and not eat chocolate – it just increases the likelihood that this will happen. What you're doing is reducing the number of steps to performing the desired habit. And increasing the number of steps needed to carry out the unhelpful habit.

If you want to write one customer proposal every day, your close down routine the evening before might include leaving a pile of unanswered customer proposals in the middle of your desk and clearing everything else off your desk.

Another tactic is to insert a new habit into an existing routine. The established routine acts as a natural trigger. If you wanted to do some strength training, you might decide that every time you clean your teeth, you'll do some press ups. You might also stick a 'Press Ups' note on the mirror. Perhaps you even stick two neon-coloured vinyl handprints on the bathroom floor. And you'd make it easy – you'd only do three. And then four. And then five.

Perhaps you decide you'd like to interact with colleagues more often. Currently you go and make a cup of coffee when you've finished a piece of work. Rather than walking directly to the brew room, you'll walk a slightly longer route and speak to someone on the way. You might leave a reminder note saying 'Relationships' on the drinks coaster on your desk. And to make it easy, you'd only initially commit to a brief conversation with one member of the team each day.

It can be helpful to have a reward for carrying out a new behaviour. Make the reward proportional. It can be as simple as a cup of coffee when those prospect calls are made; saying 'well done' to yourself when you've acknowledged a member of staff; or putting a pleasing 'tick' on your daily press-up tick sheet. A monitor or tick sheet is a good mechanism for tracking and rewarding the performance of a new behaviour. Once you've completed your new behaviour a few times, you'll like the look of that string of ticks and you'll want to keep the pattern going. Your tick sheet can become a strong driver of your new behaviour so keep it somewhere visible. Occasionally you'll miss a day. And that's fine – you're only human. Just start again tomorrow.

Tick sheets are not just a good tracking and reward mechanism, they're visual evidence that you're changing. You might not see any improvements in your results yet, but that doesn't matter. The results will come.

After environment, the second most powerful tactic for creating new habits is planning where, when and with whom you'll do your new activity and scheduling it in your calendar. Again, it's not a guarantee you'll do it – but it increases the odds that you will. Scheduling reduces the need for motivation and willpower. You're more likely to keep commitments that are in your calendar.

If it's an activity that can be done with someone else, having an accountability partner also increases the likelihood you'll follow through. If someone you know in a different team is also going to phone five prospects before eleven each morning, you can agree to meet for a coffee mid-morning and share how you got on. And it doesn't have to be same activity. You could have your one proposal to write and they could have their five potential customers to call.

When planning anything, it's good to think about what might go wrong. Tell the story of how you didn't do what you intended. Identify specifically what tripped you up. Once you've flushed out the potential stumbling blocks, think about how you'll reduce the likelihood of those things happening (your mitigating actions); and what you'll do if it does happen (your plan B). You want to write a customer proposal first thing every morning. Perhaps team members regularly pop their head around the door with a problem or crisis. You could keep your door closed. You could tell the team you'll be available to answer questions and deal with issues at ten thirty. You could write your proposal at a (quiet) coffee shop on your way to the office. If it really is a crisis that requires you, your plan B could be to also schedule proposal writing between two and three each afternoon. If you don't need that time, you have an extra hour in your afternoon to do something else – perhaps working with your team on crisis prevention strategies.

It's likely that changing one habit has a knock-on impact on other aspects of your behaviour. For example, you start going for a half hour walk every lunchtime; you start eating better and drinking more water; you feel more relaxed and more energised; you're more positive and encouraging in your interactions with people in the office, etc. You'll find that some new habits become a catalyst for the adoption of other helpful habits. These are foundational habits.

At what point can you say that your new daily behaviours have become habitual? That will depend on what the behaviour is, the circumstances or environment, and you. Most habits certainly take longer than the often cited 21 days – probably two to three months is more likely. Personal experience suggests that good, new behaviours never become 100% habitual. It's possible to slip after many years of doing something on a daily basis. It's best to remain aware and vigilant at all times.

Other self-management techniques

Being driven to maximise your potential and being ambitious are worthy objectives but they may bring stresses and strains to life if not kept in check. In closing this section, here are three tools that will help in stabilising and sustaining your growth and strengthening your resilience.

Resilience

Resilience is that ability to prevail through a difficulty or setback. You inherently have greater depths of toughness than you imagine. The irony is that you don't know what resilience you have until you're in a situation where you need it. You've got this far in life and survived.

> *Shit happens.*
>
> CONNIE EBLE

Exercise: Remember the tough times

- What tough times have you faced in business and in life so far?
- Did you survive?
- What have you learnt about yourself when you look at those situations?

Having the evidence that you've survived and come back from difficulties in the past will empower you to cope with difficult situations in the present and the future.

You can think of resilience at the business level and the personal level.

The world is a tough place and periodically bad stuff happens that is not of your making. A recession or a global pandemic are not of your making but will make business life extremely tough. Accept that large scale business interruptions will happen in the future. One of the central themes of this book is 'take action now'. It's vital to react quickly and decisively when a crisis hits. However, being prepared is more important.

Part of being prepared means having a plan B – the result of thinking through what you'd do in the face of major business interruption.

Another part of being prepared comes from having a business built on solid foundations. An aim of this book is to encourage you to put foundations in place that will support you when the waters rise and the flood comes. Foundations such as strong leadership, robust systems, good people, clear vision and purpose, lived-out values, healthy numbers (and cash reserves), etc. It takes time and some of it isn't glamourous.

In the case of a personal crisis, the situation can be made far worse by having a weak business that quickly flounders without your close attention. By contrast, a strong business built on rock won't alleviate your situation directly, but it won't exacerbate it either.

Exercise: Your crisis team

- Which of your team would you like to have around you in a crisis?
- Through incompetence, a weak character or malevolence, which of your team might actually make the situation worse?
- What might you want to do about that?
- Which of your family and friends would you like to have around you in a crisis?
- Who could you confidently and confidentially talk to in a business or personal crisis?
- Have you taken out critical illness or key man business insurance?

In the same way that business resilience is built day by day and step by step, so too is personal resilience. Parents may have helped in the process by exposing you to danger and risk in a controlled setting, preparing you for life in a risk-filled world.

When your child runs towards a tree, do you shout, "Be careful. Don't fall." Or do you shout, "See how high you can climb!"?

Regardless of your upbringing, as an adult you can now deliberately start to climb your own trees.

Exercise: Building resilience

- Sit down for a few minutes each day and think about what feels difficult or fearful at the moment. (e.g. phoning a customer who owes you money; speaking to a team member about not meeting your expectations; thanking a colleague for doing their job well; calling a supplier and asking for better terms; rather than instinctively saying yes, explaining to a client why you can't do something; saying no to a colleague; going home at four o'clock; admitting to someone that you're struggling with something; admitting that you got something wrong; complimenting a stranger.)
- Bite the bullet and, as an experiment, just do it. Notice how it felt and what the outcome was. How did it compare to the thoughts you had beforehand?

Whilst you have a natural quotient of resilience, this asset can be developed and strengthened. These approaches will help build your personal resilience:

- Become an optimistic realist. If things are bad, they're bad. Don't put a positive spin on it or think that the situation is suddenly going to resolve itself. However, know that you will get through it, regardless of how long it takes.

- Don't avoid the tough conversations. Deal with things when they're small and manageable.

- Keep things in order and well maintained. Don't put off until tomorrow the things that need sorting today. If there's lots that needs dealing with, each day start with something that's small and easy and build from there.

- Keep yourself in good physical shape. Pay proper attention to your nutrition. Get proper rest on a regular basis.

- Build up some savings. Delay gratification – sacrifice some of the present for the future.

- Keep enhancing your skills. Learn to be adaptive, changing your mind and your plans.

- Get into the habit of setting goals, both big and small. Have an aim for yourself – and for your life. A bigger picture goal can help put periodic crises into proper context.

- Develop the habit of taking action.

- Surround yourself with supporters – people who want the best for you; people who'll be there for you in a crisis. Cut the people out of your life who don't build you up.

- Find some people you can be honest with and can confide in. Practise sharing your fears and vulnerabilities with them.

- Practise asking for help on a regular basis.

- Don't be scared but be vulnerable. Tell people what you find difficult and challenging and how you're working through it. And if you don't know how you're going to work through it, be honest and tell them: "I don't know. Yet."

- When things are really, really bad, everybody prays. If there really is a powerfully benevolent and loving force in this universe, ask for strength and guidance. Asking for help is a characteristic of the strong.

If other people have survived, so can you. And most worries and fears never come to pass. Remember to encourage your children to climb trees. And find your own trees to climb.

Humans have a unique and amazing ability to picture a future and to then create that future. This powerful faculty is useful when it focuses on a good future. However, when it focuses on a bad future, it can cause distraction, paralysis, and even illness. It may even bring what is feared into reality. Persistently held thoughts have a habit of becoming real.

Another benefit of becoming more self-aware is to catch the concerns that float into your head. Then you can do something about them. Activity will starve many of your fears of the oxygen they need to survive and grow. Simply 'getting back to work' is a good strategy.

Writing down your fears is a useful exercise. You can then categorise them and generate a solution for each. The mere act of writing them down is often sufficient for some of them to evaporate. Next time that thought pops into your head, imagine writing it down, staring at it, and watching it evaporate away – or whatever works for you.

Certain concerns are real but are out of your control (e.g., a recession). You can dedicate a proportion of your planning time to creating a contingency plan for this eventuality.

Other concerns are real and are in your control. You can dispel your fears by doing something about it: State what the issue is; diagnose the root cause; create a solution; implement. Name it and deal with it. Take action.

Feel the fear and do it anyway.
SUSAN JEFFERS

Catch yourself thinking negatively about the past. The past is the past. Take the lesson – and then leave the past in the past. You should have one foot in the present and one foot in the future.

Gratitude

It's a natural human instinct to make things better. However, society and culture have taken this to another level. Accelerated and fuelled by advertising in its many forms, the pursuit of more and better has become intoxicating. Being ambitious is healthy. Blindingly pursuing more, in the vain hope that it will bring more happiness, isn't.

Learn to be both ambitious and content.
JIM ROHN

Scientific studies show that being grateful makes you happier. A by-product of looking at what you're grateful for also highlights things that bring you deep-down joy. (Happiness can be thought of as the ocean surface, susceptible to winds and storms; joy is much deeper and less disturbed by the ups and downs of life.)

In terms of boosting your happiness, being grateful is a remarkably easy thing to do. Far easier than earning enough money to buy a new car – although that can be fun too. Being grateful can also increase your ability to delay gratification. i.e. more able to invest in the present for a benefit in the future, rather than doing what is easy, expedient and pleasurable in the present but not as beneficial in the longer term.

You simply need five minutes a day, a pen, and a piece of paper. Actually, investing in a small notebook would be good. It's useful to periodically flick back through your gratitude notebook, especially when life's storms are battering you. If it helps, schedule your five-minute gratitude exercise in your calendar, with a reminder. Or use the trigger technique. When you're having your morning coffee, spend five minutes jotting down what you're grateful for. Or incorporate the exercise into your work close down routine.

Thinking about what you're grateful for is good. Writing down those things is more powerful and profound. As with other ideas in this book, try this exercise for a month. You have to give new things a sufficient period to determine if the results are beneficial. Trying something just once doesn't cut it.

Exercise: Gratitude

Spend five minutes answering one of these questions. Perhaps pick a different question each time you sit down to write in your notebook.

- What good things happened today?
- Which relationships are you grateful for?
- Who said thank you to you or smiled at you today?
- What are some of the things you take for granted that people in other parts of the world don't have?
- Within five minutes of waking up this morning, what were you grateful for? (perhaps 'waking up' is the first thing on your list!)
- What did you see (or hear, or smell, or taste, or touch) today that was beautiful?
- What would you miss if it disappeared from your life?
- What do you appreciate about your job (in addition to the fact that you have one)?
- What are you grateful for about your health?
- When has good fortune shone on you recently?
- What are you grateful for about your home?
- What are you grateful for about your family?

CONTINUED

- As you sit here now, what can you see or hear that you're grateful for?
- What made you laugh or smile today?
- What are you grateful for about the country you live in?
- What are the things you got done today that you're grateful for?
- What things are you grateful for that didn't cost you a penny?

Alternatively, you may just want to answer the following question:
- The three things I'm grateful for today are...

This is a powerful exercise to also play around the dinner table, especially with children. Introducing them to the concepts of gratitude, appreciation, and thanks is a wonderful life skill. Children are also good at turning questions on their inquisitors so it's a neat way of introducing some accountability for you. Perhaps your children might also benefit from the regular habit of noting down what they're grateful for too. Start good habits early.

Exercise: Review your gratitude notebook

- When you look back through your notebook, what are the things that bring you real joy?
- How might you show appreciation for these things?
- How might you increase the intensity or frequency of these things?
- How will you protect the things you're grateful for and not lose sight of them?

Whilst you're reflecting on what you've written, or even as you're writing on a regular basis, you might want to show your gratitude for what you already have. You might want to make a regular donation to a water sanitation project in a poor country, or simply say thank you to someone who has helped you or who is always there for you. Saying thank you is good. Writing 'thank you' has far more impact for the recipient and for you, so send them a note or card.

Exercise: Thank you

- Send a postcard to someone who's done something for you and say thank you. Tell them how they've helped you and what the impact has been.

Again, another good life skill for children.

Rest

Whilst it's important to punctuate the hours in your day with regular energy-boosting breaks and to have a good night's sleep, it's also important to have at least one day's rest each week. Whoever came up with the idea of working for six days and resting for one was on to something good.

If you must get the laptop out over the weekend or pop into the office to clear a few things up, schedule it and keep it time bound – don't just drift into it and do bits and pieces all over the weekend. Perhaps get up early on a Saturday, get in the office for seven and work until eleven. Set a timer so you leave on time. And then leave your laptop at work. Perhaps you dedicate 60 minutes every Sunday at 7:30pm to preparing for the week ahead. That will reduce the likelihood of you lying in bed on a Sunday evening thinking (worrying) about the week ahead.

A break of at least 24 hours from doing, talking about, and thinking about work will help restore your energy levels and give you a clearer, fresher mind when you return.

Ideally your day of rest isn't a day of utter collapse and hibernation because you're exhausted. It could be a day of celebration; a day of activities that feed your soul; a day to look back with satisfaction on a week where you've worked hard and given your best. Your day of rest could be a day that you look forward to as if it was a birthday or anniversary or Christmas Day. A day like that needs a little bit of forethought and planning. Spontaneous things can be fun but generally planned things are better. You don't want to be nipping to the supermarket because there's not enough food in the house or discovering that your friends can't come around for a barbecue because they've already got plans. Remember that the purpose of your rest day is to restore body and soul, not to see how many adrenalin-fuelled activities you can cram in. You want more energy, not less. It's likely that activities will be simple, family orientated, and home based. Good food, chatter and laughter; reading a good book; garden games or board games; walking or cycling; family film night. As time goes on, less planning will be required. You (and your family) will have discovered the things that bring joy and restore your souls, and your day of rest will become a wonderful routine. (Depending on where you live, it's probably good to have dry and wet weather options.)

Occasionally you might have to throw an all-nighter or work over a weekend, but if you're doing this on a regular basis there's something wrong – something wrong with your business model or something wrong with how you've got things set up.

Exercise: Planning a day of restoration

- Plan a great one-off day (24-hour period – it can start one evening and finish the following evening if you wish) for a particular weekend this month.
- What simple things would you really look forward to?
- What will you definitely not do?
- Who else will be involved? What will they love to do? Should they be involved in planning this day?
- What will you need to prepare in advance?
- What rules might you need in place to ensure your day is not disturbed and you're not distracted? (phones, television, etc.)

As is mentioned throughout this book, it's best to start modestly. Ironically, for you and your family, doing fewer things, but more exciting things, will get you off to a good start. It's also good to have a review a few days later: What did everyone like? What might you do differently next time to make it even better? Commit to doing three or four. By then you should have developed sufficient momentum to keep going.

Meditation

Stress is not only energy-sapping, it can be debilitating and physically and psychologically harmful. Meditation is an antidote to stress and it can be used in a preventative way.

Some stress is good. You need stress and tension to form and develop your character. You need something to push against to get stronger. Stress becomes a problem when it's incessant, excessive and out of your control. Then it becomes strain – something that depletes you and may even break you.

There have now been many clinical trials to show that meditation has restorative physiological benefits that counteract the harmful effects of stress. Check out the work of Dr Herbert Benson (a cardiovascular surgeon and Harvard professor) and The Relaxation Response meditation.[1]

You'll need 15 minutes (daily ideally), a quiet space, one word or phrase, and the ability to breathe. Ironically, breathing isn't quite as simple as it sounds – but it is the solution to many problems.

Exercise: Eliciting the Relaxation Response (Herbert Benson)

- Sit quietly in a comfortable position.
- Close your eyes.
- Relax all your muscles, beginning at your feet and progressing up to your face. Keep them relaxed. Relax your tongue and thoughts will cease.
- Breathe through your nose. Become aware of your breathing. As you breathe out, say a word or short phrase silently to yourself. For example, breathe in, and then out, and say a phrase or word. (Thank you, peace, love, compassion, etc.) Breathe easily and naturally.
- Continue for 10 to 20 minutes. You may open your eyes to check the time, but do not use an alarm. When you finish, sit quietly for several minutes, at first with your eyes closed and later with your eyes opened. Do not stand up for a few minutes.
- Do not worry about whether you are successful in achieving a deep level of relaxation. Maintaining a passive attitude will permit relaxation to occur at its own pace.
- When distracting thoughts occur (and they will), simply say silently, "oh well". Let the thoughts go and return to repeating your word or phrase.

---

1 https://hbr.org/1974/07/your-innate-asset-for-combating-stress

Summary

You are your most important job and your business's biggest opportunity. Prioritise learning how to manage yourself well and develop your leadership skills.

> *Don't wish it was easier. Wish you were better. Work harder on yourself than you do on your job.*
>
> JIM ROHN

As a business leader, you're principally concerned with the future. Yes, you'll have urgent and important things you need to address today, but in principle your role is about seeing, creating, and planning for the future of your business. Your people want to know that they'll have a job this time next year, ideally one that involves engaging work that makes a positive impact on the world, but first and foremost they want to know they'll have a salary and can pay their bills.

Schedule regular and repeating sessions in your calendar when you'll focus on your development. When you carry out your quarterly business planning sessions (as detailed in the Planning chapter), it's helpful to review your personal development and create a quarterly personal development plan as part of that process.

Dedicate time outside of the working day to learning – reading books, listening to audios, attending webinars, speaking with other entrepreneurs and businesspeople who are more experienced than you.

Work with a business coach who will increase your knowledge, challenge you, and hold you accountable. Alternatively, find an accountability partner. Consider joining a group of like-minded, ambitious businesspeople – a mastermind group.

You will become like the people you spend most time with. Choose consciously and carefully who you spend time with.

Put a commercial value on what you do. Over time, increase your commercial value by letting go of low-value tasks and focusing on higher value tasks.

Decide on the date when your business will be complete. And smile to yourself when you realise you've made the mental transition from technician to business owner.

Discover what your strengths are and focus on developing those. Within the context of your role and responsibilities, understand what you're not so good at and learn to manage those areas.

Become aware of your energy levels. Direct your focus and energy towards your most important tasks. Learn what and who restores your energy. And who depletes it. And manage yourself accordingly.

Recognise that success often isn't down to grand strategies – it comes down to being disciplined about consistently and diligently doing simple things well on a daily basis. Recognise the power of habits. Become self-aware. Recognise which habits are helpful and serve you well – and which ones don't. Start the process of replacing the unhelpful ones with helpful ones.

Like everyone else, you are not the finished article. You have potential. Your most important job is to draw out that potential and keep growing as a leader and a business owner. Keep that image of your future ideal self alongside you.

You live in an abundant world. Embrace and serve it with confidence and to the best of your ability. There's more money out there than you can ever imagine. And there's a great need for more joy and less suffering in the world. There's plenty of opportunity for you to realise your full potential as you strive to make your contribution.

Checklist Exercise: Leadership

The following checklist exercise will be helpful in identifying the progress you've made and in selecting the areas you want to focus on next. Review this checklist once a quarter as part of your quarterly planning process.

- Put a tick in the 'DONE' column for those items you already do or are happy with.
- Make a second pass through the checklist and highlight those things that you'd 'LIKE TO' work on next.
- For each 'LIKE TO' item that you've highlighted:
  » What benefits that will come from completing it (or what consequences will be avoided)? Jot down the benefits (in your planning notebook).

CONTINUED

» How excited do you feel about cracking on with this activity? Score your level of excitement out of 10 and put your score in the third column of the checklist.

» Prioritise your 'LIKE TO' activities based on their beneficial impact and how excited you feel about taking action now.

» Pick the one or two items from the top of your prioritised list and commit to making them a reality.

» What's the simplest action you can take right now to get moving?

• Put this book down and make a start (or if impractical at the moment, schedule the activity in your calendar).

Some of the items on the list are relatively straightforward and self-explanatory. Others will need a plan behind them and assistance from other people. The purpose of this exercise is to identify what improvement initiatives you feel motivated to commit to, and to encourage you to find a first, small, simple action step to get you going.

	LEADERSHIP	DONE	LIKE TO	EXCITED
	MINDSET	✓	✓	Out of 10
1	I'm aware that what I have in my life reflects my past thoughts, decisions & actions.			
2	I take 100% responsibility for what happens. I don't complain, blame or make excuses.			
3	I'm aware of my thoughts & beliefs and am replacing unhelpful ones with helpful ones.			
4	I push myself & accept that mistakes are an essential part of learning & growing.			
5	I constantly look to raise my standards and improve. I am a life-long learner.			
6	I have personal & professional ambitions & objectives which I've written down.			
7	I have shared my ambitions & objectives with my partner/family.			
8	I always ask, "What's my aim here?"			
9	I regularly ask for help.			

	YOUR ROLE	DONE	LIKE TO	EXCITED
10	I have a written a 'Result Expectations' statement for each role I fulfil in the business.			
11	I have reviewed & scored how I'm performing as a Leader in my business/work.			
12	I have a Leadership Development plan I'm working on.			
13	I'm aware of & am developing my strengths (and managing my weaknesses).			
14	I surround myself with inspiring people & mix with people I want to emulate.			
15	I have a coach who encourages, challenges, supports & holds me accountable.			

	SELF-MANAGEMENT	DONE	LIKE TO	EXCITED
16	At the end of the day, I create a short, prioritised list of key activities for tomorrow.			
17	The first 90-minutes of my day are spent working on my most important project.			
18	To avoid distractions, I have turned off notifications, email & phones.			
19	My important activities are scheduled in my calendar.			
20	I have scheduled time in my calendar to maintain my health, fitness & energy.			
21	I batch activities like email, calls & question-answering into certain timeslots.			
22	I have audited my activities & know how I spend my day/week.			
23	I've put a £ value against the activities I do (based on the cost to outsource them).			
24	I only do what only I can do & outsource or delegate less important tasks.			
25	To drive my productivity, I set a time-target for each activity.			
26	I 'grasp the nettle' & deal with unpleasant things early in the day (Eat that Toad).			
27	At the end of each week, I create a plan for the following week.			
28	I spend one-on-one time with my best performers & interact with others in meetings.			
29	I am becoming more self-aware & working on improving my self-management skills.			

	ENERGY MANAGEMENT	DONE	LIKE TO	EXCITED
30	I take regular breaks throughout my working day.			
31	I get at least seven hours' sleep and get up early.			
32	I take time off from work to rest, recuperate & reenergise.			
33	I drink water throughout the day and eat good nutritious food.			
34	I exercise regularly and make sure I get out into the fresh air.			
35	My physical environment is inspiring & distraction-free.			
36	I avoid people who drain me of energy & associate with people who give me energy.			
37	I minimise tasks that drain me of energy. I major on tasks I enjoy and am good at.			
38	I do the most important, high-value tasks when my energy levels are highest.			

	HABITS	DONE	LIKE TO	EXCITED
39	I'm aware of the unhelpful habits I'd like to replace with helpful ones.			
40	I've noted the long-term consequences of carrying on with my unhelpful habits.			
41	I've noted down the benefits of adopting new, helpful habits.			
42	I have a simple plan with small steps to establish my new helpful habits.			
43	I have a simple daily tick chart to record completion of my new behaviour/activity.			
44	I've created an environment that hinders unhelpful habits & encourages helpful ones.			
45	I have someone I respect & trust supporting me.			
46	When I stumble & fall, I know I can simply get up & start again tomorrow.			

	RESILIENCE, GRATITUDE, REST & MEDITATION	DONE	LIKE TO	EXCITED
47	I deal with small matters daily and avoid them accumulating into big issues.			
48	I live by the daily mantra that "Prevention is better than cure".			

49	I am developing a network of supportive friendships.			
50	When I need help, I ask for help. I've asked for help, even when I can struggle through.			
51	I take time on a regular basis to write down what I appreciate and am grateful for.			
52	I regularly say "thank you" to people.			
53	I regularly give time, money and support to people who need help.			
54	I have a planned day of personal restoration once a week.			
55	I meditate for 10 to 20 minutes each day.			

CHAPTER 2
Planning

Plans are nothing. Planning is everything.

DWIGHT D. EISENHOWER

On what date will the business you're building be complete? Most people don't know the answer. Or if they do answer, they mention the date of their 65th birthday – the date they're going to retire.

Many people are accidental entrepreneurs – they fell into business because it seemed like a good idea at the time or they were fed up with their boss or they were made redundant. The thought that they were creating something that would one day be completed didn't cross their minds. And if they did have that long-term ambition, it soon faded as the overwhelm of day-to-day business life crowded in and suffocated that dream.

You get so personally and emotionally invested in your business it can be difficult to separate you and it. But a business should be a separate entity. It should be something that you breathe life into, nurture as you might a child, and then set free to thrive in the world independent of you. You should be passionately invested in your business – but you should realise that your job is to equip it and develop it so that it can stand on its own two feet. And the job can – should – be done in less than the 18 years it takes to raise a child.

What does a business standing on its own two feet look like? Firstly, and critically, it can operate independently of you – or any other individual kingpin. Much of what it does is therefore driven by systems and processes. Much – but not all. You still need people operating those systems; people who will drive it forward, adapting its strategies and operations to changing market conditions and customer needs. It's profitable. It generates cash. It's running on a sound, credible business model (there's a market need for its products and/or services which can be sold for a profit). It's sustainable. It has potential – and a system for continuing to grow and realise that potential. It has an engaging and purposeful culture that attracts and retains good people.

What might you do when the business you're building is completed? Anything you like. You could sell it and sail around the world. You could appoint a General Manager, enjoy a passive income from it, and become non-executive Chairman. You could continue to direct and develop it. You could climb right back in where you started and engross yourself in the technical aspects of the business if that's your passion. Having built one business, you might just fancy doing it all again – incorporating all the lessons you learnt from building the first one. Once you've built a few businesses, you may become really good at it.

EXERCISE: Beginning with the end in mind

- On what date will the business you're building be complete? (Pick an actual date.)
- And what will your business look like when it is completed? Spend 10 minutes over coffee sketching out your dream finished business. (When you've finished sketching it out, perhaps fold up that piece of paper and tuck it away at the back of a drawer. When you find it one day, you might be surprised that your idle 10-minute thought experiment has become a reality. You wouldn't be the first.)

Take some time over the coming days and write exactly what your completed business will look like. This will put you ahead of 99% of business owners. You now know what you're aiming to create, and you'll recognise it when you see it.

This Planning chapter is a foundational block that will achieve two things:

Firstly, it will help you take the first steps in building an organisation that stands out from the crowd; that may even be unique in its chosen market niche, serving its specific customers, in its inimitable way. This will also help in attracting committed people who want to join you in building a business that has meaning and purpose at its heart.

Secondly, it will introduce you to a structure and system for translating your dreams and ambitions into action plans that will form a framework for sustainable growth.

More specifically, this chapter covers:

- **Vision:** Creating a company vision.
- **Purpose:** Articulating your organisation's purpose.
- **Values:** Defining your business's core values.
- **Business engine:** The economic model that will drive your business forward.
- **Business strategy:** The key practices that steer the long-term course of your business.

- **Organisational alignment:** Sharing your vision, purpose, values and business strategy with your people, engaging everyone and aligning the whole team to a common overall aim.

- **Organisational brainstorming:** A tool for engaging your team to generate the action plans that will deliver your business strategy and achieve your aims.

- **Planning:** The long, medium and short-term planning and implementation systems that translate a vision into tangible services, which are effectively and efficiently delivered, with the resulting and essential by-products of profits, cash and a good return on investment.

- **Meetings:** The place where you review progress, keep on track and clear roadblocks.

It's best to gain an overview of these elements initially – you don't have to immediately adopt and work through them all over the next few weeks.

Before getting into the nitty gritty of vision, purpose, values, business models and action planning, think about how you'll communicate these things to your team and at what point you'll involve them. Whilst you may write the score and conduct the orchestra, it's your team of players who'll do the implementing and turn your plans into a profitable reality. Therefore, you may wish to involve them in the process, particularly when it comes to the more tangible aspects such as action planning. Once these elements are complete, you'll want to align the whole team to ensure that everyone is bought into the same vision, purpose and values and signed-up to the same action plan.

Aligning your organisation

As leader, part of your role is to look outwards, understanding how the world is changing, what new challenges are rolling towards you, and what fresh opportunities are emerging. Your responsibility is to adapt your strategies and plans accordingly. As leader, your role is also to look inwards, winning hearts and minds to adopt and implement those new strategies and plans.

If you (and your senior team) have worked through an extended exercise of determining your vision, purpose and values, and have perhaps embarked on your first quarterly plan, you'll want to bring the rest of your organisation on board and align them in the direction you're now heading. Whilst you may not have changed course, you'll certainly be more focused and deliberate about the future course of your business. To maximise progress, you'll want everyone pulling together, and everyone doing so to the best of their ability.

Bring your whole organisation together and share your vision, purpose and values. Delivered with passion, this will have a profound impact on your team. It's unlikely they'll have been involved in this kind of session before. A stimulating alignment session is a great opportunity for people to get involved and contribute. Over and above that, you can't do this by yourself. You need everyone involved. Business is tough and you can't afford to carry anyone.

Having shared your business vision at the beginning of your alignment session, you may then want to use a facilitator to get the rest of the team engaged in feeding back on what they've heard; discussing how your vision translates into day-to-day organisational life; and how they can get involved in making it a living, breathing reality. When people come up with their own ideas and are allowed to be involved in the implementation of those ideas, they're more likely to be engaged and pick up the responsibilities for making things happen. The people at the sharp end know what real life is about and are therefore in the right position to contribute meaningfully in translating your vision into everyday actions.

How readily your people engage will depend on your organisational culture and their previous conditioning. It's sad but true; many people in many organisations have been conditioned to do what they're told and not to think or take initiative. It may take time to thaw ingrained attitudes. And it's your actions and behaviours that will do that, rather than your fine words, regardless of how genuine and authentic they are.

Having said that, some scepticism can be a good thing. If everyone sits there and nods, you might have a problem. Challenge is a good thing. And don't profess to have all the answers – you don't. If you don't know, say you don't know. Acknowledge the importance of the question. And ask the questioner what they think. However, if you're sincere about creating an inclusive and engaging workplace, you will win out over time.

The key output from the alignment session is a commitment from the people (actual names) in the room to run with some initiatives that will start turning thoughts (vision, purpose and values) into things (actions and results). It'll be important to understand what support and resources they'll need to help them. And there needs to be scheduled follow-up sessions to feedback on progress and to plan next steps. As mentioned elsewhere, start with a few, simple things.

Be aware of what you're unleashing through this initiative, and your responsibility for supporting your team. Your life will change but change for the better. You won't be doing this alone anymore.

When you decide to hold organisational alignment sessions will depend on your circumstances. As you embark on this journey of putting in place the foundational business blocks of vision, purpose and values, and establishing a routine of business planning, your team will sense that things are changing. It's best to share with them relatively early on what your intentions are and where you're up to. In essence, you're embarking on a journey to improve the business and make life better for everyone – that's a good news story for everyone. You don't need the perfect plan and you don't need all the answers, but you do need to be open, honest, and authentic and share your intentions with everyone. The aim of this exercise isn't just to align, it's to engage – whatever you may think and however they may have behaved in the past, deep down your team wants to be part of (and contribute to) something that's meaningful, challenging, and exciting.

Organisational brainstorming is an effective mechanism for engaging your team in generating improvement initiatives and taking responsibility for implementation. You can see how to do it at the end of the chapter.

A vision for your business

This is your picture of what the future looks like for your business. It pulls together how your organisation will look, who it'll be serving and benefiting, and how it'll be operating. It needs to be compelling and exciting. It should make the hairs on your neck stand up. It will serve to draw you towards it. In the eyes and ears of people who share the same values as you, who want to be part of something meaningful and purposeful, it will serve as a rallying call to be part of something far greater than a monthly pay cheque.

The job of creating the vision is initially yours. However, you may then wish to invite your team to respond and add more colour and brightness to your vision. Even if you don't invite them, you may find that at your organisational alignment session, your team are inspired and can't help but contribute to your picture of the future. Your vision has become your organisation's vision – which is what you want.

Vision is not about money, although turning your vision into a commercial reality and ultimately into cash is a necessity. But that's not why you're doing this. No one's going to join you and commit their best efforts for the purpose of making you rich. You may become rich, but one of the major reasons people will join you is because they want to be part of something exciting, something bigger than themselves.

The more you talk about your vision, the clearer it will become. The more you write your vision down, the clearer it will become. Something magical happens when you take ideas out of your head and put them down on paper and say them out loud.

How do I know what I think until I see what I say?

E. M. FORSTER

When it comes to sharing your vision with others, particularly your team, your passion and belief are vital ingredients. This will come across in how you share it. It is what you say – but it's also how you say it that communicates your authenticity, belief and conviction.

EXERCISE: Crafting your business vision

- Personally, why do you want to build this business? (When a well-paid job would be far easier.)
- How far ahead can you see? 5 years, 10 years, 20 years? (It needs to be far enough ahead that no one can argue with the impossibility of your dream.)
- What will be distinctive about the business you build?
- Who will it serve? With what products and services? How many customers will it serve? What will those customers look like?
- How will the business make your customers' lives better?

CONTINUED

113

- What will be special about how you do business?
- What will you be known for by your customers and competing businesses?
- Where will you be operating from (locally, regionally, nationally, internationally, globally)?
- How many people will be working in the business? What sorts of people will you employ? What do you want your employees to say about the business? How would you describe your culture?

These questions are designed to get you thinking. You can add whatever you like into your vision – it's your vision. After you've answered these questions, draft out a paragraph or two that starts to capture it. If it spills out over several pages, that's fine. You can refine it later.

After you've had a go at the other exercises in this section, come back to your draft vision and recraft it. Keep thinking about it and amending it until it feels...exciting. If you're not excited, it's unlikely that anyone else is going to be excited. And excitement and enthusiasm are fuel additives that will propel you forward further and faster.

You don't need to think about the 'how' of turning your vision into a reality – that comes later. This is the dream; the vision; the ideal.

The purpose of your business

Also known as mission, or cause, or core focus, or raison d'être. How do you make the world a slightly better place? More specifically, what do you do, who do you do it for, and how does it make their life better and brighter – even for just a moment? It is this that your customers value – what they will be willing to pay for. This exercise will build on the vision exercise you've been working on and will help clarify your purpose.

EXERCISE: Developing your purpose

- What specifically is the product and/or service you provide?
- What is the need, want, desire or opportunity that it satisfies?
- Who will benefit from using your product/service?
- More specifically, who are your ideal customers? And why? How would you describe your ideal customers?
- Why is your product and/or service such a good choice for your (ideal) customers?
- What's special or preferable about the way that you do business?
- Why will people choose to give you their hard-earned cash?
- What is it that makes you feel passionate about serving these people with your product/service in your own particular way?

Having sketched out answers to these questions, complete the following paragraph with a few draft sentences:

The business exists to...

After a break, come back to it and see which form of words resonate with you the most.

Be assured that your business has purpose and meaning. It exists – but currently its purpose may be hidden and require unearthing. The aim of this exercise is to discover it. If you start to feel it in your gut, it's a good indicator that you're on the right track.

Some businesses don't see their purpose because they're focused on the money. Paradoxically, money can be elusive when you focus on it. In business, money is a by-product of providing a valued service. When you provide a valued service, money is what you get in return. Focus on the service (valued by your customer); don't focus on the money. A customer values a service if it makes their life better in some way. Simplistically, this is usually relieving pain or increasing pleasure or happiness — in the present or the future. Understanding why someone wants to buy your products and service can help you determine your purpose.

There's a chance you feel that you don't have a worthy purpose or feel it's a little thin. You may want to establish a more significant purpose for the business you're creating. That's a bigger undertaking but will result in a bigger transformation of your business, and ultimately a better business that you enjoy far more.

Hold onto your purpose tightly, and your plans lightly.

Your business values

Also known as guiding principles, or culture, or ethos. It's highly likely that your organisational values will mirror your personal values. Your blend of values determines how you'll do business and how your organisation will be run. Think of values as the unchanging stars in the night sky that you steer your ship by. Or as true north, forever reliable when your need to set a course or make a directional decision. Where organisational values are ingrained and lived out authentically, there is hardly any need for rules and regulations.

Your values can be seen most clearly through what you say, the decisions you make, and how you act and behave. Once you've distilled and articulated your values it will become easier to make comfortable decisions and act in alignment with your values.

Becoming aware of your values and deliberately strengthening them – or becoming more aligned to them – has numerous benefits: increased mental strength, more energy, better attitude, more self-control, more connection, more compassion, less worry, increased pain tolerance, and increased perseverance.

If something is valuable, by definition, it's costly. Staying true to your values may be costly at times. It may mean letting go of a highly skilled member of the team, or ceasing doing business with a profitable customer, if it compromises a value that's integral to who you are as a person and as an organisation. If your top salesperson is less than honest in winning new business, do you reward them or let them go? If your best manager gets superb performance though fear and intimidation, do you reward them or let them go?

The next exercise will help you identify your values.

Exercise: Determining your values (part 1)

- Here are two lists of values — the first is a list of words which will serve as a prompt. However, values are best expressed as sentences. The second list gives you some examples. When you've completed the exercise, you can turn your values into sentences that are meaningful to you.
- Highlight the values in this list that immediately stand out for you.

List 1: Values (not definitive but a decent list.)

	Accountability		Curiosity		Harmony		Perceptiveness
	Accuracy		Daring		Health		Perseverance
	Achievement		Decisiveness		Helpfulness		Persistence
	Acknowledgement		Delight		Heroism		Personal growth
	Adaptability		Dependability		Holiness		Pleasure
	Adventure		Desire		Honesty		Poise
	Affection		Determination		Honour		Positive attitude
	Agility		Devotion		Hopefulness		Power
	Alertness		Dignity		Hospitality		Practicality
	Ambition		Diligence		Humility		Precision
	Anticipation		Discipline		Humour		Preparedness
	Appreciation		Discovery		Imagination		Presence
	Assertiveness		Discretion		Improvement		Preservation
	Attentiveness		Diversity		Independence		Privacy
	Audacity		Drive		Influence		Proactivity
	Awareness		Duty		Ingenuity		Progress
	Balance		Eagerness		Inner peace		Prosperity
	Beauty		Education		Innovation		Punctuality
	Belonging		Effectiveness		Insightfulness		Quality
	Blissfulness		Efficiency		Inspiration		Quiet
	Boldness		Elation		Integrity		Rationality

Bravery	Elegance	Intelligence	Recognition
Brilliance	Empathy	Intensity	Relationships
Calm	Encouragement	Intimacy	Reliability
Candour	Endurance	Intuitiveness	Religion
Carefulness	Energy	Inventiveness	Resourcefulness
Caring	Enjoyment	Investing	Respect
Certainty	Enthusiasm	Joy	Responsibility
Challenge	Equality	Justice	Righteousness
Change	Excellence	Kindness	Risk-taking
Charity	Excitement	Knowledge	Romance
Cheerfulness	Experience	Leadership	Safety
Clarity	Expertise	Learning	Security
Cleanliness	Exploration	Liberty	Self-esteem
Collaboration	Expressiveness	Logic	Selflessness
Comfort	Fairness	Longevity	Seriousness
Commitment	Faith	Love	Service
Communication	Fame	Loyalty	Simplicity
Community	Family	Making a difference	Sincerity
Compassion	Fidelity	Mastery	Skill
Competence	Flexibility	Maturity	Speed
Competition	Flow	Meaning	Spirit
Concentration	Focus	Merit	Stability
Confidence	Forgiveness	Mindfulness	Strength
Connection	Fortitude	Modesty	Style
Consciousness	Freedom	Money	Systemisation
Consistency	Friendship	Motivation	Teamwork
Content over fluff	Frugality	Nonviolence	Timeliness
Contentment	Fun	Openness	Tolerance
Continuity	Generosity	Opportunity	Tradition
Continuous	Giving	Optimism	Tranquillity
Contribution	Going the extra mile	Order	Trust
Control	Goodness	Organisation	Truth
Conviction	Grace	Orientation	Unity
Convincing	Gratitude	Originality	Variety
Cooperation	Growth	Outcome	Well-being
Courage	Guidance	Outstanding service	Wisdom

List 2: Examples of value definitions

1. **Creativity**: New ways of thinking and acting.
2. **Curiosity**: Exploring and seeking for its own sake.
3. **Open-mindedness**: Seeing things objectively and fairly, from all sides.
4. **Love of learning**: Constantly developing skills and knowledge.
5. **Perspective**: Seeing in ways that make sense and giving wise counsel.
6. **Courage**: Not shrinking from threat, challenge, difficulty, or pain; acting on convictions even if unpopular.
7. **Persistence**: Seeing things through, despite difficulties.
8. **Integrity**: Presenting oneself in a genuine way; taking responsibility for one's actions.
9. **Vitality**: A zest and enthusiasm for life and living.
10. **Love**: Valuing, sharing and caring for others.
11. **Kindness**: Doing things for others without requiring reciprocation.
12. **Citizenship**: Being socially responsible and loyal.
13. **Fairness**: Treating everyone in a similar way. Being just and without bias.
14. **Leadership**: Driving achievement whilst maintaining harmony.
15. **Humility**: Not putting oneself above others. Letting achievements speak for themselves.
16. **Self-regulation**: Controlling one's emotions and actions in line with one's values.
17. **Wonder**: Appreciating beauty and excellence.
18. **Gratitude**: Knowing, feeling and being thankful for all the good things in life.
19. **Hope**: Positively expecting the best and working to achieve it.
20. **Humour**: Enjoying laughter and making people laugh. Seeing the lighter side of life.

The purpose of the following exercise is to draw out the values that you already have. It's likely that you'll recognise them when you see them and be able to share plenty of examples from the way you live your life.

Exercise: Determining your values (part 2)

These questions will help you think about the values that are important to you.

- Which two or three well-known people, past or present, do you admire? Why? What are their values?
- Which family member do you admire? Why? What would you say their values are?
- Which friend do you admire? Why? What would you say their values are?
- Which boss or work colleague do you admire? Why? What would you say their values are?
- Which business or organisation do you admire? Why? What would you say their values are?
- Which values would a close family member say you lived by?
- Which values would a close friend or colleague say you lived by?
- At your funeral, what values would you like people to say that you lived by?
- If you were giving a talk to a class of students, what values would you advise them to embrace as they ventured out into the world?
- What values would you like to pass on to your children?
- If you were financially independent and didn't need to work, what values would you still hold?
- What values will still be relevant in 100 years' time?
- If you were going on a 3-month adventure with someone you didn't know, what values would you like them to have?
- If you were recruiting someone to work for you, what values would you like them to have?
- For which strongly held and displayed values would you promote someone?
- For which broken values would you fire your best performing employee?
- Looking back at your answers, what are the 10-20 values that seem most important to you?
- If you could only have 10 of those values, which ones would you pick?
- And if you could only have 5, which would you pick?

If you're struggling to narrow down your list, put the values in a rough order of importance. Then run a tie-breaker exercise. Pair off number

1 and 16, and determine which value goes through to the next round; then pair number 2 and 15, and determine which value goes through to the next round; etc. If you don't have 16 values, number one gets a bye to the next round.

Tie Breaker Tool

1 _____

16 _____

5 _____

12 _____

7 _____

10 _____

14 _____

3 _____

4 _____

13 _____

8 _____

9 _____

6 _____

11 _____

15 _____

2 _____

Exercise: Determining your values (part 3)

When you've focused in on your five (give or take one or two) values, write a couple of sentences that capture the essence of what each value means to you. Perhaps use an example of what it looks like – and an example of what it doesn't look like.

Having been through the vision, purpose and values exercises, now go back and reread what you've written. Your thinking will have become clearer, and you may now want to craft refined versions of each.

Researching the constantly evolving market you operate in

You will want to carry out market research periodically. The world in which you operate constantly changes and you want to keep abreast of those changes. Based on your own business experiences and what's changing around you, take a view of what may happen in the future and position your business accordingly.

Part of your investigation will be desk research (secondary research), studying information and analysis that's publicly available and covers your area of business. These reports may be free or may have to be purchased.

You may also want to carry out or commission some original research (primary research) to understand how your market is changing and what the future implications and opportunities are for your business. You might commission a market research company, a consultancy or even a group of business students.

As a business owner, it's critical to spend a portion of your time out of your business, observing and listening to keynote speakers at conferences, to suppliers, to other businesses in your sector, to customers, former customers, potential customers, to business journalists and to sector specialists. You'll then be able to build a picture of how the market is likely to change over the coming years and adapt your business model, strategies and plans accordingly.

The commercial model for your business & setting a 10-year aim

This is where your purposeful aim to serve a particular group of people with a beneficial product or service translates into a viable commercial enterprise. It takes your vision and good intentions and translates them into numbers. First and foremost, you need to convince yourself that your business will generate a good return for the energy, time and money that you'll invest.

If you already have a business, revisit your business model. You now have real trading data to work with, and combined with your market research findings, your model will be more robust and realistic. You'll be able to make more informed assumptions about the future.

Assumptions will include:
- Changes in market size and make-up of the market.
- Changes in the competitive environment.
- Changes in supply.
- Regulatory changes that impact how business is conducted.
- Likely technological changes that will impact how business is conducted.
- Your projected growth rate.
- Selling price, cost price and wage inflation.
- Customer retention rates.
- Average customer spends.
- Number of customers.
- Enquiry conversion rates.
- Staff productivity levels.
- The ratio of frontline staff to sales levels.
- The ratio of back-office staff to support front line staff.

If you have a trading history, include your actual trading results as part of your model. You'll be less tempted to introduce unrealistic growth projections for the 10 years ahead. If you've achieved two or three percent growth for the last four years, you're unlikely to jump to 20% per year. You may gradually improve your growth rate but it's unlikely that your performance will change suddenly. Not impossible – just unlikely.

Typically, when we talk about growth we're talking about sales growth. High levels of growth can bring problems if your business can't absorb that growth. Quality can start to dilute. Customer service may deteriorate. Lead times may lengthen. Overstretched staff may leave. Quite quickly, rapid growth can turn into rapid decline in reputation, customers and profits. It's interesting that a celebrated and highly successful company like Southwest Airlines limited their annual growth to 10%. Whilst projected sales growth may be modest, profit growth may be far greater. As discussed in the business development chapters, there are levers you can pull to increase your profits and cash position – which is the aim of the game.

When it comes to setting financial targets,
set you profit target first.

As part of your 10-year projection exercise, you can expand out the first two years to show a 24-month profit & loss projection by month. In effect, this can become your operational budget. Once you have a working model, updating it will be a relatively straightforward exercise. Consider rolling forward your projections every six or twelve months. You'll also want to turn your profit & loss projection into a cash flow projection. Your accountant will be able to help you.

EXERCISE: Building a business model

Think about and answer these questions to help build your business model.

- If you're starting a new business or relaunching/reinvigorating your existing business, how much money will you need? What expenses will you have and for how long before money starts coming in? At what rate will sales increase and over what period? Will you need to invest money in stock and working capital?
- If you already have a business, is an additional injection of money required?
- How many customers will you serve?
- How much will those customers spend?
- How much will it cost you to acquire those customers (your marketing costs)?
- What's the cost of the products/services those customers will buy from you?
- How much will it cost you to serve those customers (in addition to buying the products to sell)?
- What other expenses will you have?
- What net increases will you see each year in customers, customer spend, expenses, etc.?
- What will the flow of cash look like? (when will customers pay, when will suppliers have to be paid, what inventory will you have to hold, etc.?)

Your projection gives you a numerical picture of what you believe your business will look like in 10 years' time. In effect, you've created a 10-year target. Go back to your draft vision and weave in the quantified picture of what your business is going to look like (how many branches you'll have; how many customers, suppliers and staff; your sales and profits, etc.). Set a 10-year target for your business and share this with your team. The good thing about a 10-year time horizon is that virtually anything is possible. No one can tell you that you can't do it.

Most people overestimate what they can achieve in 12 months, but underestimate what they can achieve in 10 years.

Your business strategy

Within the context of serving a particular market with specific products and services, successful organisations will have evolved certain ways of operating and competing. Those ways of operating can be thought of as *business strategies*. (Tactics are short-term manoeuvres, enacted within the boundaries of broad strategies.) Strategies can be unique to a particular organisation but don't have to be. In fact, businesses operating in the same sector often adopt similar strategies – because they're effective. However, the execution of those strategies can vary greatly, producing very different business performances. Strategies are relatively fixed, but may need to change with the emergence of technical disrupters or regulatory change, etc. You can discover the strategies of successful companies by studying leading companies in your sector via annual reports, websites, academic papers, trade journals, and news articles. With a little digging, those sources will reveal the industry challenges and strategic solutions needed to thrive and grow.

*You don't necessarily need unique strategies to succeed.
Excellent execution is the real differentiator.*

Examples of company business strategies:

- Knowing our coffee, service and ambience is exceptional, and to ensure high customer traffic flows and favourable comparisons, we will only locate our coffee shops within 200 metres of a national coffee chain outlet.

- We will price work based on the value our solution delivers to our partner clients. We will not quote work based on hourly rates or how long jobs take. We will never offer discounts.

- We only offer bespoke products that are made with natural materials that are supplied from 100% sustainable sources. We will deal directly with producers at source, even if other third parties are subsequently involved in our supply chain.

- We work with clients who have a minimum annual budget of £100,000 and who have an internal marketing team in place.

- We accept individual projects with a minimum spend of £10,000 and a minimum gross profit of 50%.

- We only work with clients who have been introduced to us from existing clients.

- To maintain an exceptional level of personal service, we will only serve clients within a drive-time catchment area of 60 minutes from each branch.

- We only employ engineers who have a minimum of five years site experience and who can demonstrate a record of continuous professional development.

- We employ customer service staff who demonstrate natural customer service talent (identified in our selection process) but who have no prior customer service experience. All customer service staff must successfully pass through our 2-month customer service academy.

EXERCISE: Developing your business strategy

External Focus:

- What are the problems and challenges for all clients in your sector? What challenges are emerging?
- What is being done to help them overcome those challenges?
- What opportunities are there in this sector? What new opportunities are emerging?
- How are organisations capitalising on these opportunities?
- How are clients purchasing products/services?
- How are organisations marketing and selling to customers?
- What do you believe are the *critical success factors* in supplying this sector?

Internal Focus:

- Looking back, what has worked well for you?
- How can you build on what's gone well to propel your business forward?
- What's not gone so well?
- What have you learned? What will you do differently next time?
- Looking forward towards your vision, what hurdles or critical issues do you see?
- How might you clear those hurdles and solve those critical issues?
- Thinking about the opportunities and challenges in this sector, how will you build and grow the business? What are your handful of critical success strategies?

A key question of your business strategies is, "If we implement this combination of business strategies consistently well, will it make us successful over time?"

Your business planning system

Planning is the process of taking the general intentions you've articulated in your vision, purpose, strategy and long-term targets, and translating them into specific actions that you and your team can implement.

You'll have different levels of planning, all of which connect together:

- **A 2-year orbit.**
  This is a one-page visual that captures progression in key areas of your business for the next two years.

- **Annual and Quarterly action planning.**
  Every 13 weeks you meet with your team to review progress over the last quarter, to identify the development priorities for the next quarter, and to create an action plan to deliver those priorities. Annual planning is an extended quarterly planning day when you set the priorities for the next 12 months.

- **Organisational alignment.**
  This is the opportunity to share the priorities and plans with the whole organisation, explaining the rationale and gaining understanding and commitment to the way ahead.

- **Weekly progress and roadblock-clearing sessions.**
  Having committed to a quarterly action plan, you meet weekly to assess progress and resolve issues and challenges that may be hindering progress.

This planning and meeting structure, operated on a repeating basis, becomes the operational framework for running and developing your business.

It's important to recognise that the real benefit isn't in your plan, it's in your planning. Planning is the scheduled, periodic and focused time you dedicate to thinking through how you'll move from your point A to your point B. You may well produce a physical plan – and that will be useful – but the real benefit is in the quality of your thinking at your planning sessions. And your thinking and planning only becomes truly beneficial if it translates into action. An excellent plan that doesn't translate into action is worthless.

Planning is a key responsibility of a business owner or managing director. Preparing for the future is your job. The rest of your organisation expects you to be looking outwards and forwards and planning a prosperous future for them – their jobs depend on your effective planning.

Whilst planning is your responsibility, you don't have to do it alone. There can be benefits to involving the whole of your management team, or even the whole of your organisation. This will depend on the size of your organisation, the culture you've created, and the availability of your team. Whilst your team may not be involved in the whole of the planning process, they may well provide you with some of the information you need. Salespeople should be aware of market trends, feedback from customers, and what competitors are doing. Customer service people should be aware of what customers like, don't like and how their tastes are changing. Production staff might be aware of the quality of materials from suppliers. Much of your pre-planning work is about observing, questioning, and listening, both internally and externally.

Communicating to your people is another of your responsibilities. As part of your planning process, think about how you'll sell your plan internally – how you'll align everyone with the overall theme and specifics of the plan. It's likely that the plan will involve change – change for the better, even if some of the actions might appear hard and painful. People are more likely to embrace change when they're involved in the process in some way and when they can see their lives will be better as a result.

A 2-year orbit picture for your business

This is a simple one-page tool that encourages you to think about all areas of your business. It allows you to articulate what you want to do in each area to achieve your two-year targets (as determined in your business model and 10-year target setting exercise).

In the following diagram, the central circle is your current business reality. The middle light-shaded ring represents life in 12-months' time; and the outer dark-shaded ring represents where you'd like your business to be in 24-months' time. For your organisation, you may wish to rename one or two segments or add or take away a couple of segments.

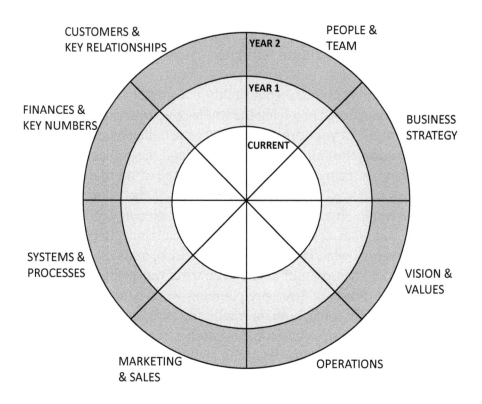

It's helpful to print out a couple of large copies (ideally A0 size) of your blank orbit. You can then put it on a wall or flip chart. This allows your planning team to see a complete representation of your business in one visual. Being on one page, you can more easily see the inter-relationship between different parts of your business. Before filling in your orbit, remind everyone of your vision, purpose and values and where you want to be as a business in 10 years' time. (Keep reminding yourself and your team of the bigger picture.)

This is a working copy, so you can scribble over it with coloured pens or use coloured sticky notes. You can use one of your spare blank copies to make a final version at the end of your session. Often, the working copy is quite adequate as it captures how your thinking progressed during the session.

Start the orbit process by capturing where you intend to be in 24-months' time based on the projections you created as part of your 10-year target exercise. Put these numbers on the outer edge of the Finances & Key Numbers segment. Depending on how detailed you were in creating your projections, you may also have numbers that can go in the Customers & Key Relationships and People & Team segments.

Next move to the centre of the orbit diagram and capture your current position.

The bulk of the meeting and your thinking is then concerned with what needs to happen over the next 24 months in the major areas of your business to move from where you are to where you intend to be. You'll also quantify some 12-month milestones. For example, to meet your sales growth intentions, your number of front-line technicians may increase from 12 to 36 over the next 24 months. Perhaps you'll put Improved Recruitment Process and Enhanced Training Programme in the Systems & Processes segment for the next 12 months and put a 12-month intention of having 20 technicians in the People & Team segment. You may also put that you'll have a Training Manager in People & Team for 12 months' time. You'll gradually build up a picture of what needs to happen in each area of your business.

Once you've built your orbit, take a short break and look again at the intentions you've captured. Given where you are today, and what you know about what you've achieved in the recent past, how ambitious are your intentions? Your intentions need to be exciting, stretching and progressive – but they also need to be grounded in reality. There's nothing as dispiriting than to look again at your orbit diagram in three months' time and feel that it's pure fantasy.

It's possible that progress will be slower than you'd like in the first 12 months but will accelerate in the second 12 months as confidence and momentum build. You may want to reflect this fact in the intentions you have for the two 12-month periods of your orbit.

Leave your completed orbit on the wall as a constant visual reminder of where you intend to be in 24 months' time. Ideally, put it on a wall in the room where you have your management meetings or where it'll be in your peripheral vision on a daily basis.

Example: Here's the 2-year orbit diagram for a technical services business:

2-Year Development Intentions

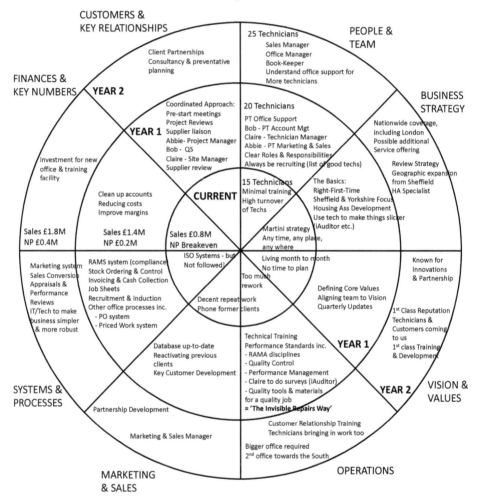

Breakthrough objectives

Having quantified your key results in the 10-year target exercise and captured your major intentions in the 2-year orbit exercise, you'll now want to be more specific and define your breakthrough objectives. These are the handful of projects or initiatives that are going to make a significant difference to the development of your business.

An objective captures your current position and articulates your future position at a point in the future. They don't say anything about the *How* of achieving those objectives. Your breakthrough objectives will likely come out of your orbit session. These are the vital few objectives that will produce a step-change over the next 12-24 months.

Example: Some breakthrough objectives from a variety of different companies:

- Move from being a business who service commercial and domestic clients to a business dedicated to only serving domestic clients over the next 12 months.
- Increase the number of technicians from 12 to 36 over the next 24 months.
- Instigate an invoicing and payment collection process and a late payment collection process with the aim of reducing the non-current trade debtor balance from over £100,000 to less than £40,000 over the next 12 months (whilst also seeing sales increase by 15% over the same period).
- Appoint a local marketing agency to create and execute an online lead generation strategy that delivers twice as many leads as the existing offline strategy within a budget of £25,000 over the next 12 months.
- Increase our gross margins from 28% to 36% over the next 12 months.
- Employ a part-time bookkeeper to reduce accountancy costs by a net £200 per month and to produce trading information within 5 days of each month-end within the next 6 months.
- Create a compelling vision for the business and share this with the team in 3 months' time.

Annual and quarterly planning

Your business world then gets broken down into quarterly blocks of 13 weeks. Every year you have four planning sessions, with one of those planning sessions focused on the year as a whole as well as the next quarter.

The annual planning session can be the first one in the new calendar year, the first one in your new financial year or can be incorporated with the last quarterly planning session of the previous year. Obviously, the key thing is that it's held every 12 months. What's most important is that you hold regular (quarterly) planning sessions. Remember that you have 10-year targets, clear intentions for the next 24-months, and a handful of defined breakthrough objectives that give you and your team a clear direction of travel and an excellent operational framework.

In addition to what happens at quarterly planning sessions, the annual planning session gives you the opportunity to review the last 12 months' performance against plan, to project your numbers and finances for the next 12 months, to revisit your 2-year orbit and consider some of the bigger questions around strategy and resource investment. Every planning session gives you the opportunity to refer to your vision, purpose and values and your 10-year target projections.

At a quarterly planning session, you will decide on a handful of key objectives that need to be achieved: who's going to be responsible for delivering those objectives, when they'll start and finish, and what action steps need to be taken to achieve them.

The action steps required to achieve an objective are typically of two types. They're either a project or a repeating activity. A project might be the recruitment of an additional engineer, the installation of an IT system or moving to bigger offices. A repeating activity might be phoning five prospective customers every day, sending clients a weekly video update on project installation, or holding monthly one-to-one sessions with your direct reports.

An important aspect of your quarterly planning session is to think about what might go wrong as you implement your plan. Planning sessions tend to be positive, upbeat, can-do occasions. You'll feel that everything is going to happen just as you've planned it. However, it's important to play devil's advocate and flush out the ways in which things could go wrong. What could get in the way of your recruitment project getting off the ground or what could distract you from having those monthly one-to-one meetings? You can then think of the mitigating actions you can take to reduce the likelihood of things going off track. And secondly, you can think through a plan B – what you'll do if a particular project or activity does crash or veer off track.

Think about how you'll recognise and celebrate milestones and achievements along the way. These can and should be built into your plan. It can be hard if you just miss a target and therefore miss out on a major celebration. Even though you've just missed a target, you and your team might have made fabulous progress over the 13-week period. Build in celebrations along the way and recognise effort and activity. If your objective is making 5 additional sales calls every day with the aim of securing 2 sales meetings, recognise the effort that someone is putting in to achieve those 5 calls, regardless of how many meetings they secure. Don't ignore unacceptable results. But recognise effort – and you'll get more of it. You'll naturally want to help someone improve their performance when you can see they're giving their best efforts.

Three particular tools that are useful at a quarterly planning session are:
- A business audit questionnaire.
- An objective-setting questionnaire.
- A wall planner.

Business audit questionnaire

The business audit questionnaire is a list of business-wide activities that will be helpful in growing your business. This tool allows you to look at each area of your business and to check off what you've already got in place and what you haven't. The summary checklists at the end of each chapter follow a very similar format to the business audit questionnaire.

Most people don't check off much in the 'DONE' column when they first use the audit questionnaire, which can be a little dispiriting. However, it's more helpful to think of the activities you've not ticked off as representing improvement opportunities – because this is exactly what they are. The fewer items you've ticked off as done, the more potential your business has! Also remember that as a business you're probably doing better than "okay" at the moment. So, imagine how well you'll be doing when you've ticked off everything. If you're committing to holding quarterly planning sessions, you're already ahead of most businesses.

You'll have a natural tendency to want to work on many of the activities in the 'NOT DONE' column. The more quarterly planning sessions you work through, the less you'll put on your plan, realising that completing just a few, meaningful objectives each time translates into sustainable, steady progress.

> *The value of a planning process is more about what you take out than what you put in. Better to achieve a few important objectives than fail at many.*

A few important things achieved is far better than many things planned but never started. A plan with too many activities leads to overwhelm, which leads to paralysis, which, more critically, leads to despondency and a belief that planning might work for other people, but it doesn't work for you.

In the early days, it's more important to develop your belief in planning through the achievement of a few modest objectives than it is to attempt great strides. Initially, develop the discipline, rhythm and habit of planning and achieving. You can lengthen your stride later.

It's helpful to think of the audit questions as prompts or ideas. Many of them will support your quarterly commercial objectives; others are more foundational to your long-term business development objectives.

Some of the audit questions are enablers, such as: "We hold regular team meetings that are scheduled and have an agenda." A relatively simple thing to do, but the discipline to do it consistently might be a challenge.

Some of the audit questions will feed into bigger commercial objectives, such as: "We are working on one or two strategies to increase customer enquiries."

Some of the audit questions are bigger tasks and may become a quarterly objective in themselves, such as: "We have a clear picture of where we're going as a business (our vision)."

Some of the audit questions are small and would take a few minutes to complete, such as: "I have a date for when my business will be finished (when I could go away for 6 months)." Setting the date only takes a few minutes – making that a reality will obviously take far longer.

EXERCISE: Business Audit Questionnaire

- Put a tick in the 'DONE' column for those items you already do or are happy with.

- Make a second pass through the checklist and highlight those things that you'd 'LIKE TO' work on next.

- For each 'LIKE TO' item that you've highlighted:

  » What benefits will come from completing it (or what consequences that will be avoided)? Jot down the benefits (in your planning notebook).

  » How excited do you feel about cracking on with this activity? Score your level of excitement out of 10 and put your score in the third column of the checklist.

  » Prioritise your 'LIKE TO' activities based on their beneficial impact and how excited you feel about taking action now.

  » Pick the one or two items from the top of your prioritised list and commit to making them a reality.

  » What's the simplest action you can take right now to get moving?

	Business Audit Questionnaire	DONE	LIKE TO	EXCITED
	Destination: Begin with the end in mind.	✓		Out of 10
1	I have a date on which this business will be finished.			
2	I have a clear & attractive picture of where we're heading as a business (our vision).			
3	I know who we'll serve & how we'll make their lives better (our purpose).			
4	I've captured the critical non-negotiable guiding principles we operate by (our values).			
5	I have a 10-year projection that demonstrates we have a credible business model.			
6	We have a 10-year business target that we're aiming for.			
7	We know our fundamental ways of operating in our segment (business strategy).			
8	I've run alignment sessions to ensure the whole team is heading in the right direction.			

	Finance: Measuring, monitoring and improving profits & cash.	DONE	LIKE TO	EXCITED
9	We have a process for actioning overdue payments which we stick to religiously.			
10	We track on-time payments and overdue payments.			
11	We have a cash flow forecast which is updated on a monthly basis.			
12	We periodically renegotiate with clients to reduce payment terms.			
13	We periodically renegotiate with suppliers to increase payment terms.			
14	We avoid discounting our prices.			
15	We're measuring at least 1 or 2 important things that we want to improve.			
16	We're tracking the key activities that will lead to the results we're aiming for.			
17	We produce & analyse monthly (or quarterly) management accounts.			
18	We operate with an annual budget & understand variance in our actual performance.			
19	We know what sales we have to achieve each day, week, month & year to breakeven.			
20	We know the Lifetime Profit Value of our customers.			
21	We know the average profit £ we make on each sale.			
22	We track customer profitability & have a minimum acceptable profitability target.			
23	We know our gross profit margin and have set a target gross profit margin.			

	Team: The right people in the right place doing the right things.	DONE	LIKE TO	EXCITED
24	Each person would say they know what is specifically expected of them at work.			
25	Each person would say they have the tools & equipment to do their job right.			
26	Each person would say they get the chance to do what they're best at every day.			
27	Each person would say they get frequent, prompt & positive feedback for good work.			
28	We have an up-to-date organisational chart.			
29	From their behaviour, it's apparent the team are clear on our vision, purpose & values.			

		DONE	LIKE TO	EXCITED
30	We have role descriptions & up-to-date contracts for all team members.			
31	We hold regular team meetings that are scheduled & have an agenda.			
32	We have short daily 'huddles' to ensure everyone knows who is working on what.			
33	I trust my team & have given them responsibility to make decisions in their area.			
34	The team don't make excuses or blame others. They own it and take responsibility.			
35	There are no passengers. We include the whole team & they all get involved.			
36	We have a programme in place for on-going training & relationship-building.			
37	Staff are cross trained so as to remove reliance on 'king pin' people.			
38	We have identified the leadership qualities needed in the business.			
39	We have a recruitment system to find people with the right attitude & skills.			
40	We have an onboarding programme in place to fully engage new team members.			
41	We have a succession plan, and a contingency plan should anyone suddenly leave.			

	Systems: Consistently good results with less effort.	DONE	LIKE TO	EXCITED
42	We have a list of all the systems that we would like to establish in the business.			
43	We have prioritised those systems based on their positive operational impact.			
44	We are creating or improving 1 or 2 systems all the time (part of our quarterly plan).			
45	We are involving the team in developing & refining those systems.			
46	We are capturing systems in a manual - in writing, with screen shots, photos, video.			
47	We are using process maps to pictorially show how systems work.			
48	We periodically review all systems to check they're still relevant & working well.			

	Business Development: Retention through consistently good service.	DONE	LIKE TO	EXCITED
49	We have defined our customer service standards.			
50	We have documented procedures to ensure every client experience is equally good.			
51	We have mapped all the touchpoints where we come into contact with customers.			
52	The team are trained to discover & understand all of our customers' needs.			
53	We forecast stock movements to avoid 'out-of-stocks' & keep stock levels tight.			
54	We regularly measure the quality, timeliness & professionalism of our service.			
55	Our service delivery exceeds our customers' expectations.			
56	We track customer retention & have a minimum retention rate target.			
57	We have a retention strategy.			
58	We have a computerised customer database which is up to date & regularly cleaned.			
59	We've graded all customers (A=Raving Fans; B=Good; C=Improve or Drop; D=Dead).			

	Business Development: Standing out from alternative providers.	DONE	LIKE TO	EXCITED
60	We have defined & identified our ideal customers & know exactly who they are.			
61	We have researched our ideal, target customers & know a great deal about them.			
62	We know what makes us different in a meaningful way to our customers.			
63	We know the combination of factors that will make us unique to our chosen audience.			
64	We know what frustrates customers & have built a guarantee around this.			
65	We know where to find our target customers in greatest concentration.			
66	We appreciate we may need multiple customer touches (a campaign) before they buy.			
67	We have staff uniforms or a standard dress code, including the use of name badges.			
68	We use a set of words to greet people on the phone & in person.			

	Business Development: Growing profits.	DONE	LIKE TO	EXCITED
69	We have an adequate marketing plan including offline & online activities.			
70	We know our customer acquisition cost.			
71	We know the lifetime profit value of a customer.			
72	We measure customers enquiries and have set an improvement target.			
73	Enquiries from each marketing source are measured.			
74	We track all prospective customers through our sales process.			
75	Conversion at each sales process stage is measured & we've set an improvement target.			
76	Customer average purchase value is measured & we've set an improvement target.			
77	Customer average purchase frequency is measured & we've set an improvement target.			
78	Gross profit margins are measured & we've set an improvement target.			
79	Overhead costs are tracked month to month & we've set an improvement target.			
80	We're working on 1 or 2 strategies to increase retention.			
81	We're working on 1 or 2 strategies to increase customer enquiries.			
82	We're working on 1 or 2 strategies to increase prospect conversion.			
83	We're working on 1 or 2 strategies to increase average value sale.			
84	We're working on 1 or 2 strategies to increase purchase frequency.			
85	We're working on 1 or 2 strategies to increase gross profit margins.			
86	We're working on 1 or 2 strategies to reduce overheads.			

	Business Development: Marketing essentials.	DONE	LIKE TO	EXCITED
87	We have a systemised Referral Strategy in place.			
88	We have a system in place for capturing Testimonials, Reviews & Case Studies.			
89	We have registered with Google My Business & are continuously asking for reviews.			
90	We contact customers at least every 90 days.			
91	We review our pricing every quarter.			

92	We have put prices up in the last 12 months.			
93	We have a professionally optimised website that is regularly update & enhanced.			
94	Everyone in the business has a role, however small, in our marketing communications.			
95	We collect good marketing ideas & collateral from other businesses & sectors.			

	Business Development: Selling - helping customers make a decision.	DONE	LIKE TO	EXCITED
96	We understand that selling is helping prospects make their best buying decision.			
97	We understand that sometimes a customer's best decision is, "No, not at the moment."			
98	We have a documented sales process which we follow.			
99	We measure & review the customer conversion rate of each salesperson.			
100	Our salespeople use a Daily Activity & Weekly Results Monitor.			
101	We practise & use sales dialogue guides to ensure we interact professionally with people.			
102	We use a list of diagnostic-style questions to discover a customer's needs.			
103	Our salespeople train regularly on their products & services knowledge.			
104	Our salespeople train regularly to keep their sales skills sharp.			
105	We hold the salespeople accountable for their activities & their results.			
106	We know the specific characteristics that go to make a good salesperson.			
107	We have an effective recruitment system for salespeople.			
108	We have a self-funding incentive scheme in place for salespeople.			

It's likely that you'll have many ideas ticked in the 'LIKE TO' column – too many to complete in one quarter. The thing to remember is that you get the chance to update this sheet every quarter and you can systematically work your way through the questionnaire quarter by quarter.

If you have too much on your quarterly 'LIKE TO' list, the first thing to do is to put those items into an approximate priority order. For each proposed activity, ask the question why? Why do you want to commit to this activity? What will be the benefits? A second question to think about is how much effort you'll have to put in to realise those benefits. What time and resources will you have to invest? On one side you've got your investment of time and effort, and on the other you've got returns or benefits. This exercise will help you objectively prioritise your 'LIKE TO' activities.

Once you have your prioritised list, the following exercise will help you define each objective and create an action plan to achieve it. It'll only be possible to complete this exercise for the handful of objectives at the top of your list.

Exercise: Objective setting exercise

Complete this exercise by yourself or with your planning/management team. If you've already decided who'll be responsible for a particular objective, that individual can complete this exercise. Your operations manager might be responsible for recruiting a stock control and ordering assistant. Your sales and marketing manager might be responsible for developing and implementing a client referral strategy.

1. Title of Objective

2. Description of Objective

3. Motivation to Pursue this Objective
   a. How important is this objective (out of 10)?
   b. What are the benefits of achieving it?
   c. What are the consequences of not achieving it?
   d. Who benefits from you pursuing this objective?
   e. How would the pursuit of this objective make you feel (excited, challenged, fulfilled, scared, etc.)?
   f. Are there any downsides to pursuing or achieving this objective?
   g. What bigger objective, ideal or dream does this particular objective feed into?

CONTINUED

4. Impact of Achieving this Objective
   a.   How would the disciplined and progressive realisation of this objective change the way you see yourself?
   b.   How would other parts of your life change?
   c.   How might achieving this objective affect the people around you?
   d.   Having achieved this objective, how might the future expectations and perceptions of people around you change?
   e.   What broader beneficial impact might your success have?

5. Strategies & Tactics to Achieve this Objective
   a.   What sub-objectives does this objective break down into? What things need to be done to achieve this objective?
   b.   What external and internal resources are needed to pursue this objective?
   c.   Whose support or involvement will you need as you pursue this objective?
   d.   What daily or weekly things need to be done (repeated) to progress towards this objective?
   e.   What behaviours are needed to achieve this objective? What habits need to be developed?
   f.   When, specifically, will you work on this objective?
   g.   How often will you work on this objective?
   h.   Where will you be when you work on this objective?
   i.   What will your schedule look like over the coming weeks and months when pursuing this objective?
   j.   What's a very small step you can take immediately towards this objective?

6. Identifying and Overcoming Hurdles to Achieving this Objective
   a.   How will you get in your own way as you pursue this objective?
   b.   The pursuit of an objective usually involves change. Who will be affected by this change? Will they help and support? Or will they hinder and sabotage?
   c.   What else might knock you off course or be a problem?
   d.   For each of these obstacles, how might you reduce the likelihood of it happening?
   e.   How will you overcome the obstacle if it does happen?

7. Monitoring Progress & Evaluating Performance
   a. When specifically would you like to achieve this objective? (You may need to modify this as you progress. The key thing is to progress and to do so in the right direction.)
   b. How will you know you are making progress? What can you measure? What evidence of progress might you see? Are there particular benchmarks or milestones along the way?
   c. How often will you check on your progress?
   d. What will you have to see and when, to feel satisfied with your progress?
   e. How will you know that you're not being too soft or too hard with yourself?

Methodically working through this exercise will generate considered and sound objectives. A third useful document at your quarterly planning session is your Action Wall Planner.

Action Wall Planner:

Major Objective:	JANUARY				FEBRUARY				MARCH				
	WEEK 1	WEEK 2	WEEK 3	WEEK 4	WEEK 1	WEEK 2	WEEK 3	WEEK 4	WEEK 1	WEEK 2	WEEK 3	WEEK 4	WEEK 5
Objective 1													
1													
2													
3													
4													

5																	
6																	
7																	

Objective 2

1																	
2																	
3																	
4																	
5																	
6																	
7																	

Objective 3

1																	
2																	
3																	
4																	

5															
6															
7															

Objective 4

1															
2															
3															
4															
5															
6															
7															

It's a very simple document. It has objectives and associated action steps down one side, and time (weeks) across the top. It allows you to indicate when a project starts and when it finishes. You might want to put the number of hours you'll spend on a particular project in each week. You can then add up the hours to see how much time you're planning on investing in all your projects. Sense check this number against all your essential day-to-day operational commitments and, if needed, adjust your plan to make it more realistic.

Here's the output from a quarterly planning session for a bathroom design & installation business:

Example: Quarterly action wall planner:

Major Objective: Whilst maintaining the same level of enquires, double our conversion rate from 16% to at least 33% before the end of March.	JANUARY				FEBRUARY				MARCH				
	WEEK 1	WEEK 2	WEEK 3	WEEK 4	WEEK 1	WEEK 2	WEEK 3	WEEK 4	WEEK 1	WEEK 2	WEEK 3	WEEK 4	WEEK 5
Objective 1: Determine an effective sales process that clearly shows the steps involved and the time between each step.													
1 Define steps in SALES process (info request to deposit)		✓											
2 Determine TIME expectations between Sales process steps			✓										
3 Write Positioning Statements for each stage in the process so clients know what to expect				✓	✓								
4 Keep Enquiry Tracker up-to-date daily and analyse weekly	✓												
5 Focus on key touches in process: 10 Tips, Measure & particularly Proposal Presentation						✓	✓						
6 Determine client communication/ touch points between deposit and start of installation								✓					
7 Remove clutter from the showroom and create a neat, clean environment for clients	✓	✓											
8 Consider applying frosting to bottom 2/3rds of the window			✓	✓									
Objective 2: Reduce time on non-urgent things, increase efficiency and put more time into important & urgent and important & non-urgent things.													
1 Allow Bob to book appointments and to manage the diary		✓											
2 Be more discerning over leads and say NO (& refer on) the ones we don't want	✓	✓	✓	✓									

#	Task												
3	Look into a 2nd phone number to be put on adverts and website and a diversion service							✓					
4	Look at opening times to ensure there are uninterrupted time blocks for important stuff	✓											
5	Stop all rep walk-ins and only have rep essential meetings	✓											
6	Agree communication protocol with installers				✓								
7	Create a cash flow forecast that is updated every fortnight									✓	✓		
8	Determine system for scheduling work	✓	✓	✓	✓								
Objective 3: Maintain a healthy and steady flow of leads.													
1	Agree 1/4 right page, front half, bi-weekly with the Llandudno Advertiser; cancel other ads; consider no other ads		✓	✓									
2	Complete website & get it launched					✓	✓	✓	✓	✓	✓	✓	✓
3	Buy an A-frame sign board and station on the main road.	✓											
4	Remove awning and replace with a new sign		✓	✓									

There are a number of advantages to it being a wall planner – as opposed to a plan that gets put in a drawer or concealed in a computer. It may seem old fashioned but having a plan visible on a wall is a powerful, daily reminder that there's some critically important development objectives that need to be delivered. It can serve as a focal point for meetings. As a team, you can congregate in front of the plan and talk through this quarter's objectives and who is going to be doing what. Even if some of your team are field-based and others are working remotely, the principle of the wall planner is still relevant. There's merit in mailing a hard copy of the plan to the relevant team members so they can put it on a wall in their home workspace.

The key thing is to keep your plan visible.

It's useful to have an overall theme for the quarter that serves to pull the plan together. A theme might be 'Right First Time' or 'Always Following Up' or 'Systems, Systems, Systems'.

You can also be imaginative about how you breathe life into your quarterly improvement theme. In addition to having a team alignment session, perhaps you produce a short, simple video that can be shared internally. Perhaps you build the theme into your internal email signature. Perhaps you send everyone a coffee mug with the theme on. Anything that will remind the team of what you're all focused on that quarter.

Even if you never look directly at your plan again, if it's in your peripheral vision, it will serve as a reminder that you've got some important stuff to be chipping away each day. Two questions to ask at the beginning and end of each day are: "What will I do today to make progress on one of my key objectives?" and "What have I done today to make progress against one of my key objectives?"

You may not complete everything on your plan. However, you'll get more done, and make more meaningful progress, having been through a planning process, than if you simply put your head down and ploughed on. Planning is a skill, and like all skills, you'll become better at it the more you do it and the more you learn about it.

The best piece of planning advice is to keep your plan light. Commit to just a handful of meaningful objectives. And get them done.

Regular quarterly planning is the key mechanism for developing your business. If you're giving yourself 10 years to *finish* your business, that's 40 quarters to get all the elements in place.

It's best to schedule your quarterly planning days in your calendar at least 12 months in advance. It's also preferable to be off-site, away from customers, problems, interruptions, phones and emails. Find an inspiring location that's free of distractions. You and your team of planners should be able to turn off your phones and emails for one whole day and let your operational team run the business. If you can't, perhaps that should be one of the objectives for your first quarter – put processes and people in place so we can have one uninterrupted planning day every 13 weeks. It can also be helpful (and pleasant) to stay over, have a meal together the night before and be able to make an early start on the day itself. Avoiding a stressful commute ensures you begin the day on full power.

Weekly progress meeting

Meetings ensure you're making progress against your quarterly objectives and allow you the opportunity to deal with issues, problems and roadblocks.

Be as accommodating as possible when choosing your meeting day and times, but once you've decided, make your meetings at the same time and same place, every time. Issue the calendar invites on an automatic repeating basis. Ask everyone to schedule the rest of their life around these immovable meetings.

Example: Here's the fixed agenda used by a successful company for their weekly meeting.

(It took time to refine the agenda and it took time to run the meeting effectively and efficiently.)

1. **Highlights:** What's gone well? Why did it go well?
2. **Key numbers:** On-track or off-track?
3. **Quarterly focus:** What's our quarterly theme and objectives?
4. **Quarterly objectives:** Are we on-track or off-track?
5. **Customer headlines:** At a high level, what do we need to know about our customers?
6. **Supplier headlines:** At a high level, what do we need to know about our suppliers?
7. **Team headlines:** Who's joined, left, been trained or made an extra-mile contribution?
8. **Actions from last time:** Done or not done?
9. **Issues:** What's the most important problem for us to solve today? And if we have time, what's the next? (At least 50% of the time should be dedicated to resolving issues, problems, hindrances and blockages.)
10. **Actions:** Who's committing to do what before the next meeting?
11. **Communication:** What needs to be shared with people outside the meeting?
12. **Liked best & next time:** What was good about today's meeting? How can we make it better next time?

Make your agenda a series of questions so that people come along with answers. With the exception of item nine in the example, all these items should be kept short – very short. For a 90-minute meeting, at least 45 minutes should be dedicated to item nine – getting stuck into the blockages that are impeding progress against your quarterly objectives. There doesn't need to be a discussion about items one to eight. If there's an issue to discuss, then it gets incorporated into item nine.

Keeping this meeting tight, focused and running to time requires a strong lead. However, when everyone understands the agenda and the purpose of the meeting, it should become self-policing. No one wants to waste their time. One person needs to run the meeting and someone else needs to take notes. The critical part of the note taking is agreeing the actions at the end of the meeting (who is going to do what over the next seven days).

Highlights

Start your meeting with everyone sharing one business highlight from the last week. It doesn't matter if it's big or small, it forces everyone to be more observant during their week and more aware of the good things that are happening in your business. This will put everyone in a positive frame of mind for the meeting. Keep it succinct and brief – this isn't an invitation to open up a discussion.

Key numbers

Get all your key numbers and measures on one document (your Dashboard). Draw attention to any sizeable positive or negative deviations from expectations. If there's issues for discussion, then drop them into item nine.

Quarterly theme and objectives

This reminds everyone of the priorities for the quarter.

Customer, supplier and team updates

Just the headlines. Perhaps share a particular story behind the key numbers you shared. A customer who has just placed a large order, a supplier who's given you a rebate, or a team member who received a glowing letter of thanks from a customer.

Actions from last time

Done or not done? No debate, no excuses. Again, if something has become an issue, drop it into item nine.

Issues (problems, hurdles, frustrations, inhibitors, distractions and opportunities)

This section forms the main part of your meeting. Keep a log of things that are inhibiting progress in an Issues Tracker (example given). Have a prioritising mechanism. Start with the most important item at the top of your list. Debate and discuss it until you can see a way to make progress. Capture the proposed action(s). Move on to the second item. Repeat. Keep going until your timekeeper points out that you have 10 minutes before the end of the meeting and stop at that point. Issues that haven't been discussed can be covered the following week.

The final 10 minutes allows you to cover the final three points on the agenda, agreeing actions, noting which non-present team members need to be informed of something, and two minutes to cover your 'liked best' and 'next time'.

Example: Here's an example of a company's Issue Tracker:

	Date	Issue	Details	Owner	Priority (High/ Med/Low)	Update/Next Step	Date Completed
1	10-Jul	Technician parking	Office Manager spending 1 hour each day sorting out parking issues	Ged	Med	Pre-paid cards for all Technicians	17-Jul
2	10-Jul	Expense forms	Technician expense claims late & inaccurate	Ged	Low		
3	17-Jul	Job adverts not working	No applicants in first week of running adverts	Jamie	High	Check what other job title other companies use for this role. Get Graham to critique job advert.	

| 4 | 24-Jul | Invoices not settled | Job sheets incomplete | Nicki | High | Helen understands what job sheets should look like. Immediately return to Technicians when wrong. | |
| 5 | 24-Jul | Quotes going out late | Day to day distractions and emergencies happening | Jamie | High | | |

Actions for next time

The key here is 'actions' that have to be completed within the next seven days. If the action holder can't make that commitment, don't capture the action. Don't allow actions that will be completed by the end of the month, or in two- or three-week's time. Break larger actions into smaller actions and determine what can be achieved within the next seven days. The key is for people to confidently commit to following through on their actions, even if they're small actions, and for you to develop the habit of making progress each and every week. Photocopy or photograph the actions at the end of the meeting and share immediately.

Actions: Who-What-When. To be completed by next meeting.

WHO	WHAT	Done/Not Done

As with quarterly planning – and many other initiatives – start by making a few, small commitments and keeping them. Prove to yourselves that you're a team who keep your commitments and can make step-by-step progress.

The action needs to be specific. There are two parts to an action: the activity and the desired outcome. The activity is within your control – the outcome is not. For example, "I will call five people every day with the aim of securing eight bookings by next meeting." The activity can be committed to and achieved; the outcome can't be guaranteed. An alternative action might be, "I will carry on making calls until I've secured eight bookings this week."

Nominate one person to capture actions. As your discussions progress, this person should ask the questions: "And what's the action we're proposing? And who's action is it?" Ask people to keep a note of their own actions. At the end of the meeting, go around the table and ask everyone to confirm their actions, comparing it to the list that your nominated action note taker has captured. There's something powerful about people verbalising their actions. Ensure clarity and agreement on who's going to be doing what. Your team should also get into the habit of reminding each other to be specific when required. "I'll call some people this week" isn't specific. "I'll block out 3 hours on Thursday afternoon and call 45 people" is specific.

Circulate the actions immediately. They can be either typed during this section of the meeting, or if they've been handwritten, they can be photographed and circulated via email or WhatsApp. It's preferable to keep actions on a spreadsheet or similar and to keep a rolling history of actions. This also allows you to look back and see how effective you've become over time at completing your actions. A trail of 'Done' actions can be encouraging and motivating.

Liked best and next time

It's useful to allow a couple of minutes for everyone to mention what they liked about the meeting and suggest things that might make it even better next time. Be open-minded to continuously improving your processes.

Brainstorming as a whole organisation

When we want things to be better, culturally we seem to have a tendency to focus on what's wrong or broken – the problems that need to be fixed. The weakness of this approach is that people can take listing shortcomings or problems as a personal criticism; they become defensive; they make excuses; or they blame circumstance or other people. Not a good place to start. Organisational brainstorming focuses on a different start point – what's going well.

If you want to be successful, don't study failure, study success.

Organisational brainstorming is a powerful tool that can be used to initiate improvements in different areas of your business. It can be used with the whole organisation, with individual teams or with cross-functional groups. It will immediately get your team involved and generating ideas. It's enlightening how enthusiastic people can become when they're sincerely invited to think and contribute. This brainstorming technique tackles problems, but it does so in an indirect way.

The technique works like this:

- Nominate a particular area of the business to focus on.
- Ask the people in the room to individually list out all the things that are going well in that area.
- Go around the room, allowing everyone to share one item from their list. It may be that someone's item prompts someone else to add another item to their list. Keep going around the room until everybody's list is exhausted.
- Ask everyone which of the things shared is most interesting to them. It's likely that there will be consensus in the room and they'll focus on one thing in particular.
- Ask them why they've focused on that particular thing; why it's important to them.
- Ask everyone to discuss why they think it's going so well.
- Ask them what they could do to make it even better or to get more of that good thing.
- Ask them to decide on some specific, practical actions they could take.
- Discuss what support and resources they'd need to take those actions.
- Empower them to have a go.

- If time permits, and you feel that everyone has the energy and capacity to focus on a second item, repeat the above process.

- Schedule a follow up session.

The first time you do this, you'll be amazed at the levels of energy and enthusiasm in the room. Most people in the workplace have rarely been asked to think about what's going well – and it's a real boost to how they feel about themselves and the organisation, over and above the fact that this tool will generate some fabulous, practical ways of making things better. Again, the key is in the follow up. If you're going to tap into the collective brainpower and commitment of your team, you have to go the whole way in supporting them and giving them the responsibility to implement their ideas. Your role is to facilitate the process – to prompt and encourage the people in the room, drawing out their ideas. Initially you may want to use an external facilitator to get it established.

Recognising progress & celebrating along the way

It's important that you recognise progress along the way. Build in time to periodically and regularly celebrate your team's wins, progress, learnings and effort. Have a celebration budget.

The best celebrations need to be planned. For a start, you need to know what you're going to celebrate so that you can look out for it.

Be wary of setting up competitions where you'll only have one winner. It's better to set a benchmark that everyone has the opportunity of exceeding. It's not necessary to set up competitions. Based on your improvement theme for the quarter, you might focus the team on an aspect of your business – but there's no need to turn it into an only-one-winner style competition. For example, you're a play centre and your improvement theme might be more customer interaction. That might mean smiling and saying hello when you pass a customer; or asking how they enjoyed their coffee when you clear their table; or commenting about their child. You might also brief the whole team to be on the lookout for colleagues who've wholeheartedly embraced the initiative. You might ask them to remember instances when they've had an unexpected response from a customer. Ahead of the celebration you might ask the team who they'd nominate for an 'extra mile award' based on that quarter's theme.

Your celebration is an opportunity to share encouraging and uplifting stories. You can have awards if you like but keep them modest. Acknowledgment from a colleague for going the extra mile or putting in extra effort is probably the best reward in the world. You'll remember it long after you've spent a £50 gift voucher.

The best celebrations involve food. The simplicity of sharing a meal with other people is powerful when it comes to developing relationships. And that's one of the key aims of your celebrations – strengthening relationships.

Getting together once a quarter is a decent interval to hold a celebration. However, as you develop a culture of mutual acknowledgement, you'll start to see celebration taking place spontaneously on a daily basis. The day when you see your team recognising the extra effort that a colleague has put in with a "Well done – good job" is a happy day indeed. Developing that sort of culture starts with you, so become observant and start recognising extra effort and progress, however small. You'll get more of what you focus on.

Exercise: Looking for reasons to celebrate

- What would you like more of?
- What are the behaviours or actions that are going to give you more of that?
- How will observe those desired behaviours?
- Who will observe those behaviours?
- How will you celebrate?
- When will you celebrate?
- How much is your celebration budget?

Summary

"Cheshire Puss, would you tell me, please,
which way I ought to go from here?"
"That depends a good deal on where you want to get to" said the Cat.
"I don't much care where—" said Alice.
"Then it doesn't matter which way you go," said the Cat.
"If you don't know where you are going ... any road will take you there."

LEWIS CARROLL. ALICE'S ADVENTURES IN WONDERLAND

This chapter encourages you to choose a destination and completion date for your business and to create a plan to get there. You can certainly keep yourself busy and earn a living reacting to whatever your day throws at you. However, you'll leave much of your potential unfulfilled, you'll look back with regret, you won't impact the world in the way that you might, and your business will be of lesser value than it might have been – possibly even being unsaleable.

Humans are goal-seeking beings. To function as you were designed and created you need something to aim for. Therefore, you need to create an objective for your business, a vision, something to aspire to, something to aim for. Know what your business will look like when it's finished.

This chapter demonstrates how to create your business vision, and to translate that into bite-sized quarterly development objectives and plans.

The first and most critical step is to create a little more time and space for you to start the planning process. Your team and your business will benefit from you investing more time and focused effort in observing, thinking, planning and directing. One of the dividends of actioning your quarterly plans is that you'll gradually free up more time to re-invest in future-orientated activities.

Checklist Exercise: Planning

The following checklist exercise will be helpful in identifying the progress you've made and in selecting the areas you want to focus on next. It will be useful to review this checklist once a quarter as part of your quarterly planning process.

- Put a tick in the 'DONE' column for those items you already do or are happy with.
- Make a second pass through the checklist and highlight those things that you'd 'LIKE TO' work on next.
- For each 'LIKE TO' item that you've highlighted:
  » What benefits will come from completing it (or what consequences will be avoided)? Jot down the benefits (in your planning notebook).
  » How excited do you feel about cracking on with this activity? Score your level of excitement out of 10 and put your score in the third column of the checklist.
  » Prioritise your 'LIKE TO' activities based on their beneficial impact and how excited you feel about taking action now.
  » Pick the one or two items from the top of your prioritised list and commit to making them a reality.
  » What's the simplest action you can take right now to get moving?
- Put this book down and make a start (or if impractical at the moment, schedule the activity in your calendar).

Some of the items on the list are relatively straightforward and self-explanatory. Others will need a plan behind them and assistance from other people. The purpose of this exercise is to identify which improvement initiatives you feel motivated to commit to, and to encourage you to find a first, small, simple action step to get you going.

	PLANNING	DONE	LIKE TO	EXCITED
	FUNDAMENTALS	✓	✓	Out of 10
1	I have a date on which this business will be finished.			
2	I have a clear & attractive picture of where we're heading as a business (our vision).			
3	I know who we'll serve & how we'll make their lives better (our purpose).			

4	I've captured the critical non-negotiable guiding principles we operate by (our values).			
5	I have a 10-year projection that demonstrates we have a credible business model.			
6	We have a 10-year business target that we're aiming for.			
7	We know our fundamental ways of operating in our segment (business strategy).			
8	I've run alignment sessions to ensure the whole team is heading in the right direction.			

	PLANNING PROCESS	DONE	LIKE TO	EXCITED
9	We've completed a 2-year orbit exercise to know where we are & where we're going.			
10	We're clear on what our major breakthrough objectives are.			
11	We're have an annual plan that includes commercial objectives & a 12-month budget.			
12	We use a business audit questionnaire to identify priorities for our quarterly plan.			
13	We identify what's going well and determine how we can build on that.			
14	We've committed to a quarterly action plan that's displayed on a simple wall planner.			
15	We've shared the theme and aims of the quarterly plan with the whole team.			

	PLAN IMPLEMENTATION	DONE	LIKE TO	EXCITED
16	We hold weekly progress & issue/problem solving meetings.			
17	We have a fixed agenda for our weekly meeting and keep to time.			
18	We make a point of recognising what's going well and the progress that's being made.			
19	We capture actions that must be completed that week – and complete those actions.			
20	We hold short daily 'What's happening' meetings to share daily progress & priorities.			
21	We recognise & celebrate progress, milestones & objectives achieved along the way.			

CHAPTER 3
Finance

*You must gain control over your money –
or the lack of it will forever control you.*

DAVE RAMSEY

If you're in business, love them or hate them, you have a responsibility to be on top of your numbers. If you hate them now, you can learn to appreciate their usefulness over time – perhaps even love them!

In any game you play, you want to know how you're doing; you want to keep score. If you're developing a business, firstly you want to know that you're operating on a sound business model and that the financial basics are in place. As you endeavour to grow the business, you'll want to know what impact your initiatives are having, and that profits and cash are increasing. That all requires the regular collection and analysis of accurate numbers.

If you're a whizz with numbers, this section will be a simple check for you. Please remain open minded though – you may pick something up that will prove useful.

If you're a little fearful of numbers, even to the point of avoiding them, please be reassured that you can learn what you need to know. This chapter will give you an introduction to some key concepts and give you some basics to get you going. If you're willing, with a little effort, you will become comfortable with your numbers over time. You'll understand how your business is doing and be able to make sound financial decisions.

Ensure you're working with an accountant (and bookkeeper) who speaks in plain English with the ability to explain things in a way that you understand. If you don't know or don't understand something, just ask – you're paying their bills. And keep asking until you understand. YouTube is a great source of answers to your basic financial questions – and YouTube is free and instantly available.

More specifically, this chapter covers:
- **Cash:** As important to a business as air is to you.
- **Measurement:** A game is a game only if you keep score – and it's integral to the game of business.
- **Financial planning:** A simple introduction to budgets and forecasts, return on investment, the time value of money and the concept of risk.
- **Financial concepts:** Understanding mark-up and margin, breakeven and the impact of price discounts and price rises.
- **Common financial terms:** Definitions of the more common accounting terms.

The importance of cash

Sales is vanity, profit is sanity, cash is reality.

Cash is the oxygen your business needs to survive. If a business fails, it usually fails because it runs out of cash – it asphyxiates. At the end of every month, you ideally want to see that your closing bank balance is higher than it was at the beginning of the month. Or if it's not higher, it's where you expected it to be – perhaps there's been a large, planned expense in a particular month. Your bank statement can serve as a simple, understandable and readily available financial statement.

Digital accounting packages link directly with bank accounts and credit cards, allowing you to readily view helpful reports. Failing that, your bank and credit card statements can be downloaded into a spreadsheet. With a little manipulation, you can summarise what monies are coming in and going out. Your accountant can help you set these things up.

Look at your cash first, then your profits, then your sales.

The basics of cash

Before looking at improving your cash position, the following examples will show how the cash position of a business can vary depending on different structural factors.

Which of these two businesses would you prefer?
- A business that has sales of £2M, earns net profits of £100k, and operates in the construction sector where clients pay their invoices 90 days after the work is completed.
- Or a business that has sales of £600k, earns net profits of £100k, and operates in the ecommerce arena where customers pay when they place their order.

Headline sales numbers can sound impressive, but profits are more important, and ultimately, it's whether or not those profits translate into cash that's vital.

A profit and loss table shows the sales income, costs, expenses and resulting profits or losses of a business. Here's the first six months of a simple business.

Scenario: Each month, 10 units are sold for £10 each. The units cost £6 to buy. Therefore, profit per unit is £4 and the sale of 10 units a month generates monthly profits of £40.

Profit & Loss Table 1: Selling 10 units per month

Month	1	2	3	4	5	6
Units Sold	0	10	10	10	10	10
Sales	£0	£100	£100	£100	£100	£100
Costs	£0	-£60	-£60	-£60	-£60	-£60
Profit	£0	£40	£40	£40	£40	£40

The company has to pay for the units it buys one month ahead of receiving them into stock. They then sell those units to customers who pay for them three months later. So, the goods that are sold in month two were paid for in month one, but the business doesn't receive payment from their customers until month four. This is what the flow of cash looks like.

Cashflow Scenario 1: Paying for goods 1 month ahead, being paid 3 months after sale

Month	1	2	3	4	5	6
Opening	£0	-£60	-£120	-£180	-£140	-£100
Incomings	£0	£0	£0	£100	£100	£100
Outgoings	-£60	-£60	-£60	-£60	-£60	-£60
Closing	-£60	-£120	-£180	-£140	-£100	-£60

You'll notice that the closing cash position in month one becomes the opening cash position in month two. By month three the business is overdrawn by £180. This overdrawn position reduces after month three (and would turn positive if the table was extended beyond month six). From month four onwards there is a positive flow of cash each month (£100 in, £60 out, equals £40 net in), and the cash gap (-£180) that has built up starts to reduce by £40 each month

A *cash gap* refers to the fact that you're paying your supplier for the goods you're selling before your customer pays you. There's therefore a need to finance that *gap*. For example, you might use an overdraft, in which case it's the bank who pays the supplier on your behalf and you repay the bank when the customer pays you.

Here's the same business but with a different payment and receipt profile. The company still receives goods in month one but pays for them in month two. Customers still take delivery of their goods in month two but pay for them when they order them in month one. This is what the flow of cash looks like.

Cashflow Scenario 2: Being paid when goods are ordered, paying for goods 1 month later

Month	1	2	3	4	5	6
Opening	£0	£100	£200	£240	£280	£320
Incomings	£100	£100	£100	£100	£100	£100
Outgoings	£0	£0	-£60	-£60	-£60	-£60
Closing	£100	£200	£240	£280	£320	£360

Exactly the same business – with the same profit & loss table – but a totally different cash position.

This is what the previous two cash scenarios look like when the business is growing at 25% per month. You'll notice that the number of units sold has more than doubled by month six.

Profit & Loss Table 2: Selling 10 units per month and then growing at 25% per month

Month	1	2	3	4	5	6
Units Sold	0	10	12	15	18	22
Sales	£0	£100	£120	£150	£180	£220
Costs	£0	-£60	-£72	-£90	-£108	-£132
Profit	£0	£40	£48	£60	£72	£88

Cashflow Scenario 3: Growth of 25%, paying 1 month ahead, being paid 3 months later

Month	1	2	3	4	5	6
Opening	£0	-£60	-£132	-£222	-£230	-£242
Incomings	£0	£0	£0	£100	£120	£150
Outgoings	-£60	-£72	-£90	-£108	-£132	-£162
Closing	-£60	-£132	-£222	-£230	-£242	-£254

Ironically, the growing business – higher sales and higher profits – is making the cash position even worse! Month six closing cash position has gone from -£60 to -£254.

This example shows why it's so important to be totally on top of your cash position, and the value of planning and forecasting your business growth (which comes later in this section).

To complete the picture, here's the cashflow for the second receipt and payment profile with 25% monthly sales growth.

Cashflow Scenario 4: Growth of 25%, paid when goods ordered, paying for goods 1 month later

Month	1	2	3	4	5	6
Opening	£0	£100	£220	£310	£418	£548
Incomings	£100	£120	£150	£180	£220	£270
Outgoings	£0	£0	-£60	-£72	-£90	-£108
Closing	£100	£220	£310	£418	£548	£710

The same sales and profit results but markedly different cash positions. By month six, a closing position of +£710 compared to -£254.

Whilst your bank statement is a useful place to start, one drawback is that it's historic – it doesn't tell you anything about the future. What will be more useful is a cashflow forecast. The previous tables show the basic layout of a cashflow forecast. It shows your opening position, what comes in, what goes out, and your resulting closing position.

Your accountant will be able to build you a cashflow model for your business and explain how it works. They'll be able to populate it with your sales income, your recurring expenses and build in formulas to calculate taxes (PAYE, VAT, corporation tax). Ironically, that's the relatively simple part. The critical element is the trading and operating assumptions that are made – and you're the person who'll have most insight into those.

You'll need to estimate:
- Your future monthly sales volumes.
- Your selling prices (now and in the future).
- The seasonality of sales across the year.

- Your likely growth in sales (depending on your marketing plans, customer service, etc.)
- When your customers pay.
- Your buying prices.
- When you pay your suppliers.
- How much you'll invest in marketing to achieve your forecasted sales growth.
- What the time lag is between marketing investment and sales receipts.
- The number of team members you'll need to produce and deliver your product or service.
- When you'll take on more people as your business grows.
- How much you'll pay those people.
- What additional equipment you might need as you expand.
- How frequently you'll need to replace equipment.

You can study historical records and patterns, but your market insights, ambitions and plans are the key.

Improving your cash position

Ways to improve your cash position:

- **Collect payments on time or early.** Have a tried and tested payment collection process and be disciplined about following it.

- **Reduce customer payment terms.** If your customer pays in 90 days, negotiate for less. You may be in a stronger negotiating position than you imagine. If you offer a valuable, responsive and flexible service to your customers, ask them to be flexible about payment terms. Alternatively, put your prices up and offer a discount for payment within 30 days.

- **Increase supplier payment terms.** Perhaps you started out on *cash on delivery* terms. If you now have a decent trading history, ask for 30 days – or more.

- **Hold less stock for less time**. If you buy goods in and they sit in stock for four weeks before they're shipped to customers, reduce those four weeks to three, or two, or one week. Perhaps you keep stock because of unknown and fluctuating demand. Getting closer to customers to better understand their business and their plans, will allow you to better forecast your stock requirements. Health warning: stock availability is more important than trimming stock to the point of being *out of stock*. You don't want lost sales and lost customers. Trim the fat but no more.

- **A reduction in manufacturing time.** You'll be able to order supplies later and will be able to supply and invoice finished goods earlier.

- **Improve your gross profits.** Increase your selling prices and negotiate lower purchase costs with your suppliers. Your higher margins will reduce any cash gap more quickly.

- **Delay expense payments.** Pay staff at the end of the month rather than weekly; make monthly payments rather than paying at the beginning of the year, etc.

Example: Actions taken by 3 different businesses to improve their cash position:

- **Example 1:** A company wrote to all suppliers at the beginning of a new year, highlighting how sales (and therefore purchases) had grown, and sharing plans on how they would continue that growth. Based on a good payment history and higher purchase levels, they asked for longer payment terms and a reduced cost price. Their payment terms moved from payment on receipt of invoice to 45 days from date of invoice. They couldn't negotiate a lower cost price.

- **Example 2:** As a trial with their next new customer, a business asked for 30-day payment terms when all their other customers were on 90-days from the end of the month. The company had a good reputation, a good level of business and the potential new customer would be nice but not critical to their continued success. They finally agreed on 60 days. They continued the same negotiating stance with all future new customers. Sometimes they gained and sometimes their negotiating efforts proved fruitless. However, their overall position improved.

- **Example 3:** Put prices up twice over a 9-month period. The company were surprised that there were no complaints from customers – and all customers stayed. (This is not unusual.)

Exercise: Improving your cash position

- When did you last put your prices up?
- List the ways your customers get value from what you do for them. What they pay and what value they get are two different things. Value always exceeds price – or they wouldn't buy.
- How could you trial a price rise (with your next new customer or with a segment of existing customers)? Or could you just put your prices up across the board?
- The more valuable your service, the more you can ask from customers. How could you ask for shorter payment terms (all customers, segment of customers, new customers)?
- Have your purchases from your suppliers increased? Will they increase over the coming period?
- Which suppliers could you contact and ask for (i) lower prices and (ii) improved payment terms?
- What actions will you commit to in relation to a price increase, shorter customer payment terms, lower cost prices from suppliers and longer payment terms from suppliers?

Financing your cash gap

If you have to pay suppliers before you receive payment from customers (e.g. a manufacturing business), you have a structural cash gap. As shown already, if your business is growing, your cash gap will also grow. Therefore, you'll need a solution to finance your unavoidable cash gap.

The funds required can come from traditional sources such as savings, a bank loan, a bank overdraft, or other financial investment. Other options are *factoring* or *invoice discounting*. Factoring and invoice discounting are two financing services provided by third parties. In essence, when you issue a customer invoice, a third party immediately gives you a high % of the invoice value as cash. This third-party loan is secured against your invoice. If you choose the invoice discounting route, you retain control of the collection process and your customer isn't aware that you're taking advance payment from a third party. On the other hand, factoring companies take ownership of your invoices and your customers pay the factoring company directly. There is a cost to using both services. Your accountant can explain more about the differences between factoring and invoice discounting and whether either is appropriate for your business.

Debtors and payment collection

When you've provided someone with a product or service, but they haven't paid for it, the customer is in your *debt* – they owe you money. They're a *debtor*. There are two types of debtor: Those who are within the agreed payment terms and those who aren't – they're late!

Collecting overdue payments is a fast way of improving your cash position. It also reduces the risk of you potentially never getting paid. You don't want a company that owes you money going out of business. Overdue payments might be a sign that the company is struggling financially. Or it might just be a sign that you're not on top of collecting what's owed to you!

Make it a priority to collect all payments that are overdue, starting with the companies who owe you the most. Simply pick up the phone and politely ask for your money. Ask each client if they're aware that they haven't settled their invoice. Often, it's a simple oversight; they apologise and organise a bank transfer straight away. Don't email. Phone. Phoning gets better results more quickly. Always have the last word. If they promise to pay, ask them when you should expect the payment. Ask if there's any reason why the transfer might not happen as promised. Follow up immediately with a brief, pleasant email stating what's been agreed. Make a note in your calendar when to expect the money and add a prompt to give them a call 24 hours later. If the money's in your account, simply say thank you. If it's not, ascertain why, and ask for payment as soon as is practicably possible. Be prepared to escalate the matter if they don't pay as promised.

Be courteous yet firm with late payers. The person at the other end of the phone is only doing their job – keep on friendly terms with them. Being pleasant and persistent will bring in more money than being aggressive.

A drop of honey catches more flies than a gallon of gall.
ABRAHAM LINCOLN

If their non-payment is not an oversight and there's a problem that's holding up payment, resolve any issues as far as you're able. This might be an error on the invoice, a missing purchase order (PO) number, a missing authorisation signature, a problem with your service, etc. Resolution may involve contacting multiple people in the customer's organisation, all of whom are busy doing more important things. It's important to be persistent, to remain courteous yet firm, to keep calm, to keep in control, and to remember that this is your cash.

> *The wheel that squeaks loudest is the one that gets the grease.*
>
> CAL STEWART

One scenario is that your customer is having cashflow issues and can't make payment. (Regularly credit checking customers is a prudent thing to do.) It's unlikely that your customer will admit this. Agreeing a repayment plan is your next best step. Even if the amount is small, get them paying something and get them into the habit of making regular payments. And put them on cash-on-delivery trading immediately.

It can be tempting to blame your customer and become cross and angry. Take the stance that this late payment is your responsibility and that it's occurred because of an inadequacy in your organisation. If you accept that it's your responsibility, you have the potential to do something about it. Yes, collect what's owed as a priority, but then look at your internal processes and disciplines and see how they can be improved.

Start improving your own invoicing and payment collection process. You want this exercise of collecting late payments to be a one off, not something you have to do every three months. As you deal with each client who owes you money, you'll want to understand how their internal payment processes work. Many clients will have their own little idiosyncrasies. In the interests of being paid on time, it's worth the effort of understanding and accommodating these. Get to know the people involved in paying your invoices so that you're on first name terms with them. If you're accommodating and can make their lives that little bit easier, you're more likely to get paid on time.

When it comes to your process, issue your invoices promptly. Have a procedure for checking that your issued invoice has been received and that your customer confirms that it's correct. Create a simple checklist of questions to ask: Was the work carried out to your satisfaction? Was the work signed off? Is the Purchase Order number present and correct? Is the accompanying paperwork (timesheets, photographs, etc.) okay?

Customers, especially the process-driven accounts-receivable departments of large customers, have a habit of not letting you know when your invoices are incorrect or incomplete, and thus not starting the payment countdown clock. The next time they look at your invoice is the day you call them to query their non-payment.

You may also have to improve your internal disciplines. Perhaps you need to be more consistent at submitting daily job sheets, or ensuring they're sufficiently detailed, or signed-off by the customer. Perhaps you need to make sure you always get a PO number, even if your customer is screaming at you to get the job done.

If there's a time lag between issuing the invoice and being paid, call just before the due date to ensure payment is scheduled. If that's difficult because of the number of invoices you issue, at least do it for the larger payments. Perhaps you can relax your process for customers who have a track record of paying promptly.

Every so often you might send a thank you card (or even a box of chocolates!) to those clients who pay faithfully on time, in full, every time. These gestures will cement good customer relations and make you stand out from the crowd.

The best time to discuss payment terms and to understand how customers operate internally is at the beginning of the relationship. It can be worth the time and effort of your accounts receivable person meeting or speaking to your customer's accounts payable person.

As well as having a payments process, you'll also need a late payments process, detailing the escalation actions you'll take when payment isn't received as agreed. The timings in this process are vital. If your process says you'll phone a customer 24 hours after the payment date is missed, call them after 24 hours – don't give them a couple of days to see if they pay. Be consistent and follow your process. Think of your interactions with your customer as a form of conditioning. If you don't keep your word (as detailed in your process) of referring late payments exceeding 30 days to a collection agency, they know you're not serious and won't see any reason to pay. Be firm, fair, courteous and stick to your process.

At the start of a new customer trading relationship, sit down together to discuss how you'll do business together. As part of that discussion, share your payment process and your late payment process. Ask them if it's fair and reasonable. They'll agree that it is and say that they have something similar – or that they should have something similar! The best way to solve problems is to avoid them happening in the first place.

Don't adopt standard payment terms just because custom and practice in your sector says that it has to be 90 days. It should always be a part of your negotiations. Make your payment terms as short as possible. The more valuable and critical the service you provide, the stronger your negotiating position. If you can get the digital equivalent of cash on delivery, go for it!

It's helpful to measure the total £ value of all your overdue payments and track that number as it reduces over time – all the way down to zero. You can also start measuring the % of revenue collected on time and make it a key measure to report on regularly.

There aren't many things that are as energy-draining, enthusiasm-sapping and stressful as chasing overdue payments. It sours the customer relationship and can even put you off being a business owner. As well as monitoring your cash position and maintaining a cashflow forecast, having a few key cash-related measures will keep your finger on your cash pulse. Regular measurement will help you monitor the health of your business.

Exercise: Collecting what you're owed

- Run an Aged Debtors report.
- Highlight the companies who are out of terms.
- Sort the list in descending order, with the company who owes the most at the top.
- Get on the phone today (yes, today) and ask for immediate payment. Get a commitment as to when the money will be in your bank.
- Follow up with a courteous email, confirming what's been agreed.
- Check that the money arrives as agreed.
- Call to thank them or to discover what the problem was. Ask to speak to a director if you're not getting anywhere.
- Repeat on a weekly basis until all late payments have been collected.
- Work on a process to ensure that payments are not received late.

Measurement and keeping score

Is your business making measurable progress against your expectations or plan? Keeping score is vital in the game of business. Your business statistics let you know what you need to do more of, what you need to do less of, where you need to improve and where to reward progress. Measurement helps you identify if you're off course or falling behind so that you can do something about it.

Collecting data, analysing it, drawing conclusions and making decisions is what this section is about.

You will want measures for different parts of your business such as:
- Financial performance
- Marketing and sales
- Customer service
- Colleagues and teams
- Quality
- Operations

Here are some examples of measures that you may have in different parts of your business:

Financial
- Sales against forecast
- Sales growth
- Gross profits, gross profit margin and change in gross profits
- Net profits, net profit margin and change in net profits
- Sales to top customer as a % of total sales
- Cash balance
- % payments collected within terms
- Average payment terms

Marketing
- Enquiries generated
- Qualified enquiries as a % of total enquiries
- Source of enquiries
- Customer referrals
- Customer reviews received (4* & 5*)

- Marketing cost per enquiry
- Customer acquisition cost

Sales
- New customers gained
- Conversion rate of enquiries into customers
- Conversion time from enquiry to first order
- Average customer purchase value
- Average customer purchases per year

Customer Service
- Customers lost
- Customer retention rate
- Customer satisfaction score (Net Promoter Score)
- Lifetime profit value of a customer
- Complaints received and complaints resolved
- Compliments received

Team
- Employee engagement score
- Employee retention rate
- Sales divided by staff costs
- Attendance rate
- Improvement ideas generated and implemented

Quality
- % deliveries made on-time and in-full
- Right-first-time measure I ([total time *less* rework time] / total time)
- Right-first-time measure II ([total orders *less* returned orders] / total orders)

Operational
- Order fulfilment time
- % products in stock and available for sale
- Ingredient costs per product shipped
- Energy usage per product shipped
- Production staff hours and costs per product shipped
- Accident-free days

The measures you choose will be specific to your business and your situation. Make sure you have a purpose for each measure – don't have measures for the sake of having measures.

Measuring activity and results

Another distinction is between activity measures and result measures, particularly in marketing and sales. An activity is something you do; a result is something you get. Sometimes you don't get the results you want when you carry out the activity. However, you **never** get the results you want if you don't carry out the activity! You can't guarantee the results you'll get; but you can guarantee the activity you'll do. Therefore, whilst measuring results is important, measuring activity is more important.

Activity measures will be business specific, but examples are:
- Former client calls per day
- Prospect letters sent per week
- LinkedIn posts per month
- Number of customer referrals asked for per month
- Number of job sheets spot checked this week
- Number of staff Thank You cards sent per month

Corresponding outcome or result measures might be:
- Former client jobs booked per week
- Prospect meetings secured per month
- LinkedIn company profile views per month
- Right-first-time correct job sheet
- Positive, enthusiastic comments from staff

How often you measure is also important. Too frequent and there's not enough time to get anything done; not frequent enough and things tend to drift.

Example: A Printing company monitored these things with this frequency:

- Daily: Prospective calls made by the sales team.
- Weekly: New enquiries generated.
- Monthly: Actual production hours against total hours available.
- Quarterly: Gross profit margins.
- Annually: Staff engagement.

Creating a dashboard of critical measures

It's neat to get all your key measures onto a one-page *dashboard* (or the digital equivalent) that shows all the vital numbers, ratios and trends for your business. In the same way that a dashboard helps you drive your car, it can help you drive your business. All dashboards should be simple. You want to keep your eyes on the road and only have to glance at your dashboard to see if everything is in order or whether you need to make any adjustments.

Your dashboard of key measures will contain a mixture of financial and non-financial information. If you're new to numbers, monitoring and dashboards, start simple with a few key numbers. Pick a few financial basics like sales, gross profit and bank balance, and one or two things you're working on to improve.

Example: A Blind & Awning company

The company was so busy that enquiries were building up and proposals were taking far too long to write. They believed that this was losing them business. If they could shorten the time, they believed they'd convert more project enquiries into business. As part of their improvement plan, they started monitoring enquiries and how long each proposal took to write and send out. They summarised this on their monthly dashboard.

CONTINUED

Monthly Dashboard

Finance	Oct-19	Nov-19	Dec-19	Jan-20	Feb-20	Mar-20	Apr-20	May-20	Jun-20
Invoiced Sales	£69,888	£72,374	£58,936	£65,935	£71,853	£79,653	£82,542		
Index	*100*	*104*	*84*	*94*	*103*	*114*	*118*		
Gross Profit	£27,256	£28,950	£22,396	£26,374	£29,460	£32,658	£34,668		
Index	*100*	*106*	*82*	*97*	*108*	*120*	*127*		
GP Margin	39%	40%	38%	40%	41%	41%	42%		
Cash at the Bank	£85,475	£92,756	£83,675	£90,465	£97,273	£88,796	£98,604		
Index	*100*	*109*	*98*	*106*	*114*	*104*	*115*		

Quarterly Improvement Initiative				Jan-20	Feb-20	Mar-20	Apr-20	May-20	Jun-20
Project Enquiries				7	9	6	9		
Won / Lost				3	4	3	5		
Win Ratio (conversion)				43%	44%	50%	56%		
Avg time for Proposal (days)				7.5	5.4	5.5	3.4		

On this dashboard you'll see that the financial numbers have been *indexed* to a base reference point (October 19 as 100). This allowed the company to quickly see how each month's results had changed relative to their reference month. For example, April 20's sales are 18% higher (Index 118) than October 19's.

It would also appear that the more promptly proposals are completed, the more business is won. There may be other factors at play, but there seems to be a positive correlation. The fact that you've started measuring and sharing how long proposals take to complete will automatically result in them being completed in less time, such is the power of measuring. If you have a backlog of proposals, before writing them, phone the prospective customer, apologise for your tardiness (no excuses necessary) and ask if they'd still like you to complete your proposal. On many occasions, the work's already been awarded to someone else and you can save your time and effort – and perhaps use the freed-up time to create a better process for dealing with enquiries.

Example: A more comprehensive dashboard.

This company has decided to monitor some information on a quarterly basis and some on a monthly basis. You can also see that there's a quarterly improvement initiative in the Team section around increasing the number of improvement ideas generated by the team.

Dashboard of Key Metrics

Financial	2019 Q1	2019 Q2	2019 Q3	2019 Q4	2020 Q1	2020 Q2	2020 Q3	2020 Q4	2021 Q1
Cash on Deposit	£117,252	£96,701	£127,981	£171,179	£222,265	£216,192	£288,356		
Index	100	82	109	146	190	184	246		
Payments collected within terms	75%	80%	82%	80%	87%	91%	89%		
Gross Profit	£92,252	£94,449	£106,280	£118,198	£126,086	£138,927	£147,164		
Index	100	102	115	128	137	151	160		
GP Margin	44%	44%	45%	45%	47%	46%	48%		
Sales / Salaries	3.5	3.4	3.5	3.4	3.5	3.4	3.3		
Biggest 3 Clients / Total	67%	63%	59%	54%	54%	49%	49%		

Marketing	Jan-20	Feb-20	Mar-20	Apr-20	May-20	Jun-20	Jul-20	Aug-20	Sep-20
Net Promoter Score	41%	40%	42%	44%	43%	45%	50%	49%	48%
Client Retention (+12 mths)	68%	70%	69%	75%	73%	76%	78%	77%	76%
Referred Enquiries	3	4	3	5	4	6	2	2	7
Total Online Reviews	65	67	70	72	76	80	82	85	89

Sales	Jan-20	Feb-20	Mar-20	Apr-20	May-20	Jun-20	Jul-20	Aug-20	Sep-20
New Customers	2	3	3	2	4	2	2	4	3
Proposals Presented	7	11	8	7	12	6	6	11	6
Conversion Rate	29%	27%	38%	29%	33%	33%	33%	36%	50%
Enquiry to Proposal (avg days)	18	20	15	15	13	13	12	12	8

Team	2019 Q1	2019 Q2	2019 Q3	2019 Q4	2020 Q1	2020 Q2	2020 Q3	2020 Q4	2021 Q1
Retention	92%	95%	94%	80%	75%	85%	88%		
Engagement Survey Score	75%				85%				
Total Charity Days Worked	10	12	12	20	4	8	15		
Q3 Improvement Initiative	Jan-20	Feb-20	Mar-20	Apr-20	May-20	Jun-20	Jul-20	Aug-20	Sep-20
Improvement Ideas Submitted							22	33	75
Ideas Implemented								15	23
% Implemented								68%	70%

Operations	Jan-20	Feb-20	Mar-20	Apr-20	May-20	Jun-20	Jul-20	Aug-20	Sep-20
(Total - Reworks) / Total jobs	88%	90%	90%	89%	92%	94%	93%	92%	93%
Unprompted Client Compliments				3	5	4	7	8	7

There are no particular rights and wrongs when it comes to creating your dashboard. It can be bespoke to your business and it may change over time. Periodically you may have to cull it back if it becomes too large and unwieldly. If you're a visual person, you may prefer to use graphs rather than index numbers or percentages to see trends. One of the key questions to ask of each measure is, "So what?" There should be a purpose to having each measure. If there isn't, ditch that measure – clear the clutter so you can focus on what's important.

Headlight measures

Most financial and accounting performance measures look backwards. They tell you something about how you performed. As a result of looking at those measures, you may want to change things going forward, but you can't go back and change what has already happened.

There may also be a time lag between taking corrective action and the better outcomes you're looking for.

Other measures look forward – *headlight* measures. These tell you something about what is likely to happen in the future in the same way that car headlights shine on the road ahead. Headlight measures will help you change or improve things *before* your results materialise. Measures related to customer surveys and staff surveys are examples. How people are feeling in the present will tell you something about how they'll behave in the future. If customers feel that things are slipping a little in terms of delivery reliability, they may remain customers today, but switch when an alternative comes along. Survey results give you a chance to correct things now.

If there's a link between how promptly you submit customer proposals and how much business you win, measuring how many proposals are submitted 'on time' might be a key headlight performance measure.

Perhaps invoice accuracy has a direct bearing on how promptly you're paid and thus on your cashflow. Measuring invoice accuracy is a key headlight measure.

Another example of a powerful headlight measure is *employee engagement* (as detailed in the Team section). If your team is less engaged today than it was 12 months ago, your results are likely to deteriorate over the coming 12 months. There can be a long lag between employee disengagement and deteriorating results. Reversing the process and reengaging your team can also be a long process, so it's important to measure employee engagement on a regular basis.

Measurement is also critical when you're introducing something new, be it a new product or service or a new marketing campaign. You'll want to run a pilot or testing programme and measure and analyse the results before making a decision about a full roll out.

Testing and measuring your ideas

You don't know what's going to happen in the future. Despite the logic of any proposed course of action, you can't guarantee your results. Therefore, you'll want to adopt a testing and measuring approach. You can run a small-scale pilot programme to determine if your initiative is going work and to what degree.

Marketing is a particularly critical area to test and measure. You spend some money on a new campaign, you generate leads, some of those leads turn into customers, and those customers generate sales and profit. However, you want to know if your resulting profits will exceed what you spent – and by how much.

Example: Company approached by a regular supplier to list a new product line.

The company weren't sure the line would be successful, but they'd been dealing with the supplier for a long time and liked doing business with them. They wrote to customers periodically with special offers. Each customer mailing costs £2. They had just over 10,000 customers. The product cost was £30 (including post & packing) and the supplier suggested a selling price of £49. The supplier wanted to know how many units the company would commit to. Mailing 10,000 customers at £2 each would have cost £20,000 – a sizeable investment. And the company didn't want to invest in stock that might not sell out. They decided to mail a representative sample of 100 customers for a cost of £200. Following the mailing, they received orders for 20 units. Their profit was: 20 units x £19 profit per unit = £380 total profit.

Their marketing investment of £200 generated a profit of £380. The test gave them a positive result. Given that the result was positive by a factor of nearly two, they decide to invest in the new line and market it to the whole of their database.

When you're faced with investment decisions, find a way of *testing* what you want to do and establish a mechanism for *measuring* the results.

Business modelling and financial planning

Your business model represents the economic engine of your organisation. When you first conceived your business project, you will have translated your concept into numbers. You will have projected your business's annual sales, costs and profits over a number of years. Based on these projections, the future looked bright! You wouldn't have gone ahead otherwise. Perhaps you needed to borrow money to kickstart your business. Your financial backers who lent you the money (your family, the bank, crowdfunders, etc.) wouldn't have invested in your business without a credible financial projection.

However, it's good to check periodically that you have a credible business model and that the future still looks bright. The trading performance of businesses won't exactly mirror the initial projections. With real trading data, and a better understanding of your business and your market, you can create an updated and more realistic projection.

Budgeting, forecasting and projecting

Budgets, forecasts and projections are all concerned with looking forward. An annual *budgeted* profit and loss (P&L) is the expectation of what your monthly sales, costs, expenses and profits will be over the coming 12 months. Once it's set, it stays set – it doesn't change. As your year progresses, you'll achieve some *actual* results, which are likely to differ from your budget. Based on your *actual* results and your more informed view of current trading conditions, you may *forecast* what you believe the results will be for the remainder of the year. Only re-forecast if there's value in doing so – don't re-forecast just for the sake of it. You may want to re-forecast to understand what your tax obligation is likely to be; or how much bonus you'll be paying to your sales team at the end of the year; or how much of a loan you'll be able to pay off.

Projections go beyond the next 12 months. You might create a financial *projection* for the next 10 years. Perhaps you're applying for a bank loan. The potential lenders want to know how the business is projected to perform over the term of the requested loan. The most important thing about your *projections* are the *assumptions* that you make – and how well researched, credible and conservative those *assumptions* are. You don't know the future, so by definition your budgets, forecasts, and projections will be inaccurate. Hopefully they're inaccurate on the downside and you perform *above* expectations.

See the *Your Business Engine & Your 10-Year Target* section in the Planning chapter for an exercise in creating a 10-year projection for your business.

Your annual budget will be a mix of non-financial and financial numbers. In the following example, the critical variables are:
- How many customers you'll serve each month.
- How much those customers will spend on average.
- How much labour will be required to serve those customers.

- What your growth in customers across the year will be.
- How much you'll invest in marketing to achieve your growth in customers.

Annual budget

Month	1	2	3	4	5	6	7	8	9	10	11	12
Customers	200	200	200	220	220	220	242	242	242	266	266	266
Avg. Sale Value	£100	£100	£100	£100	£100	£100	£100	£100	£100	£100	£100	£100
Sales	£20,000	£20,000	£20,000	£22,000	£22,000	£22,000	£24,200	£24,200	£24,200	£26,600	£26,600	£26,600
Gross margin %	50%	50%	50%	50%	50%	50%	50%	50%	50%	50%	50%	50%
Gross Profit	£10,000	£10,000	£10,000	£11,000	£11,000	£11,000	£12,100	£12,100	£12,100	£13,300	£13,300	£13,300
Direct Costs												
Labour	£7,000	£7,000	£7,000	£7,000	£7,000	£7,000	£7,000	£7,000	£7,000	£7,000	£7,000	£7,000
Operating Profit	£3,000	£3,000	£3,000	£4,000	£4,000	£4,000	£5,100	£5,100	£5,100	£6,300	£6,300	£6,300
Overhead Costs												
Salaries	£2,000	£2,000	£2,000	£2,000	£2,000	£2,000	£2,000	£2,000	£2,000	£2,000	£2,000	£2,000
Rent & Rates	£1,000	£1,000	£1,000	£1,000	£1,000	£1,000	£1,000	£1,000	£1,000	£1,000	£1,000	£1,000
Marketing Costs	£400	£450	£500	£550	£600	£650	£700	£750	£800	£850	£900	£950
Energy Costs	£100	£100	£100	£100	£100	£100	£100	£100	£100	£100	£100	£100
Professional Fees	£100	£100	£100	£100	£100	£100	£100	£100	£100	£100	£100	£100
Total	£3,600	£3,650	£3,700	£3,750	£3,800	£3,850	£3,900	£3,950	£4,000	£4,050	£4,100	£4,150
Net Profit	-£600	-£650	-£700	£250	£200	£150	£1,200	£1,150	£1,100	£2,250	£2,200	£2,150
% to Sales	-3%	-3%	-4%	1%	1%	1%	5%	5%	5%	8%	8%	8%
Cumulative	-£600	-£1,250	-£1,950	-£1,700	-£1,500	-£1,350	-£150	£1,000	£2,100	£4,350	£6,550	£8,700

Earning a return on your investment

As well as wanting your business to be profitable and cash-generative, you also want it to represent a good investment (of your money and your effort). A financial investment is an asset you put your money into in the expectation that it will grow into a larger sum. You could put £1,000 in a bank account for a year and earn a 1% return (£10); or into the shares of a stable, blue-chip company and earn a 5% return (£50); or into an independently owned small business and earn a 100% return (£1,000). However, each of those investment opportunities carries a different level of risk.

This example shows an *investment* of £1,000 generating a *return* of £1,500 over a 5-year period.

Return on investment

Year	0	1	2	3	4	5	Total
Investment	£1,000						£1,000
Return		£300	£300	£300	£300	£300	£1,500
						Profit	£500
				Overall Return on Investment (ROI)			50%
					Profit per Year		£100
						Annual ROI	10%

You might view a business as a collection of mini investments transacted daily. You might buy a product (your investment) and then sell it for a profit (your return). The same is true of services, even if your investment takes the form of the service-delivery staff you employ. Here's a simple example of how powerful buying and selling can be as an investment. Imagine buying an item for £1 on January 1st and selling it for £2 on the same day. You then put your £1 profit in a savings tin and buy another item with the other £1 – which you sell for £2 on January 2nd. If you repeat this activity every day, you'll have £365 in your savings tin by the end of the year. Your original £1 has turned into £365 – a return on investment of 36,500%! Buying and selling can be a profitable business and a great investment. If you become good at buying for £1 and selling for £2, you might graduate to items that cost £10 – and then £100!

A business may be profitable and good at generating cash. However, that doesn't necessarily mean that it's generating you a good return on investment.

In the next example, the business generates profits of £300 for 5 years. It's a simple business – customers pay in the month they get their goods, and you pay your suppliers in that month too.

Example: Simple business generates £300 profit per year

Year	1	2	3	4	5	Total
Sales	£800	£800	£800	£800	£800	£4,000
Costs	£500	£500	£500	£500	£500	£2,500
Profit	£300	£300	£300	£300	£300	£1,500

In this example, imagine two different scenarios. In the first scenario (A), you invest in a one-off license fee costing £500 for the privilege of selling these products. Your £500 investment generates you profits over the five years. In a second scenario (B), you invest £1,000 in a machine to produce the products you sell. Your £1,000 investment generates you profits over the five years. The machine has no value after five years as it's worn out. On a trading basis, both businesses are identically profitable and cash generative. However, the business in scenario A generates a far better *return on investment* that the business in scenario B.

- **Scenario A:** £500 investment generates annual profits of £300 per year (ROI of 60%)
- **Scenario B:** £1,000 investment generates annual profits of £300 per year (ROI of 30%)

If you had £1,000 available to invest, you'd want to find two scenario A businesses to invest in.

The time value of money

£1,000 in your pocket today is more valuable than £1,000 in your pocket in a year's time because you can spend or invest it now. If you forego having money in the present, you want to be compensated or rewarded in some way – you want future money to be greater in value than present money.

In the following example, both investments and the five-year returns are identical. However, you intuitively know that it's better to get £300 a year for five years rather than £1,500 at the end of the five-year period.

Scenario A & Scenario B investment comparison

Year	0	1	2	3	4	5	Total
Investment A	£1,000						£1,000
Return		£300	£300	£300	£300	£300	£1,500

Year	0	1	2	3	4	5	Total
Investment B	£1,000						£1,000
Return						£1,500	£1,500

In order to compare like with like, it can be useful to turn future income streams (£300 a year for five years or £1,500 in five years' time), into their present-day value. In that way, you can compare your proposed investment to your potential future income. You do that by reducing the value of future money and convert it into its present-day equivalent – in effect, you *discount* it by a certain amount or percentage.

For example, if you were promised £1,500 in 12 months' time you might discount it by 10% to arrive at a present-day value £1,350 (£1,500 x 90% = £1,350). A discount rate of anything less than 33% would return a present-day value that was greater than £1,000. For example:

- £1,500 discounted by 10% = £1,500 x 90% = £1,350
- £1,500 discounted by 20% = £1,500 x 80% = £1,200
- £1,500 discounted by 30% = £1,500 x 70% = £1,050

The actual money you'd get in 12 months' time is £1,500. You're only doing a like-for-like comparison of your investment and your return in *today's* money so that you can make a more informed decision.

The key question then becomes what discount rate to use. One way to do that is to use a discount rate equivalent to the cost of borrowing the money. For example, a bank might charge you 8%; a crowdfunding platform might charge you 15%.

If promised a return of £1,500 in two years' time, you'd use the annual discount rate twice. If the discount rate you wanted to use was 10%, the present-day value of £1,500 in two years is:

£1,500 x 90% x 90% = £1,215.

If you weren't going to get your £1,500 for 5 years, the present-day value would be:

£1,500 x 90% x 90% x 90% x 90% x 90% = £886. i.e. less than the £1,000 investment in the previous example.

Understanding different levels of risk

Investments also carry risks – there is no 100% guarantee you'll receive the return promised. Some investments carry more risk than others. In the following example, it appears that investment B offers a better return than investment A.

Investment A

Year	0	1	2	3	4	5	Total
Investment A	£1,000						£1,000
Return		£300	£300	£300	£300	£300	£1,500

Investment B

Year	0	1	2	3	4	5	Total
Investment B	£1,000						£1,000
Return		£500	£500	£500	£500	£500	£2,500

If A was an opportunity to invest in a stable blue-chip company, you might deem it to be low risk. If investment B was an opportunity to invest in your neighbour's first-time business venture, you might deem it to be high risk. You can think of taking a *risk* as similar to applying a *probability* that something is going to happen in the future. You might give your blue-chip investment a *probability* of 95% of becoming a reality. You may give your neighbour's venture a *probability* of 50%.

Investment A: Blue Chip company investment

Year	0	1	2	3	4	5	Total
Investment	£1,000						£1,000
Return		£300	£300	£300	£300	£300	£1,500
Probability		95%	95%	95%	95%	95%	
Adjusted Return		£285	£285	£285	£285	£285	£1,425

Investment B: Your neighbour's new business venture

Year	0	1	2	3	4	5	Total
Investment	£1,000						£1,000
Return		£500	£500	£500	£500	£500	£2,500
Probability		50%	50%	50%	50%	50%	
Adjusted Return		£250	£250	£250	£250	£250	£1,250

Applying a probability to a potential outcome helps you make a decision on where to invest your money for two opportunities that carry different levels of risk. The adjusted returns in these examples aren't the actual returns you'd receive, they're merely an attempt to compare two future potential income streams that carry different levels of risk on a like-for-like basis.

On a macro level, you want to know that the money you invest in your business stands a good chance of delivering a good return on investment for the risk you're taking. For many business owners, the *good return* only materialises when the business is sold. Understanding what makes a business saleable and what makes it valuable are important concepts to understand whilst you're building your business. A Corporate Finance specialist can help you with this. They help people buy and sell businesses, raise development finance, change banks, etc. It's forward thinking to have a corporate finance specialist as part of your network of professional advisors.

On a micro level, understanding the concept of return on investment is important for all financial planning decisions. Any money you spend on marketing should be thought of as an *investment* – you're expecting a *return on your investment* in the form of profitable sales that exceed your initial investment. Similarly, if you're making a decision about a salesperson, you can consider that an *investment* decision as you're expecting a *return on your investment* in additional profitable customers in excess of your salesperson's salary.

Usually you have limited funds available, and you have to make a decision between several alternative options. This quarter, you may have to choose between a new machine or a salesperson. Understanding the *return* that you achieve from each will help you make that decision.

Mark-up, Margin and Breakeven are other helpful concepts to understand.

The difference between mark-up and margin

Mark-up and margin often get mixed up. Mark-up is profit as a % of cost price. Margin is profit as a % of selling price.

You buy an item for £20 and sell it for £30, generating a profit of £10.

You have *marked-up* the item by £10 and your *mark-up* percentage is 50% (£10/£20).

Your *margin* is also £10, but your *margin* percentage is 33% (£10/£30).

The following table shows how different the two measures are.
- A 100% mark-up is a margin of 50% (cost of £10, selling price of £20).
- A 200% mark-up is a margin of 67%. (cost of £10, selling price of £30).
- A 300% mark-up is a margin of 75% (cost of £10, selling price of £40).
You'll notice that margin never gets to 100%!

Mark-up and margin comparison

Cost	£10	£10	£10	£10	£10	£10	£10	£10	£10	£10
Sell	£15	£20	£25	£30	£35	£40	£45	£50	£55	£60
Profit	£5	£10	£15	£20	£25	£30	£35	£40	£45	£50
Mark-Up	50%	100%	150%	200%	250%	300%	350%	400%	450%	500%
Margin	33%	50%	60%	67%	71%	75%	78%	80%	82%	83%

Calculating breakeven points

Breakeven is the point at which you move from loss to profit. It's useful to know what level of sales you need to cover all your monthly outgoings. This is your breakeven point. Once you pass your breakeven point, you start making profit.

You have a mixture of costs. Some costs will vary as your sales vary. On a simple level, if you buy goods to sell, the costs of buying goods will go up – will vary – the more goods you sell. Other costs will be fixed (such as rent, insurance, director salaries, etc.), regardless of how much you sell.

As an example, you buy goods for £10 and sell them for £30, making a gross profit of £20. You have fixed monthly costs of £10,000. You want to know how many units you have to sell each month to breakeven? £10,000 / £20 = 500 units. If you sell 600 units in a month, the first 500 units cover your £10,000 overhead costs, and the next 100 units generate net profits of £2,000 (100 x £20). You may find it useful to translate your *breakeven volume* of 500 units into a daily volume. In a month of 20 working days, you have to sell 25 units every day (500 units / 20 days) just to breakeven. If your aim is to sell 600 units, then your daily sales target is 30 units (600 units / 20 days). If you hit your daily sales target and sell 30 units per day, you only breakeven and start making profits during the final week of the month! Monthly breakeven of 500 units / 30 units per day = 17th working day (out of 20 working days).

In the early days of a new business you may be making losses each month. Once you start making profits, those profits will accumulate, and at some point, offset your losses. Your breakeven month is when your accumulated profits equal your accumulated losses.

Breakeven month and cumulative breakeven point

Month	1	2	3	4	5	6	7	8	9	10	11	12
Sales	£600	£700	£800	£900	£1,000	£1,100	£1,200	£1,300	£1,400	£1,500	£1,600	£1,700
Margin	50%	50%	50%	50%	50%	50%	50%	50%	50%	50%	50%	50%
Gross Profit	£300	£350	£400	£450	£500	£550	£600	£650	£700	£750	£800	£850
Overheads	£500	£500	£500	£500	£500	£500	£500	£500	£500	£500	£500	£500
Net Profit/Loss	-£200	-£150	-£100	-£50	£0	£50	£100	£150	£200	£250	£300	£350
Cumulative	-£200	-£350	-£450	-£500	-£500	-£450	-£350	-£200	£0	£250	£550	£900

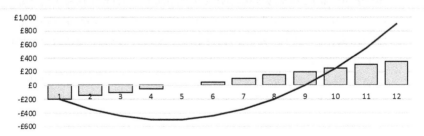

In this example, on a monthly trading basis you breakeven in month five – your sales income of £1,000 generates a gross profit of £500, which covers your overheads of £500. On a cumulative basis, you breakeven in month nine (your net profits in months 6, 7, 8 and 9 equals your net losses in months 1, 2, 3 and 4.) It's happy days after month 9!

Example: A Fabrication company's recruitment investment decision

- The business owner took responsibility for all selling activity. As the business grew, he could only dedicate 4 or 5 hours a week to sales. He decided he wanted a dedicated salesperson but wasn't sure if it would work out financially.
- He knew (because they tracked their numbers) that he signed up 2 new customers a month (on average).
- So, 5 hours x 4 weeks = 20 hours sales effort per month = 2 new customers,. i.e. 10 hours = 1 new customer.
- On average, each customer spends £3,130 each year. They earned a 46% margin. Therefore, each new customer generated £3,130 x 46% = £1,440 per year.
- A salesperson was going to cost them £36,000 per year.
- He wanted to know how many new customers they'd need to breakeven and cover the cost of the new salesperson.
- Breakeven = £36,000 / £1,440 annual customer profit = 25 new customers per year.
- Breakeven is just over 2 new customers per month.

He then took this one step further and wanted to know how likely it would be that a salesperson would sign up two new customers every month. To answer that question, he looked at three scenarios:

- **Scenario 1: Expected performance.** The salesperson is as good as the owner. i.e. 10 hours selling = 1 new customer. Therefore, 30 hours per week x 4 weeks = 120 hours / 10 hours = 12 new customers per month. (Assuming that only 30 hours would be available for selling as the salesperson would need 10 hours for administration.)
- **Scenario 2: Optimistic performance.** The salesperson might be twice as good as the owner! 5 hours selling = 1 new customer.

---

30 hours x 4 weeks = 120 hours / 5 hours = 24 new customers per month.

- **Scenario 3: Pessimistic performance**. The salesperson is as only half as good as the owner. 20 hours selling = 1 new customer. 30 hours x 4 weeks = 120 hours / 20 hours = 6 new customers per month.

He calculated breakeven as 2 new clients per month. Even in the pessimistic scenario the new salesperson is signing up 6 new clients each month. On that basis, they set about recruiting a new salesperson. Disappointingly, the salesperson only signed up 5 new customers per month on average. It turned out the salesperson just didn't have the same passion, drive and intimate knowledge that the business owner had. However, they were still better off, and the business owner had an extra 5 hours every week.

The gross profit generated by the new salesperson each year was 5 new customers x 12 months x £3,130 sales x 46% gross margin = £86,388 (on an annualised basis) for a salary investment of £32,000 (actual salary was less than estimated). Customers also remain customers for close to three years rather than 12 months!

Example: A Branding & Design company making a marketing investment decision

- The company were presented with the opportunity to invest £5,000 in a one-month radio advertising campaign. They wanted to understand what would need to happen to breakeven on that investment.
- They knew that on average the annual profit generated by a customer was £220. Therefore, they would need 23 new customers to breakeven: £5,000 / £220 = 23 new customers.
- Their other marketing efforts typically generated 4 new customers a month. So, they'd need the radio campaign to generate six times the number of new customers they normally generate. The campaign might have been successful, but they deemed it a big ask and declined the opportunity.

Calculating a breakeven figure and putting it in the context of your past experience will help you in making an informed decision.

The impact of discounting your prices

You might contemplate reducing your prices to win more business. This is another area where understanding breakeven can be helpful.

Example: A price discounting decision

- You import and sell raincoats. Your landed cost is £15, and you initially sell your coats for £75, making £60 gross profit per coat (a margin of 80%). In a 30-day month you sell 300 coats, making a gross profit of 300 x £60 = £18,000.
- The following month you decided to reduce the price of your coats by 33%. Your customers now pay £50 (£75 x 67%) and you make £35 gross profit per coat (£50 *less* £15 cost).
- **Question:** How many coats will need to sell, as a minimum, to make the same profit as the previous month (i.e. to breakeven)?
- **Answer:** Last month's profit of £18,000 divided by this month's profit per coat of £35 = 520 coats, which is a 73% increase on last month's sales of 300 coats.
- **Outcome 1:** By reducing your selling price to £50, if you increase sales by 100% from 300 coats to 600 coats, your profit will be 600 x £35 = £21,000 – you've beaten the previous month and make an extra £3,000 in profit (£21,000 - £18,000).
- **Outcome 2:** If you only increase sales by 50% to 450 coats, your profit will be 450 x £35 = £15,750. You're worse off than the previous month. You still make a profit, but £2,250 less than the previous month.

There are other considerations too. It'll take more effort and cost to handle those extra customers. Also, last month's customers might be disgruntled if they discover they've missed out on a 33% reduction – perhaps they'll hold off next time they see things at full price, waiting for your discount. Selling more coats may mean that you run out of stock before the end of the season, disappointing customers and losing out on potential full-price sales. And over and above the financial aspects of discounting, you should also be aware of the potential

---

damage to your reputation and brand that discounting does. Perhaps customers perceive £50 coats too cheap to be any good and your lower price results in fewer sales!

And what if your raincoats were stocked on one of those retail outlets that frequently have 70% off sales?
- New selling price = £75 x 30% = £22.50.
- Profit per coat is £22.50 *less* £15.00 = £7.50.
- To make £18,000 in profit you'd have to sell £18,000 / £7.50 = 2,400 coats!

70% discounts should be about selling out the last few remnants of a season's stock.

The following Discount Table shows the percentage your sales need to increase by if you discount your prices. The increase in sales will depend on two variables: Your gross margins and the price discount you apply. In the highlighted example, if you make a 40% margin and discount your prices by 20%, you'll need to increase your sales by 100% (i.e. double) to make the same profit.

Required increase in sales to give the same profit when prices are discounted

Price Discount	Gross profit margin							
	10%	20%	30%	40%	50%	60%	70%	80%
5%	100%	33%	20%	14%	11%	9%	8%	7%
10%		100%	50%	33%	25%	20%	17%	14%
15%		300%	100%	60%	43%	33%	27%	23%
20%			200%	100%	67%	50%	40%	33%
25%			500%	167%	100%	71%	56%	45%
30%				300%	150%	100%	75%	60%
35%				700%	233%	140%	100%	78%
40%					400%	200%	133%	100%
45%					900%	300%	180%	129%
50%						500%	250%	167%
55%						1100%	367%	220%
60%							600%	300%
65%							1300%	433%
70%								700%

Avoid discounting! It's bad for your financial health.

The impact of raising your prices

The other side of the discounting coin is putting your prices up. Many smaller businesses underestimate the value of the services they provide and also fear the consequences of putting prices up – surely all their customers will leave on mass! Yes, some customers may leave, but you may be better off.

Example: A boiler installation and servicing company

- They charged £50 for a boiler service which takes two hours.
- Heating engineers were paid £16 per hour.
- Heating engineers did four services per day (which was a stretch).
- Daily profit per heating engineer was 4 services x £50 *less* 8 hours x £16 = £200 - £128 = £72 per day.
- The £50 charge was a special offer when the business first started four years ago. The business owner never got around to putting their prices up. The company is good at what they do and has a good reputation locally.
- Other companies are charging between £69 and £125 per service.
- The owner was persuaded to think about putting the price of a service up to £95.
- **Question:** They wanted to know how many services they'd need to carry out to make the same profit as before (i.e., to breakeven)?
- **Answer:** New profit per service = £95 *less* 2 hours x £16 = £95 - £32 = £63. One service at the new price of £95 would generate nearly as much profit as four services at the current price of £50!
- **Decision:** They didn't quite believe the numbers, were a little nervous but went ahead and put their prices up.
- **Outcome:** When their prices went up, demand did drop a little – from four services to three services per day on average.
- Their new profit was: 3 services x £95 *less* 8 hours x £16 = £285 – £128 = £157 (a 118% improvement over the original profit per day of £72).
- Also, their engineers are now less rushed, less stressed, enjoy the job more, and have a little more time with each customer. They've even been taught to schedule in the customer's next annual

---

> service and talk about other services that will make the customers heating systems run more efficiently.

The next table shows by how much your sales volume could reduce if you increased your prices to give you the same gross profits as you had at the lower prices. In the highlighted example, a company making a 20% gross profit margin, who decided to increase their prices by 8%, could stand a 29% reduction in sales and still make the same gross profits.

Acceptable reduction in sales to give the same profit when prices are increased

Price increase	Gross profit margin							
	10%	20%	30%	40%	50%	60%	70%	80%
2%	17%	9%	6%	5%	4%	3%	3%	2%
4%	29%	17%	12%	9%	7%	6%	5%	5%
6%	38%	23%	17%	13%	11%	9%	8%	7%
8%	44%	29%	21%	17%	14%	12%	10%	9%
10%	50%	33%	25%	20%	17%	14%	13%	11%
12%	55%	38%	29%	23%	19%	17%	15%	13%
14%	58%	41%	32%	26%	22%	19%	17%	15%
16%	62%	44%	35%	29%	24%	21%	19%	17%
18%	64%	47%	38%	31%	26%	23%	20%	18%
20%	67%	50%	40%	33%	29%	25%	22%	20%
25%	71%	56%	45%	38%	33%	29%	26%	24%
30%	75%	60%	50%	43%	38%	33%	30%	27%
35%	78%	64%	54%	47%	41%	37%	33%	30%
40%	80%	67%	57%	50%	44%	40%	36%	33%

Put your prices up! You're worth it.

Exercise: Stop discounting and put prices up

- Are you giving discounts, perhaps just because people are asking and it's a force of habit?
- What will you say next time someone asks for a discount that results in you not giving them a discount?
- Can you mention in your sales process that you don't offer discounts because you're already offering excellent value?
- How much business can you afford to lose if you don't offer discounts?
- Where is your pricing relative to your competitors?
- Do you offer better value and merit higher prices?
- By how much will you put up your prices?
- How much business can you afford to lose if you put your prices up by this amount?

Introduction to management accounts and statutory accounts

The closing section in this chapter introduces you to some of the more formal financial terminology that you'll want to become familiar with over time. If you regularly consider and discuss the accounts and information your accountant (and bookkeeper) provides, you'll start to become familiar with and understand the terminology. It's like learning a new language and culture – but not as hard! Remember to ask if you don't understand something. There are no dumb questions – apart from the ones you don't ask. So here goes!

Statutory accounts (financial accounts) are the formal statements that have to be prepared for outsiders, principally Companies House and Her Majesty's Revenue & Customs (HMRC) in the UK. Management accounts are more detailed and operationally orientated and are designed to help you run your business on a monthly or quarterly basis.

You want to be reassured that your financial accounts are accurate, filed in a timely manner and tell a positive story, but you want to be far more interested in and on top of your management accounts. It's a good idea to have monthly accounts produced by your accountant or bookkeeper as soon as possible after the end of each month. Perhaps in your early days you can produce your own monthly accounts. Digital accounting packages certainly make this simpler. Bear in mind how you want to spend your time though – creating your management accounts or developing your business? You need to understand your management accounts and know what questions to ask, but you don't necessarily need to produce them yourself.

There are three main accounting statements:
1. Profit & Loss (P&L) statement
2. Cashflow statement
3. Balance Sheet

Depending on the size of your business, you'll have to submit different statements (and levels of detail) to HMRC. A *micro* business can submit a simplified balance sheet. A *small* business can submit a simplified P&L and balance sheet. Your accountant can explain your HMRC submission obligations. It's unlikely you'll have to submit a cashflow statement. Ironically, as discussed previously, your cashflow statement and cashflow forecast are the statements that are most useful in managing your business.

A few, short definitions will help.

Profit and loss (P&L)

Your profit & loss statement shows what you sold, what you spent, and your resulting profit or loss over a particular time period.

Cashflow

Your cashflow statement shows the actual flow of money in and out of your business over a particular period. As discussed earlier in this chapter, your profit and loss (P&L) and your cashflow are unlikely to mirror each other.

Balance sheet

Your balance sheet shows two things in balance at a particular point in time: the owner's (your) equity on one side, and the assets and liabilities of the business on the other. Your company is always in *balance*, every single day. If something happens on one side of your balance sheet equation, an equal and opposite thing happens on the other side, to keep it in balance.

Equity

Equity is the owner's (you and your other investors) stake in the business. On day 1, you might deposit £10,000 in your new business bank account. Your stake in your business (your *equity*) is £10,000, whilst your business has an *asset* of £10,000 in cash.

Asset

An asset is an item of value owned by the business. This could be £10,000 cash in the bank; a machine that you bought for £10,000; stock that you purchased for £10,000; or a computer or vehicle that you bought.

Liability

A liability is something that is owed by the business to someone else. On day 2, perhaps you bought a machine for £10,000 but didn't pay for it immediately. You have a machine that's worth £10,000 and still have £10,000 cash in the bank. Therefore, you have assets of £20,000. But you also have a *liability* to the machine supplier of £10,000.

Therefore, assets of £20,000 (cash + machine) *less* liabilities to the machine supplier of £10,000 = net assets of £10,000, which balances the owner's equity of £10,000. Owner's equity and the business's net assets are in balance on day 2.

Depreciation

When you buy a machine, the full £10,000 leaves your bank account and hits your cashflow. However, it won't appear as a cost in your P&L in the month you buy it. You'll make a charge to the business for using the machine each month. There are different ways for how the machine is charged to the business and different ways of treating the charge for tax purposes. (Your accountant can give a fuller explanation.) Let's say that the machine will last for five years and will have no value at the end of that time. You can *depreciate* the machine at the rate of £2,000 per year (£10,000 / 5 years) and charge the business £167 per month for using the machine (£2,000 / 12 months). £167 does not leave your bank account each month, but the company's profits are reduced by £167.

Debtors and creditors

When someone owes you money, they are a debtor. When a customer owes you money for a product or service you've provided, they are known as a trade debtor. On your balance sheet, trade debtors are classified as assets – something that is *positive* for your business. When the debt is paid, it becomes cash, and remains an asset. Whilst a trade debtor is viewed as an asset, remember that cash in the bank is far more valuable. Reducing your trade debtors to as close to zero as possible and maximising your cash in the bank should be a priority, as discussed earlier.

When you owe someone money they are known as a creditor. When you take delivery from a supplier, but don't pay for the goods immediately, the supplier is known as a trade creditor, and becomes a liability – that is something *negative* for your business. When you pay that creditor for their goods, the liability disappears and your cash decreases by the same amount. Again, everything on the two sides of your balance sheet stays in balance. Increasing creditors will improve your cashflow – but remember that creditors still have to be paid.

Accounts payable and accounts receivable

A customer's Accounts Payable team are the people who'll process and pay your invoices. A good relationship with these people is important. Your suppliers will have an Accounts Receivable team and they'll want you to pay what you owe in full and on time. In smaller businesses, it's likely that one person handles both functions.

Fixed and variable costs

Fixed costs are costs that stay the same each month, such as rent, rates, insurance, etc. If your level of sales goes up and down, your fixed costs stay the same. Periodically, they may change. For example, your business doubles in size and you need larger premises – there is a resulting step change in your fixed costs if you move to bigger premises and start paying higher rent.

Variable costs vary as your sales vary. If you're a decorator, the cost of paint will vary in direct proportion to the amount of painting you do. As painting sales goes up, so do your paint costs.

Summary

An essential part of being in business is keeping score and knowing your numbers. You might not currently see numbers and finance as a personal strength. However, they're something to get to grips with for your long-term health and wealth. In time you'll find them useful and perhaps discover one day that you like them.

If you're number phobic, one of the best ways to start is simply to schedule regular time slots in your calendar dedicated to 'numbers'. Perhaps at your first numbers session you phone your accountant or your business coach and tell them that you're dedicating an hour every week to numbers. Tell them you're not quite sure where to start and ask them how they can help.

If you're not strong with numbers, there's no value in maintaining a veneer of competence. You could be heading for a fall – or worse – if you can't see what's happening. If it's any consolation, you'd be shocked by how many businesspeople aren't comfortable with their numbers. But they are too important to ignore. There's really no stupid question related to numbers. Find some numbers-orientated people you trust and feel comfortable with, and use them to build your competence and confidence.

There is nothing quite so motivating as seeing your numbers heading in the right direction. To have the quantifiable evidence that you're making measurable, profitable progress towards your goals and vision is a great feeling.

Checklist Exercise: Finance

The following checklist exercise will be helpful in identifying the progress you've made and in selecting the areas you want to focus on next. It will be useful to review this checklist once a quarter as part of your quarterly planning process.

- Put a tick in the 'DONE' column for those items you already do or are happy with.
- Make a second pass through the checklist and highlight those things that you'd 'LIKE TO' work on next.
- For each 'LIKE TO' item that you've highlighted:

  » What benefits will come from completing it (or what

consequences will be avoided)? Jot down the benefits (in your planning notebook).

» How excited do you feel about cracking on with this activity?

Score your level of excitement out of 10 and put your score in the third column of the checklist.

» Prioritise your 'LIKE TO' activities based on their beneficial impact and how excited you feel about taking action now.

» Pick the one or two items from the top of your prioritised list and commit to making them a reality.

» What's the simplest action you can take right now to get moving?

• Put this book down and make a start (or if impractical at the moment, schedule the activity in your calendar).

Some of the items on the list are relatively straightforward and self-explanatory. Others will need a plan behind them and assistance from other people. The purpose of this exercise is to identify which improvement initiatives you feel motivated to commit to, and to encourage you to find a first, small, simple action step to get you going.

	FINANCE PLANNING	DONE	LIKE TO	EXCITED
	CASH	✓	✓	Out of 10
1	We know what payments are overdue & are collecting what is owed as a priority.			
2	We have a process for actioning overdue payments which we stick to religiously.			
3	We have a process for promptly raising invoices & ensuring on-time or early payment.			
4	We adapt our processes to accommodate customer payment idiosyncrasies.			
5	We are on personal terms with our customers' accounts payable teams.			
6	We track on-time payments and overdue payments.			
7	We check our bank balance at the beginning and end of every month.			
8	We have a cashflow forecast which is updated monthly.			

		DONE	LIKE TO	EXCITED
9	We're aware of the impact of infrequent cash outflows like tax, new equipment, etc.			
10	We understand our business's cashflow & have finance to cover any 'cash gap'.			
11	We periodically renegotiate with clients to reduce payment terms.			
12	We periodically renegotiate with suppliers to increase payment terms.			
13	We're constantly looking to increase the margin between our selling and cost prices.			
14	We avoid discounting our prices.			
15	Whilst maintaining adequate stock cover, we minimise stock holding.			
16	We have a just-in-time manufacturing & assembly process.			

	MEASURING	DONE	LIKE TO	EXCITED
17	We're measuring at least 1 or 2 important things that we want to improve.			
18	We're tracking the key activities that will lead to the results we're aiming for.			
19	We have put our key activity & result measures together on a single-page dashboard.			
20	We assess all new initiatives by measuring & analysing the results of a pilot or trial.			
21	We know what 'measurable progress in reasonable time' looks like for key activities.			
22	Everybody in the business has a few key activity & result performance measures.			
23	Everybody in the business has at least 1 or 2 improvement targets they're aiming for.			
24	We run an annual team engagement survey as a vital indicator of future performance.			

	FINANCIAL PERFORMANCE	DONE	LIKE TO	EXCITED
25	Our accountant is proactive, knows our business aims & explains things in plain terms.			
26	We produce & analyse monthly (or quarterly) management accounts.			
27	We operate with an annual budget & understand variance in our actual performance.			
28	We have a 10-year projection that shows we have a credible business model.			

29	We know how to calculate the financial return on any investment we make.			
30	We calculate the expected, pessimistic & optimistic return for a proposed investment			
31	We understand the difference between mark-up and margin.			
32	We understand the concept of breakeven.			
33	We know what sales we have to achieve each day, week, month & year to breakeven.			
34	We know what additional sales are required to breakeven if we discount our prices.			
35	We know how many sales we can lose to breakeven if we put our prices up.			
36	We regularly assess if our prices should increase because we're adding more value.			
37	I am constantly improving my understanding of financial & accounting terms.			
38	If I don't understand something, I ask my accountant to explain it to me.			
39	In the game of business, everything we do has numbers associated with it.			

CHAPTER 4
Team

*If you don't like your job, you don't strike. You just
go in every day and do it really half-arsed.*

HOMER SIMPSON

Whilst you are the most important person in your business, the second most important people – ahead of customers, suppliers, and other stakeholders – are your team.

Even if you've been trading for some time, you're probably still personally involved in many different aspects of your business – production, delivery, marketing, customer service, chasing payment, IT emergencies, etc. Perhaps you're even hands-on and fully responsible for several of those things. However, your aim is to recruit, deploy and develop competent and committed people to deliver the day-to-day technical aspects of your business (so that you can take a step back, raise your gaze and invest your time in directing rather than doing). It's your team who'll be at the coal face delivering excellent customer service and all the supporting back office activities. In turn, it's those customers, served and nurtured by your team, who become the long-term clients who value your services and love working with your team. Those customers look after your business by settling their invoices on time, by doing more business with you, by speaking well of you, and by referring other customers to you. Those business returns then reward you (for setting up and developing a well-run business that adds value to society).

In effect, you need to transition from you looking after everything to 'The Cycle for Growth' where your primary focus is on recruiting, organising, developing and retaining a great team.

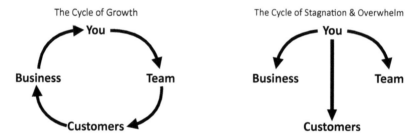

This chapter covers:
- **Recruitment:** Attracting, integrating and keeping the right people.
- **Organisation:** Getting everyone in the right positions to deliver excellent service and grow the business.
- **Performance management:** Helping people perform at their best and creating a high performing team.
- **Communication:** Ensuring everyone's heading in the same direction, knows what's expected of them, and knows how they're performing.
- **Motivation:** What gets people out of bed in the morning, enthused for the day ahead and engaged in a common purpose?
- **Celebration:** Remembering to have some fun along the way and to recognise progress.

Recruitment

Recruitment is probably the most important thing you do as a business owner. Get it right, happy days. Wrong, and it can turn into a costly nightmare. Here's a process that has been refined over many years that will increase the odds of attracting and selecting the right people.

Always be recruiting

The worst time to recruit is when you're under pressure and maxed out. You're too busy to do it; you're stressed, desperate, and there are "just no good people out there". The danger is that you compromise and pick the best of a mediocre cohort of applicants. A better strategy is to be always on the lookout for good people. Keep roles posted on your website vacancies page and on job boards. Look for good people when you're out and about and when you're networking. Have meetings with the people you like, assess them, and keep a shortlist of people you can call up as your business expands or if one of your team leaves. Meeting someone about potentially joining your business doesn't commit you to recruiting them.

Your role is to look ahead. You'll need to determine when someone will be needed and what the trigger will be to make that decision. It may link back to understanding the impact that your marketing campaigns have or understanding the time lag between enquiries and actual product sales or how seasonality works. It's a difficult judgement call but it's pretty neat if you can bring on the new person just as your current team is becoming a little stretched, but before they become strained. To the team it will seem as if they've been operating at 120% (perhaps with everyone doing a few extra hours) and then they drop back to 80% when the new person joins, and capacity rises again. It guarantees that your new person has real work to do immediately but they've also got time and space to adapt to their new environment and get themselves up to speed.

If it's an additional person joining your team rather than a replacement, as mentioned in the previous chapter, it's useful to know how much additional gross profit you need to cover their salary. For example, say you plan to take on someone and pay them £20,000 per year. If you make a 40% gross profit margin, you'll have to make extra sales of £20,000 / 40% = £50,000. If your current annual sales are £500,000, then you'll need to increase your sales by 10% to cover their £20,000 salary. It's always useful to put any investment decision into context.

Do you really need to recruit?

If someone leaves, you may be reasonably tempted to go for a like-for-like replacement. If your team seem really busy, your first instinct is likely to be to recruit more people. At those moments, take a step back and see if there's an alternative solution. Perhaps you can get the same result by putting some better processes in place; or by adopting some new technology that's become available over the last year; perhaps everyone needs to become better coordinated and organised. There may be alternative, better, and less costly solutions than reverting to recruitment. Recruitment is a time-consuming affair that carries the risk that you'll get it wrong – and perhaps just end up with another mouth to feed. If you do need someone, perhaps a freelancer is an option or perhaps the function can be outsourced.

Have a recruitment process

Processes make life easier. They produce better results on a more consistent basis and absorb less time and energy. Work on developing a series of recruitment steps that results in attracting and securing people who are great producers and thrive in your organisation. As with a sales process, measure the results at each step in your process and always be looking to improve. How many of your recruits make the grade? How many do you have to let go? What's your strike rate in terms of appointing great people, relative to okay people? This data allows you to review and improve your process. Your aim is securing great people with minimal recruitment effort and deterring and sifting out the people who aren't going to produce and thrive.

A simple system, with measurement, always beats no system. A review of CVs followed by one-on-one interviews is the traditional recruitment method – but this can be greatly improved upon.

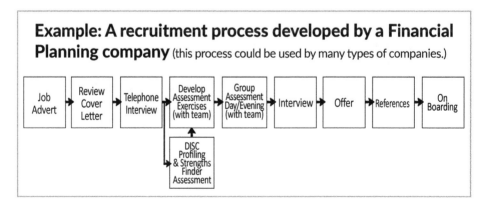

Example: A recruitment process developed by a Financial Planning company (this process could be used by many types of companies.)

Don't rely on CVs

Everyone should be able to produce an impressive looking CV. Similarly, it's possible to learn good answers to standard interview questions. Scanning CVs followed by a 60-minute interview with shortlisted applicants rarely produces the best outcomes.

The aim of your process is to allow the most suitable applicants to shine whilst filtering out unsuitable or mediocre candidates.

When posting a recruitment advert, ask applicants to send a cover letter/email, explaining (i) what attracts them to the role, and (ii) why they think they'll do well in the role. It's not so much what they write, it's that they make the effort to write. You can then rule out the people who just send a CV, demonstrating that they can't follow a simple instruction or can't be bothered to put in a little extra effort. This technique will weed out 80% of applicants. From the cover letter, you'll also see if people can construct a decent letter – if that's important to the role.

> *Don't choose people by their CVs but by their*
> *TVs; their Talents and Visions.*
> BERNARD KELVIN CLIVE

Speak to candidates on the phone

An initial phone conversation is an effective and efficient recruitment step. This should only be a five to ten-minute conversation. You'll probably know within two minutes if you want to meet the candidate in person. If you skip the call and go straight for an interview, you'll spend at least an hour with each person – because you're a nice person and it's the polite thing to do – even though you know after the first five minutes that they're not the right person.

On the initial phone call, you're assessing their ability to hold a decent conversation. Depending on the role, you can ask them to briefly expand on their experience that they feel is relevant to the role. Or what excites them about the role – you need excited and enthusiastic people. It's also telling if they call you at the designated time or not. People leave little clues about themselves everywhere. Learn to listen and look out for them. After this phone conversation, if the candidate sends you a follow-up email, they score bonus points.

Every contact leaves a trace.

DR EDMOND LOCARD

Determine candidates' strengths using a standard assessment tool

You'll want to know what your candidates are good at – their strengths. Always ask them to substantiate their claims with real life stories.

An additional approach is to ask them to complete an online strengths assessment. A superb and simple one is Gallup's Strengths Finder, which is also very modestly priced. Each StrengthsFinder 2.0 book contains a unique code that allows you to take the online assessment.[2] It will determine a candidate's top five strengths and explain how each of these plays out in daily life. Ask candidates to complete this ahead of meeting you. The results will be insightful and useful to the candidate, even if you don't take their application any further. Ensure that you and your team have used the same strengths assessment tool and that you're familiar with how it works, the language it uses and any potential limitations – there is no such thing as a perfect assessment tool. As part of your preparation process you will want to determine what strengths are likely to be needed to perform well in the role. You can then see the degree of overlap between the strengths you're looking for and each candidate's strengths profile.

The Strength Finder assessment will identify talents as well as strengths. A talent is a potential strength. Strength comes from diligently developing an innate talent. It may be sufficient that someone has the *potential* to be great at something – or you may need someone who has already developed that talent and is highly skilled and accomplished in that area already. Bear in mind that someone with *potential* will need time to develop and produce at full capacity and will absorb support and development time from your team and/or you.

Determine candidates' behavioural preferences using a profiling tool

However good your selection process, it's difficult to determine how well a candidate will fit into your organisation. Despite your best efforts, it's an artificial environment and candidates may modify their behaviour to increase the likelihood of being selected. Using a proven and well-establish behavioural profiling tool like DISC[3] will add important

---

2 https://store.gallup.com/c/en-gb/books

3 There are many online DISC tests available. https://www.mydiscprofile.com/en-gb/

information to your decision-making process.

When used as a recruitment aid, the first step is to create an 'ideal DISC profile' for the role. Next, candidates complete their own individual assessment. You can then compare their profile to the ideal profile for the role. The tests take less than 15 minutes and are inexpensive.

DISC assesses people's behavioural preferences along two axes. One axis determines to what degree someone looks at a situation in a people-focused way or in a task-focused way. The other looks at whether the person is outward looking or inward looking. Crossing the two axes produces four quadrants, as shown in the following diagram. Everyone is a mixture of all four quadrants, but to different degrees, resulting in one quadrant prevailing.

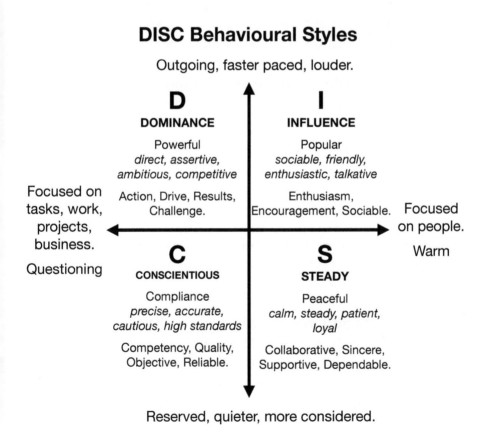

DISC Behavioural Styles

Outgoing, faster paced, louder.

D
DOMINANCE
Powerful
direct, assertive,
ambitious, competitive
Action, Drive, Results,
Challenge.

I
INFLUENCE
Popular
sociable, friendly,
enthusiastic, talkative
Enthusiasm,
Encouragement, Sociable.

Focused on tasks, work, projects, business.

Questioning

Focused on people.

Warm

C
CONSCIENTIOUS
Compliance
precise, accurate,
cautious, high standards
Competency, Quality,
Objective, Reliable.

S
STEADY
Peaceful
calm, steady, patient,
loyal
Collaborative, Sincere,
Supportive, Dependable.

Reserved, quieter, more considered.

It's important to remember that all profiling tools are just that – tools. A DISC profile can't ever fully describe or predict how someone will behave in every situation, but it's remarkably powerful in giving strong indications. As with all profiling tools, there isn't a right or wrong profile or one that's better or worse than another. In terms of recruitment, it's getting a profile that broadly matches the profile for the role.

However, DISC is situational, meaning that people can modify their behaviour. In fact, it's important that they do modify their behaviour in order to effectively and efficiently communicate and cooperate with colleagues with different DISC profiles. Your outgoing, go-getting high DI salesperson can do their necessary detailed administrative work, but only for short periods of time.

In addition to being a valuable tool in your recruitment process, DISC profiling can be used with all your team to help them better understand themselves and their colleagues. This knowledge will help in improving communication, cooperation and supervision.

DISC profiling will help you to understand someone's:
- communication style
- decision making
- organisation and planning
- motivation
- managing style
- style of management required.

If you've not used DISC profiling before, use an experienced facilitator to introduce you to it and run a session for you and your team if possible.

Focus on the right attitudes and alignment with your values

Whilst both skills and attitude are important, the latter is more important. Skills can be taught. Attitude is generally fixed and unlikely to change. You may want certain skills but it's more important that the candidates' values resonate with yours and that they have the right attitude (reliability, work ethic, willingness to learn, admitting mistakes, taking initiative, etc.). As part of your recruitment preparation, list the values and attitudes you're looking for. This can become a selection process check sheet and a place to jot down the evidence. Think how you'll identify a candidate's values and attitude. Past experiences reveal more about a candidate than hypothetical questions. Ask people to share their relevant experiences that illustrate attitudes and competencies.

> ### *The best predictor of future behaviour is past behaviour.*
> PAUL MEEHL

Use some imagination to elicit whether the applicant has what you're looking for. For example:

- **Initiative:** Whilst they're waiting for you, get someone to call the phone in the interview room to see if they pick it up – and how well they handle the call and take a message.
- **Organised:** When they're in the building, you could nip out to the car park and check out how clean and tidy their car is.
- **Reliability:** Did they call on time? Did they turn up on time? If early starts are important, hold your interviews at 7am.
- **Learner:** What was the last book they read? What did they take away from it? How did they apply it practically?
- **Improver:** What have they seen of your business so far that they could make better? What did they improve yesterday?

Make the process increasingly tough so that the best candidates get the opportunity to shine and differentiate themselves.

Involve your team in the selection process

Despite all the hours you invest in the selection process, when someone new joins the organisation, your team will know within a couple of days (hours even) if they're going to make it or not. They're doing the job day-in, day-out and know what it takes to do it well. So, involve them in designing the recruitment process and the selection exercises.

After the candidates have been through the selection process and, with the help of your check sheets, discuss the strengths and suitability of the candidates with your team. You can even ask your team which of the candidates they'd appoint and why. If you feel they've chosen someone you'd be happy to have on board, you can go with their choice. This does two things: firstly, by giving them the responsibility, it boosts their engagement in the business; secondly, they take the responsibility seriously – this becomes *their* appointment. The new person is immediately accepted and integrated by the team, and they work incredibly hard in making sure the new person works out well.

Meet all your short-listed candidates at the same time

This is efficient for you and your team and introduces a degree of healthy competition amongst your candidates. Don't tell the candidates that they'll all be attending at the same time. It may take a little logistical effort to organise, but it saves a huge amount of time and gives better results.

Create a selection process that mirrors the day-to-day job

This may require ingenuity and effort but it's worth it. Set up exercises that are as real as possible to determine if candidates can do what they say they can. Make each exercise gradually harder and give applicants more than can be done in the time available. No candidate should be able to get to the end of any particular exercise. Again, you're giving the best candidates the opportunity to differentiate themselves. If everyone gets 100%, how will you know who the best person is?

If someone has to use the phone as part of their job, get them on the phone. If they have to run meetings, get them running meetings. If they have to create spreadsheets, get them creating spreadsheets. If they have to make coffee and clear tables, get them making coffee and clearing tables.

Asking candidates to deliver a presentation is a good tactic. Most people don't like giving presentations. Before taking a break in the selection process, tell the candidates that after the break, you'd like them to give a five-minute presentation on how they overcame a challenging situation or how they've learned from a particular mistake. Is their desire for the role greater than their fear of making a presentation to a group of strangers? Again, you're giving the most committed candidates an opportunity to differentiate themselves. If they don't come back after the break, you've got your answer.

And remember that the break also forms part of the selection process. The candidates may not think it does, but you and your team want to see how they behave in a semi-social situation. If this is a senior management appointment, meet them for lunch or dinner, ideally with their partner if they have one. Senior people will be interfacing with customers and suppliers in social situations so your selection process should reflect this fact.

Example: For part-time, hourly-paid shelf-stacking roles, a retail company used to ask for candidates to submit their CVs.

They then interviewed shortlisted candidates. They had mixed results of the people they took on. Some stuck the job out, some didn't. Some were good, some were terrible. They modified their process to include some shelf stacking, presenting each candidate with a cage of mixed goods and asking them to put them on some empty shelving. Some candidates froze and didn't know what to do. Others got stuck in and started sorting out the goods, organising them by size and product type, and displaying them in a neat and tidy way with the labels facing forward. Some candidates even organised them by date, with the oldest at the front. Occasionally, some even pulled out the out-of-date goods and also mentioned that some of the products should be stored in a chiller. They still had an interview but kept it short. Its purpose was to see how clean and smart the candidates were, how well they could speak and hold a conversation, why they wanted the role and whether or not other commitments might get in the way of them fulfilling the days and hours required.

Be attractive as an organisation

Recruitment is a two-way process. You want to recruit great people – and those people will want to join a great organisation. You need to demonstrate this is a vital role; that you've got an important and exciting purpose to fulfil; and that this is a great place to work. When you have all your candidates together with your team, take the opportunity to share your vision and talk about your purpose and values. (Whenever you get the chance, share your vision!) Perhaps you could ask a couple of your team members to share a few stories that demonstrate what your purpose and values look like in practice.

Candidates will be attracted by your authenticity, passion and healthy ambition. However, it's not so attractive to people who want the job just for a pay cheque. Again, the involvement and participation of your team will boost their engagement and willingness to fully commit to your purpose and vision. Their sense of responsibility will increase, which is good for them, good for the organisation and good for candidates to see. Candidates will see that their contribution is going to count if they're successful.

Ask candidates to share stories

When it comes to interviewing candidates, "Tell me about a time when..." is a great opener for discovering relevant experiences. What you're looking for is top-of-mind responses and recent stories. There are no right or wrong answers.

"Tell me about a time when you worked under pressure."

"Urgh. Hmmm. Well, let me think...oh yes, last year I..." compared to, "Last week, two important client projects coincided...". If it's an important element of the role, ask for more than one story. "Great. Tell us about another occasion when you were under pressure?" If someone can give you plenty of recent stories of when they performed well under pressure, it's likely they'll perform well under pressure in the future. List the characteristics the person will need to perform well in the role and then preface each with the phrase, "Tell me about a time when..."

Stories are memory aids, instruction manuals and moral compasses.
ALEKS KROTOSKI

Exercise: Your next hire

- What will be the next role you'll need to recruit?
- What attitude and skills are most important in this role?
- When might you need that person? What's the worst-case lead time to recruit them? When will you therefore start the process?
- Where are these individuals currently working? How might you find and engage them?

- What will your recruitment process look like?
- Which members of your team will you involve in the process? How will you involve them?
- What selection exercises might best mirror the day-to-day job role? How will you assess their attitude and skills?

Onboarding your new colleagues

When someone new joins the business it's useful to have a 'getting to know you' session. You can tee it up so that everyone shares some personal stories about themselves. Your people can also share what they do in the business, what they enjoy about their role, what they think about the organisation and what it's aiming for. This is another opportunity to talk about vision, purpose and values.

Ensure that the person joining the team is clear about what's expected of them, what the key metrics of the role are, what support they can expect, and when their formal review sessions will be held.

Make sure they have the equipment they need to do their job on day one. If they need a fully equipped van, make sure you can give them the keys. If they need a laptop, make sure it's available, with all the relevant software and security in place.

You might want to buddy them up with someone who can show them the ropes and help them with all the little idiosyncrasies of your organisation. Depending on the position, it can also be useful to give them access to an external coach for a few months. Having access to external confidential support can help with the integration process.

If there's something they can get their teeth into straight away, that's a great way for them to quickly feel like a contributing member of the team. The earlier they can make a contribution the better.

Be on the lookout for an early opportunity to give positive feedback on any contributions made by the new person. This will build their confidence and it should be custom and practice for all your people, and not just during the first few weeks.

You can become blind to the things you and your team do on a daily basis. A new person looks at your business and operation with fresh eyes. Tap into this and ask new people to note down the questions and ideas they have. Encourage them to be curious. They should be asking lots of questions.

Build your business around your people

In recent years it's become harder to find good people than it is to find good customers. Demand is outstripping supply in many sectors. When you find a great team member, if you have sound business development processes, you can recruit the person knowing you can find the additional customers to justify the investment. Counterintuitively, you can even go and find the work that suits the skill set of the person you're employing. Perhaps you're an engineering services business and you ideally want to take on experienced electro-mechanical engineers, but you keep getting electrical engineers applying. Next time you come across an experienced electrical engineer with a great attitude, you can take them on and gear your sales team to focus on bringing in electrical work. It's a slightly different approach and requires confidence and good business development processes. Be brave and imaginative.

Retaining your good people

Having worked hard to attract and recruit good people, you want to keep them. As with customers, there can be a tendency to focus more on recruitment than retention. Recruitment is important but retention is more important (for both customers and team members). The other tendency, as with customers, is to focus more effort on your below average performers than on your best performers. Put most of your effort into your best team members and your best customers.

Most of this chapter is dedicated to sharing the specifics of how you create an environment that'll bring out the best in your people and keep them as engaged and high performing team members for a long time.

It's increasingly hard to find and retain good people – not impossible, just harder. Depending on how many people you employ, you'll want to track your staff retention rate.

Example: Staff retention for a domiciliary care company

Domiciliary Care Givers	Q1	Q2
A. Number at start	20	23
B. Number at close	23	28
C. % Increase (B-A)/A	15%	22%
D. Average Number (A+B)/2	22	26
E. Number Joined	10	16
F. Number Left	7	11
G. % Retention (D-F)/D	67%	57%

Row C shows a healthy increase in Care Givers in quarters one and two. However, row G shows staff retention is relatively low. Row E shows a high recruitment level, but row F shows a high number of leavers. The owner was pleased with the overall increase in Care Giver numbers yet concerned that they were also losing high numbers.

They also wanted to know who was leaving. Was it the new recruits or the existing staff? They added an extra layer of data, as shown in the following table:

Staff retention monitor for a domestic care business (Q3 – expanded analysis)

Domiciliary Care Givers	Q1	Q2	Q3
A. Number at start	20	23	28
B. Number at close	23	28	30
C. % Increase (B-A)/A	15%	22%	7%
D. Average Number (A+B)/2	22	26	29
E. Number Joined	10	16	4
F. Number Left	7	11	1
G. % Retention (D-F)/D	67%	57%	97%
H. Number From Start Still Employed	19	19	25
I. % Retention H/A	95%	83%	89%

Row I shows that the original staff were staying. It appeared that the new recruits were leaving after a short period. The company decided they wanted to improve their recruitment and onboarding processes in Q3. Row C shows that Care Giver numbers increased by a more modest 7% in Q3. However, both retention measures were then at a high level (rows G & I).

Greater attention to attracting and selecting more suitable staff is likely to give you more sustainable business growth – and less stress, cost and a better reputation, as well as a more enjoyable working environment.

> *Take time to appreciate employees and they*
> *will reciprocate in a thousand ways.*
>
> BOB NELSON

Exercise: Keep your best people

- Who are your best people and why?
- What specifically do you appreciate about them?
- How frequently do you sincerely let them know what you appreciate about their contribution?
- Over their lifetime as an employee, what financial contribution do your best people, directly or indirectly, make?
- What would be the impact if they left? How much time, effort and money would be involved in replacing them?
- If you committed to a retention strategy, what would be in it?
- How will you measure retention?

What to do if someone just isn't up to it

You need to do something about poor performance or poor attitude (covered later in this section), but you also need to look at how you're doing your recruitment, training and supervision. It's important to remember that the people who aren't performing are the people that you recruited, trained and currently manage. Sometimes you need to look in the mirror and determine if it's you that needs to take a different approach.

The organisation chart – your team sheet

Before putting people in places, determine which main organisational roles you need. Even if you're the first and only person in the business, you'll be carrying out different roles.

The simplest organisational chart

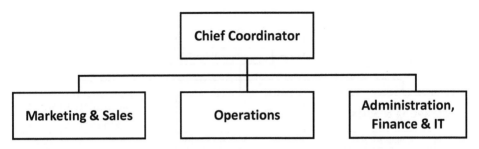

The second task is to determine and state (i) the key responsibilities, and (ii) the expected outcomes for each role. Thirdly, you can then put names to roles.

Exercise: Organisation and accountability chart

- List all the roles in your business and put them into a simple chart.
- Write out the key deliverables (outcomes/results) for each role. Be as specific as possible. Initially start with the three most important deliverables for each role. Spend no more than three minutes on each role – this will reduce the likelihood of them becoming too wordy. Write succinctly and in plain English.
- Put names against each role so that you can see who is responsible for what. The same name may appear against several roles.

As your business grows, the number of roles and how you organise those roles will change. At your annual planning session, you can create a future organisation chart for 12 months' time. Looking at your current chart and your future chart, you'll see what your recruitment objectives need to be over the coming year. You may also be aiming to reduce the number of multiple roles that certain individuals (you in particular) currently hold, and this too feeds into your recruitment plan.

Example: Current Structure

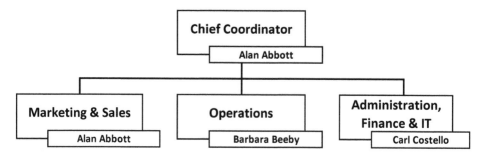

Example: Structure in 12 months

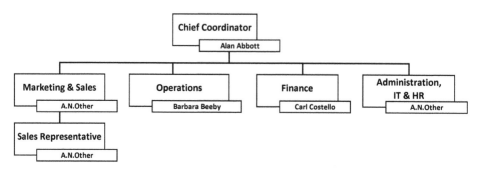

You also want to determine how each individual is performing in their role, and determine their potential, suitability and desire for taking on additional responsibilities.

You can rate individuals in a particular role against five criteria:
- Performance based on results.
- Skills to carry out the role.
- Attitude in carrying out the role.
- Potential for promotion or more responsibility.
- Future aspirations (someone may wish to move into a different area).

You can simply give each individual a score out of ten but justify your score with evidence. A nine or ten is great; a seven or eight is okay; but a six or less and you need to be addressing the issue. Perhaps you're not able to be as objective as you would like. If so, perhaps assessing your team over the coming quarter could become one of your quarterly objectives.

If someone isn't performing as expected in a particular role, determine the cause. If it's an attitude issue, they need to address it. If it's a skill issue, the solution could be training and more experience. Or perhaps it's a suitability issue – whether you train them or not, they just don't have the inherent talent to be great in that role. If that's the case, is there an available role that better suits their talents? If not, let that person go. It's the right thing for them and it's the right thing for your organisation. You can manage the process by helping them see what their talents and strengths are and helping them find something that better suits them. They might not like you in the short term, but in the longer term they're likely to say that it was the best thing that could have happened to them.

The world is a competitive place. You can't afford to have the wrong people in the wrong positions, even if they have a great attitude. If they have a fabulous attitude, hopefully you can find a place for them.

Succession planning

One role that you should be looking to fill in the long term is your replacement. Your job as business owner is to develop the business to the point where your role becomes redundant – the business can function without you. You therefore need to be cultivating someone internally who can take on the role of General Manager or Managing Director (the Chief Coordinator). You can appoint from the outside but far better to appoint someone who's grown with you and who resonates strongly with the organisation's values and culture.

On a more general point, you should be thinking about how you'd fill every role in the organisation if the incumbent suddenly wasn't there. Some roles might not need filling immediately – the rest of the team could pick up the slack until a replacement was found. This is acceptable if replacements can be readily recruited. Alternatively, you may need to cross-train people so that if someone suddenly leaves or is ill, someone else can carry out their role on a temporary basis. Don't just train them, but periodically have them carrying out the role to ensure they're relatively 'match fit'. For senior roles, a longer-term strategy of internal development needs to be adopted. As mentioned in the recruitment section, you also need to be identifying and making contact with potential future recruits in the marketplace.

Your external team

As well as your internal team, think about the support and services you need from your external team. These professionals will include:

- Investors
- Trade suppliers
- Marketing agency
- Financial and management accountant
- Business coach
- Human resources advisor
- IT support
- Insurance broker
- Wealth manager or financial planner
- Banker
- Corporate financier
- Solicitor

In addition to choosing people who are competent at what they do, ensure that these people are also willing to act as referrers and introduce potential clients to you. If they do, what you spend on their services could be exceeded by the additional gross profit you earn from serving the new clients they introduce. Obviously, you should look out for them too and promote their services. The stronger and deeper your relationships the better.

It's not essential but is preferable to choose professionals who are geographically close to your office. It's often useful to be able to meet up at short notice, and you'll be able to promote each other's services in the local community.

Example: An architect's practice had used the same accountants for their first eight years of trading.

The accounting practice was 125 miles away and only had one fully qualified accountant plus a support team of four people. The architect had 'chosen' the accountant because someone they met on holiday had recommended them! They'd got to know this person well over two weeks, liked them and this person was also in business, so not quite as random as it sounds. The accountant was fine. They did what they had to do, but they weren't proactive, they were slow, they always seemed to be mad busy, and they certainly never made any referrals. The architect decided it was time to partner with an accountant who would be proactive and would contribute over and above, making sure the accounts were completed accurately and submitted on time. They approached the exercise in a similar way to how they'd recruit an architect to join their practice – having a clear list of requirements, not rushing, and being methodical. They decided that they'd start networking locally, with the intention of finding a local accountant. They also reasoned that an accountant who went networking would be someone who was proactive and someone who'd likely make referrals to them. It took them the best part of nine months and their new accountant's charge rates were higher. However, in addition to a far superior service, their new accountants reduced their tax bill and introduced them to some research and development credits they were entitled to. In the first six months of working with the new accountants, they also received two referred pieces of work – which covered the annual account bill three times over.

Choose professionals that classify you as an important client. Avoid becoming a small customer to a large organisation. Conversely, ensure that they have sufficient support in depth. The day your servers crash, you don't want to discover that your IT support business is in fact one individual who is currently on holiday in Cuba.

You might not think you need a wealth manager – because you don't have any wealth yet. But that's your intention. So, start the process early. Start mixing in the circles where wealthy people mix. You become like the people you spend time with so start mixing with people who build and sell businesses. You've got your finance in place and you're not planning on selling your business for ten years at least, so why do you need to hook up with a corporate financier? Well, it's never too early to start thinking about what it takes to maximise the value of your business. And besides, both these individuals are likely, if you keep in touch regularly, to introduce you to new business opportunities.

Exercise: Choosing your external support team

- Which roles do you need on your external support team?
- Which roles are currently filled and by whom?
- Out of 10, how would you rate each of those people?
- For those who are below par, what will you do to improve their contribution? Or what will you do about replacing them?
- How will you go about finding people to fill any vacant roles?
- What will be your strategy for managing your external support team?

Managing for high performance

Here are several actions you can take that will get you a long way in ensuring good performance from your people.

Make sure everyone understands what you expect of them

This is the most important thing you can give someone at work: A clear understanding of why they're on the payroll. What is it, exactly, you want them to deliver? What are the key outcomes for this role? What, specifically, would be a great result? What does a job, done excellently, look like?

Performance management is less difficult when you've defined what excellence in the role looks like. For the job holder, if they have the understanding of what's expected of them, even in the absence of any formal feedback, they'll know if they've done their job well – and that sense of achievement is a vital motivational ingredient.

Setting expectations doesn't have to be a lengthy exercise. Quite the opposite – it's better if you can make it short and succinct. Avoid business jargon. Write in plain English. Write in terms of outcomes. What are the results that you want? Whilst you may have processes and procedures in place – which is good – you can leave the individual to work out the 'how' of achieving those outcomes.

Example: An events company role description

A commercial events company had grown to a size where they decided they'd invest in a dedicated salesperson. They were on the money in terms of being target driven and expecting their salesperson to be proactive. They devised an activity-based (*how*-based) role description:

- Make at least ten sales phone calls every day.
- Set up at least one sales meeting every week.
- Make sure the potential client receives a sales brochure at the meeting and always leave them with a branded mug and notebook.
- Follow-up every sales meeting with a letter, making sure that the potential client knows the benefits of working with us.
- Sign up at least three clients every quarter.
- Make sure the database of potential clients is being added to constantly and is being kept up to date.
- Keep in touch will all potential clients on a regular basis. Develop a sales newsletter that can be sent out every month, highlighting special offers.
- Keep a sales monitor updated daily and share this with the team every week.

Whilst these activities seemed sensible, things weren't going well. One salesperson had left after only a short period of time and a second one wasn't producing the goods either. There was lots of form filling and endless discussions about why certain elements of the process wasn't working. Management decided to take a different approach, partly through frustration rather than insight, and changed to a simple, short, outcome-based job description.

- Every quarter, sign-up at least three new Northwest based clients with annual purchases of at least £30,000.
- How you do it is up to you. But just do it.

Quarter three delivered two new qualifying clients, whereas the first two quarters had delivered just one new client. The salesperson was still below target but had significantly improved their performance – and was making a profit contribution well above their cost of employment.

When you've clarified the outcomes you expect, the next step is ensuring they're understood by the job holder. Just because you've written them down and spoken them out loud, it doesn't mean that they've been understood, agreed and accepted. Believing your expectations have been understood when they haven't can be frustrating, time wasting and constitutes 'poor communication'.

Twenty-four hours after sharing your expectations, or after a weekend, invite the job holder back and ask them to explain their understanding of their role in their own words. Encourage them to create a short (handwritten) presentation so you can hear and see what they believe their deliverables are.

If you've defined the specific outcomes you want and you've checked that they're understood and achievable, there's a good chance those outcomes will be achieved, even if you're not around for the next twelve months.

You may perceive this exercise to be time consuming and you just want your new hire to crack on. However, getting this step right can save you much sorrow and aggravation down the line and deliver better performance more quickly.

Periodically ask each team member, "Why are you on the payroll? What key outputs are you here to deliver?" If they can't answer, or answer fully or correctly, that's valuable feedback that you've not carried out a key aspect of your role successfully. Don't get cross or frustrated, take a breath, and find a better way of clarifying the specifics of the role.

> *Treat a person as they are, and they will remain as they are. Treat a person as they can and should be and they will become as they can and should be.*
>
> STEPHEN R. COVEY

Senior people need role descriptions too

It's also important to define the expectations of senior people in the business, including yourself. Set the example to your team. Perhaps encourage them to periodically ask you why you're on the payroll. Seriously. You want/need people who'll kick back and challenge (for the right reasons).

Include everyone and expect everyone to be involved

Part of your responsibility is to include all your team members in the business. Part of their responsibility is to step up to the plate and get involved. Here are two additional expectations worth adding to everyone's role description: Firstly, expect everyone to look for development opportunities for the business and to bring in potential enquiries. Secondly, expect everyone to look for and share ideas on how the business could work more effectively and efficiently. Regularly (at team meetings and individual performance review meetings) ask people about these two things.

Encourage and expect people to take risks

You should expect and allow team members to take risks within their areas of responsibility. You need to foster a spirit of curiosity and experimentation as you and your team explore ways of doing things better. Continuous incremental improvement needs to become part of your cultural DNA.

> *Don't be too timid and squeamish about your actions. All life is an experiment. The more experiments you make the better.*
>
> RALPH WALDO EMERSON

Taking risks will result in mistakes and things going wrong. Therefore, you need to think about your attitude to mistakes. As the boss, with a smile on your face, eyes raised to the heavens and a hand on your forehead, you'll be able to recount some of the mistakes you've made over the years – and also what you learned from them. Are you as accepting and generous with your team? Or do they get it in the neck when they get things wrong? If so, they'll learn not to take risks. And without taking risks, it's difficult to get better or grow. If your people aren't making mistakes, they're probably not trying hard enough. Do you secretly celebrate your team making mistakes in the pursuit of making things better?

Risks should be proportionate. As discussed in the marketing section, test and measure before rolling out big time. Don't allow people to take risks that put your operation in jeopardy. But do encourage your team to be curious and experiment within their areas of responsibility.

Provide the tools and equipment to do a great job

Having clarified expectations, the next task is to ensure that people have everything they need to be able to do their job excellently. It might be a reliable, clean, liveried, well-equipped van and a fuel card; it might be a superfast desktop computer with dual screens; it might be a quiet, distraction-free workspace; it might be a phone and a Customer Relationship Management (CRM) system; it might be a top-of-the-range sander and ultra-sharp chisel set. Ensure that people have the right tools to do the excellent job you expect of them.

Play to people's strengths

If you recruited someone with the right skills, strengths and passion for doing a particular role, let them do that role. Play to their strengths and let them do what they're good at doing. Avoid deploying them in areas that don't play to their strengths. Yes, there can be parts of a role that people aren't brilliant at, but as much as possible deploy people to tasks they enjoy and are good at. (Enjoying something and being good at it usually run along together.)

Feedback promptly and regularly

In business, there's a need to measure and create feedback loops for the purposes of continuous improvement. You need to know where to focus improvement efforts and what impact those interventions are having. People are no different. They need to know how they're doing. Regular, positive feedback from a supervisor or manager for doing a good job stokes the fires of motivation. Managers need to become good observers. You need to be on the lookout for people doing their job well. And be ready and alert to give sincere feedback. Keep it short and simple. 'Good job' or 'I liked the way you handled that call' or 'You make a really thorough job of clearing and cleaning those tables' or 'I love the way you smile at customers and say *Hello*'.

> *Feedback is the breakfast of champions.*
>
> KEN BLANCHARD

Feedback is best delivered as close to the action as possible. Don't save things up for the monthly review – especially things that aren't right.

TEAM

Observe the good performance and comment immediately. Feedback for good performance can be delivered in public or in private. Some people like to be complimented in front of their peers, others don't. Get to know your people and deliver feedback in a way that's best for them. Deliver feedback on poor performance in private, as soon as possible.

By pointing out good behaviours and good performance, you will get more of the same – and it reduces the likelihood of complacency creeping in. You'll also discover that it's one of your more enjoyable tasks. Receiving regular and prompt feedback for doing a good job – yes, even though it's the job they're paid to do – is another important way of engaging staff and tapping into their vitality. Giving feedback is easy and free – you just have to make a conscious effort to become a good observer.

Don't tolerate poor performance for a moment

Give people sufficient time to have a go. If they're not doing things right, not performing to the expected standard or are displaying a poor attitude, do something about it. By not saying anything about someone's less-than-desired performance, you are condoning and reinforcing it. In effect, you're silently communicating that their performance is acceptable, and the person is likely to continue operating at that level. Their performance may even deteriorate as they, consciously or subconsciously, test out where the boundaries are.

Act before things exist; manage them before there is disorder.
LAO TSU

When addressing poor performance, make the conversation a positive and constructive one. Make them do the talking by asking questions:
- What's their understanding of the standards expected in their role?
- Have they got the right tools to do a quality job?
- Have they completed adequate training?
- What do they think of their performance?
- How does their performance measure up against their absolute best?
- Do they see how they can get better?
- What can they commit to doing to close the gap?
- Do they need any help from you?

- How will they know they're closing the gap?
- When should you get together next to see how they're progressing?

You want them to recognise the performance gap – and then to come up with improvement ideas. Keep it positive. Reassure them you believe they can close the gap. The sooner you address less-than-expected performance, the sooner it can be fixed. Don't compromise. Expect the best.

Give people a high standard to live up to.

DALE CARNEGIE

Exercise: Ensure understanding and gain agreement on what's expected of each individual

- List the three most important deliverables for each role in the business. Of those three, which is the most important?
- Starting with yourself and your direct reports, ask everyone why they're on the payroll.
- Engage in a two-way dialogue with each person to clarify and agree on what their key deliverables are.
- Periodically, ask people why they're on the payroll.
- At least once a year, check that those deliverables are still relevant.

Turning groups of people into high performing teams

One mindset hurdle to clear is the realisation that a handful of people performing at 75% of your ability and capacity will achieve more than you can achieve alone – you have to let go. (Ideally you want to surround yourself with people who will achieve 125% of your performance.) A second realisation is that whilst you may have recruited competent and motivated individuals who are keen to impress and charge ahead, slowing them down to work together collaboratively as a team will, over time, produce better results.

You may be familiar with the stages involved in creating a high performing team as modelled by psychologist Bruce Tuckman: forming, storming, norming, performing (and adjourning).[4]

Forming

Perhaps you have a collection of individuals who are good but who you wouldn't describe as a high-performing team – perhaps you wouldn't even describe them as a team. Forming sessions are opportunities to announce your desire for everyone to start working together more collaboratively.

Getting to know each other personally is still a good place to start, as is sharing your vision, purpose and values. Whilst frustration and even annoyance may have brought you to this point, keep this 'forming' session positive – find the things that are being done well, and build on those. Facilitate discussion and get the team coming up with the ideas and actions. Include and involve everyone. You may feel the need to introduce new rules – boundaries that people can't cross and that have real consequences if they are crossed. This approach is acceptable and works, as long as you follow through on the consequences. Alternatively, you can facilitate a discussion whereby the team come up with the new rules and consequences. This is harder and takes more time, but your team is more likely to follow and self-police the rules they've created themselves and accept the consequences they've stipulated.

Anticipate and talk about things that might go wrong with team dynamics. Discuss how the risk of those breakdowns can be mitigated. Also discuss what you'll do if things start to fray at the edges or even breakdown. Importantly, discuss how you'll bring up awkward situations (someone not pulling their weight, someone dumping work on someone else, someone becoming overly dominant, etc.). Gain agreement on how these things are raised.

Ensure that each member of the team carries out a DISC behavioural profiling assessment. Each individual will become more aware of their own preferences in terms of communication, style of interaction, organising, planning and decision making. When facilitated (by an experienced practitioner) as an interactive session, team members become more aware of the preferences of their colleagues, learning how

---

4   https://web.archive.org/web/20151129012409/http://openvce.net/sites/default/files/Tuck-man1965DevelopmentalSequence.pdf

to modify their interaction styles in order to make those interactions more meaningful and productive.

Understanding individual strengths and weaknesses (through a Strengths Finder assessment) also serves to enhance awareness and understanding amongst team members. When individuals can talk knowledgeably about what they're good at and like doing, and what they find difficult and don't like doing, it helps engender an honest, open and supportive environment that aids team harmony.

Have these team development sessions on a regular basis. Remember the agenda isn't business performance (that's a separate meeting), it's about functioning well as a team.

Storming

Think of forming as a team honeymoon period. Storming is when real life kicks in, people's annoying idiosyncrasies start to grate, and individual egos can start inhibiting cooperation. If you're aware of what can happen, you can design the forming period to minimise the negative impact of this second phase. You might not be able to eradicate conflict, but you can agree how you'll resolve them when they do happen. Conflict can be emotionally charged, therefore an agreed resolution process is a useful tool.

The speed with which you effectively move through the storming phase can be accelerated by the structures that you put in place. As mentioned elsewhere in this book, regular, well-run team meetings and one-to-one development meetings are vital. As well as meeting to discuss performance and remove obstacles, schedule in team development and refresher sessions. Communication (DISC), strengths, vision, purpose, values and rules of the game can all be revisited and built upon.

Work at developing a culture where individuals appreciate the contribution of colleagues and where they recognise extra effort. Initially you may have to stimulate this awareness, but the aim is that it becomes a habitual daily practice.

Norming

After the storming period, you enter the norming phase. People start to understand and appreciate each other: their strengths, their contributions, their weaknesses, their idiosyncrasies, their preferred ways of working. Your team is starting to work well together, to cooperate and coordinate well – but keep having the team development meetings.

One of your roles is to help your people develop. Ideally, you want them to adopt personal responsibility for their development. A key aspect is to help them see themselves, to become self-aware. When people become increasingly self-aware, they can take active steps to manage and develop themselves. If that groundwork has started, it also gives individuals better clarity (and the right) to become other-aware – to see their colleagues in a clearer light and understand how they can work with them more collaboratively.

Performing

This is when you can step away and the team keeps moving – even accelerating. You only have to touch the tiller lightly to keep them on course. Not only are they individually motivated and performing at a high level, but they're supporting each other, holding each other accountable, bringing out the best in each other, and working collaboratively to produce great results.

It is the long history of humankind (and animal kind, too) that those who learned to collaborate and improvise most effectively have prevailed.

CHARLES DARWIN

If you want to know if you have a high performing team, look at the results they're producing. The name of the game is results and that's the acid test.

When you're developing a high performing team, investing in a professional to facilitate your team development sessions – especially the first one – can deliver great returns.

Adjourning

(Doesn't quite rhyme!) In the context of an on-going business rather than a project that comes to an end, think of this element as a review. Schedule time for you and the team to assess how the team has been performing. What are the things that have gone really well? What stories can be shared? What can you celebrate? What did you like and enjoy? What are you grateful for? What might you have lost – and need to acknowledge and grieve over? What have you learned? What can you take forward and make even better in the future? What are your aspirations? What are you aiming for?

The main four stages are likely to overlap with each other. You may not even get the storming stage and you might go from forming directly to performing. The forming stage is the most important phase, though hard work, discipline and occasionally some tough decisions are all required throughout the process.

When you've created a great team, choose wisely when adding new members, and all will be well. Once you have the teams in place, it is important to manage performance to ensure everyone continues to work at their best level. Don't become complacent. Stay humble.

Communication

In staff surveys, poor communication is cited as a problem in most organisations. Although most organisations believe they go overboard in terms of communication, talking or writing to people doesn't mean that they've heard and understood. Good communication is more about listening and responding than it is about talking, telling or writing. Don't assume that communication means internal newsletters – they're way down the 'good communication' list.

The single biggest problem in communication
is the illusion that it has taken place.
GEORGE BERNARD SHAW

On the other side of the coin, staff have a responsibility to ensure they find out what's happening and to clarify their understanding. They also have a duty to communicate upwards when things aren't right or when things could be better. Those responsibilities should be woven into their role descriptions.

At a high level, three essentials of good communication are understanding:
- personal role expectations
- the company's vision and purpose
- the specific expectations of internal and external customers.

When someone understands what's expected of them, that's excellent communication. If someone isn't performing as expected, the first port of call is to check they understand what's expected of them. Understanding the needs of your customers adds context to a role. Explaining how an individual contribution fits into the vision and purpose of the organisation enhances its value. People also need to understand their part in shorter-term improvement initiatives.

Communication isn't a one-off event. Effective, on-going communication takes place through a linked series of well-run meetings – the subject of the next section.

Purposeful and well-run meetings are the heartbeat of your business

Another common complaint in staff surveys is too many meetings. There aren't. Meetings are your principal forum for communication. What there might be are too many long and badly run meetings.

Meetings are your job. Regular, scheduled meetings are the heartbeat of your organisation.

Key meetings
1. Annual and quarterly planning meetings.
2. Quarterly 'State of the Nation' and alignment sessions.
3. Weekly progress meetings.
4. Daily huddles.
5. Monthly one-to-one performance reviews with direct reports.

Annual and quarterly planning, 'state of the nation' and alignment sessions, and weekly progress meetings are covered in detail in the Planning chapter. Daily huddles and monthly one-to-ones are covered later in this section.

We bring together the best ideas – turning the meetings of our top managers into intellectual orgies.

JACK WELCH

Running a good meeting

Before looking at each of these meetings, here are the basics of running a meeting:

- **Purpose:** Have a clear, written purpose for every meeting. Everyone needs to know the meeting's intended outcomes. This simple step will determine whether there's any need for a meeting. No purpose, no meeting.

- **Agenda:** Have one and circulate it ahead of time.

- **Time-bound:** Have a start and finish time. Stick to the start and finish times. It's a small point, but it can be helpful to start meetings at an odd time. Rather than 10:00am, try 9:55am or 10:20am. People are more likely to be on time for meetings that start at 9:55am rather than 10:00am. One organisation I know of allows people to get up and walk out at the designated finish time. That tends to keep things brisk and business-like! Another company locks the door at the designated start time. You might deem these measures draconian, but punctuality might be a core value. Would you be late for a train or a doctor's appointment or a customer meeting? Your punctuality *communicates* how important you consider your colleagues.

- **Expectations:** Clarify individual and general expectations. If people need to present or share something, check they've understood and agreed to what they're presenting.

- **Rules:** At the outset, discuss and agree some rules around etiquette and expectations (attendance, participation, interruptions, timings, attitude, how to disagree well, note taking, etc.).

- **Notice:** Inform everyone well in advance – purpose, desired outcomes, agenda, individual expectations, start & finish times, etc.

- **Regularity:** If it's a regular meeting, have it on the same day at the same time and get it in everyone's diary for the rest of the year.

- **Close:** Finish the meeting 10 minutes early in order to capture the actions – who's going to do what and by when. Ask everyone to verbalise the actions they're committing to. Only capture the actions that will be completed before the next meeting. If it's a longer-term action, break it down until there's an action step that can be completed before the next meeting.

- **Actions:** Handwritten actions are fine. Take a photo of the action sheet and message it to everyone. The key is clarity and gaining agreement and commitment to complete the actions.

- **Improve:** Liked Best, Next Time (LBNTs). In the interests of continuous improvement spend a couple of minutes highlighting what you all liked about the meeting and what you can build on to make it even better next time.

- **Finish:** If you can, finish the meeting early. Everyone likes that.

It's harder having meetings than not having them. They take energy, they're time-consuming, they can precipitate disagreements and, when you cost in everyone's time, they're expensive. However, expect a return on that investment in terms of better decisions, better actions and better results. A well-run, purposeful meeting with committed-to actions constitutes good communication.

Example: A solicitors' practice decided to work out the hypothetical annual cost of their weekly management meeting.

- The attendees are managing partner, office manager, and three department heads.
- Total hours worked per year for each person: 50 weeks x 40 hours = 2,000 hours.
- Hours in weekly meeting: 50 weeks x 2 hours = 100 hours. 100/2,000 = 5% of the year.
- Total annual salaries = £85,000 + £30,000 + (3 x £55,000) = £280,000.
- Annual cost of meeting = 5% x £280,000 = £14,000. Not an insignificant sum of money.
- More critically, the charge out rate of the managing partner and

CONTINUED

the three department heads was £185 per hour. The potential *lost revenue* (the opportunity cost) for being in that meeting for those four people was £74,000 (4 x 2hrs x 50 wks. x £185).
- These numbers really focused their mind. They still believed the benefits of the meeting outweighed the costs, but they kept the meeting extremely business-like, and it rarely went over 90 minutes.

Make your meetings count.

Start every meeting with a highlight

The core purpose of most meetings is to discuss and resolve problems. When meetings focus on problems they naturally have a negativity bias. Problems are often seen as someone's failing. This can precipitate excuses, finger pointing, defensiveness, and escalate into arguments and stubbornness – even denial that there is a problem. To solve problems, you want a meeting atmosphere that's open, creative and constructive. Start your meeting by asking everyone to share a brief story of something that's going well. This simple ritual creates a positive, confident, can-do atmosphere for your meeting. Follow this short structure:
- What's your highlight?
- Why did you pick this particular highlight?
- Why did it go so well?
- How might you get more of this good thing?

The final question about getting more of that good thing indirectly gets people thinking about overcoming problems – but from a different and more open-minded perspective.

With everyone contributing a highlight at the beginning of a meeting, your team gets into the habit of observing what's going well. Most of us seem to be naturally good at finding what's not working or going well, and less good at finding, recognising, and learning from what is going well. Stick with this routine for opening your meetings and you'll experience its power.

Your short, daily *What's Happening* team huddle

This is a simple, stand up team meeting that only lasts five to ten minutes. You may have several of these stand-up meetings happening across your organisation.

It allows everyone to succinctly share:
- their major achievement from yesterday.
- what they've got on today.
- what their biggest challenge is today.
- what they might be struggling with.
- how they're feeling.

It's not a blow-by-blow account of what you're going to be doing throughout your day. "Today I'm going to complete the slides for the new client presentation we'll be using at Friday morning's pitch" would be appropriate. However, on a different day you might say, "Today I'm going to complete the slides for the new client presentation we'll be using at Friday morning's pitch, but I'm really up against it as I've also got a tender that has to be submitted by 4pm this afternoon" which allows someone else to offer a potential solution. "I've got some flexibility in my day so perhaps I can help with those slides. Let's have a chat in a minute." This is not a solution-generating meeting. Those conversations can take place after the meeting.

It's assumed that if people work in an open plan office, then everyone knows what everyone else is up to. They usually don't. This short, daily meeting is a meaningful aid to good communication. It allows people to join the dots to see what's happening across the team and understand where they can help their colleagues, and vice versa. Holding this daily meeting will help in engendering a healthy, collaborative working environment and a desire for colleagues to help each other out. It's also helpful to stand up and vocalise your key task for the day – it introduces a degree of self-accountability, especially as you're going to report back on it the following day on how you got on. No notetaking is necessary for this short meeting.

The meeting should happen early on in the day. Some companies have what they call a 10 at 10 – ten minutes at ten o'clock. If you operate shift working, you can have your meeting shortly after the shift starts. Experiment and discover what works best for you and your team. Even if you have remote workers, it's important to involve them in the meeting.

It doesn't have to be the most senior person who calls the meeting. In fact, it helps if responsibility for running the meeting rotates around the team each week. Running the meeting simply means:

- Telling everyone the meeting's going to start in five minutes.
- Going around the circle and asking people to speak.
- Reminding people to keep it succinct.
- Asking people to keep discussions for after the meeting.
- Thanking everyone for sharing.

Nothing more than that. Same time, every day. Don't book appointments that are going to clash with your daily huddle. It's important so don't compromise it. The key is to keep it short and succinct.

One-to-one meetings with your direct reports

Of all your business relationships, the ones with your direct reports are the most important. They therefore merit a dedicated portion of your time and effort. The better your people get, the better your business gets. Even if you spend a great deal of time with these people on a daily basis, there's value in sitting down formally for a one-to-one to review, reflect and plan.

In terms of frequency, no less than quarterly and ideally once a month. With a new person, it's good to catch up at the end of every day in the first week; at the end of every week during the first month; and, assuming everything is progressing well, monthly thereafter.

Here's an agenda for your monthly one-to-ones:

- What's gone well? Why did it go so well? How can you build on that?
- What's not gone so well? What have you learned from that? What might you do differently next time?
- How've you done on the commitments you made last time?
- What challenges have you overcome? What challenges haven't you overcome? What have you learned? What's the next step you might take?
- What specific intentions would you like to commit to over the coming month?
- How could I support you over the coming month?

- What did you like about this meeting? How was it helpful? Anything that would make the next one better?
- How motivated are you feeling (out of 10)?

Get your monthly one-to-one meetings scheduled in your diary for at least the next six months. Schedule them when you're unlikely to have competing demands on your time. And think about having them when you won't have districting thoughts running around your head. First thing in the day is a good time.

Encourage and allow your colleague to do most of the talking. Your question-based agenda will help. Speaking for no longer than 20% of the time is a good guide. This is more likely to happen if you've positioned the meeting well, there's a meeting structure, and you've asked them to prepare ahead of time. Whilst it's good practice to have a meeting structure, don't stick to it rigidly. You're entering into a conversation, and you can't predict where it will go. You have to listen and respond to what's shared.

Give your colleague a notebook and encourage them to record their observations daily. This overcomes the law of recency effect whereby you tend to focus on what happened in the recent past and forget all the things that have happened over the whole month. A five-minute review at the end of every day is a good discipline – an activity that could form part of a daily closedown routine.

Your aim is that your colleague leaves the meeting feeling motivated, empowered, and supported, with a clear idea and specific actions as to how they can develop themselves and enhance their performance over the coming month. You will also clarify any supporting actions that you've committed to take.

It's most effective if you can help your colleague become increasingly self-aware and steer them towards making their own decisions about how they can improve and grow. If the words come out of their mouth, they're far more potent than if they come out of yours. Sometimes you just have to say it, but work on your skill of getting them to see for themselves.

If an issue has occurred during the month, it shouldn't be saved for the monthly one-to-one meeting. It should be dealt with, in private, as soon after the event as possible. Similarly, don't hold back on saying 'thank you' or giving praise where it's due.

Arrive early for the meeting. Rushing and arriving at the last moment will increase your stress levels and reduce your ability to concentrate and listen attentively. Avoid postponing the meeting. Being late for the meeting or cancelling it subtly communicates that the person isn't that important.

If you're carrying out regular one-to-ones with your direct reports, there isn't any need to have an annual appraisal. You can nominate one of your monthly meetings as an opportunity to discuss your colleague's longer-term aspirations and development desires.

Exercise: Managing and developing your people

- Who are your direct reports?
- How frequently will you meet with them on a one-to-one basis?
- What will be the purpose of those meetings? What will the agenda look like?
- Speak to each direct report individually, explaining the purpose and benefits of meeting. Gain agreement on when it's best to have those meetings.
- Schedule in all those meetings for the next quarter, extending a calendar invite to each person.
- Build in a review session after the quarter to determine how well they're working and how they might be changed and improved.
- Make those scheduled meetings sacrosanct.

Motivation – creating the right conditions

Motivation remains a generally misunderstood management topic. It's often believed that money motivates people – or the threat of losing their job if they don't perform well. Dangling carrots in front of people and beating them with sticks does generate movement and may produce results – but it doesn't generate motivation. You can't motivate someone else. Only they can do that.

Motivation is an inside job.

Your job as a leader and a manager is to create conditions that increase the likelihood of your team members being motivated. The carrot and stick approach to management has two major drawbacks. The carrots and sticks keep having to get bigger to get improving results. And if you stop using them, results can evaporate.

The power of money to motivate and demotivate

It's essential that people's pay is decent and fair, that they're paid the agreed amount, and they're paid on time. However, money's ability to motivate is limited. Ironically, mess around with people's money and you'll discover that money has far greater potential as a demotivator.

As a broad rule, if you're a top quartile business, with top quartile people, who are top quartile producers, you should pay top quartile wages. Avoid being in a position where people leave to take up similar positions elsewhere because of money. Make sure you're ahead when it comes to recognising what your people contribute and when they merit higher wages.

Get money right and it generates a little bit of motivation; get it wrong and it has a huge ability to demotivate.

A wise person should have money in their head, but not in their heart.
JONATHAN SWIFT

Factors that motivate people

In priority order, six things that motivate more than money are:

1. a sense of achievement
2. recognition for doing good work
3. work that the individual sees as interesting and worthwhile
4. increased responsibility
5. advancement
6. personal growth.

These factors were distilled from extensive research of various sectors in multiple countries carried out by Harvard psychology professor Frederick Hertzberg and his team of researchers. [5] Ironically, whilst this and other similar studies have been around for decades, many

5 https://hbr.org/2003/01/one-more-time-how-do-you-motivate-employees

organisations remain wedded to carrot and stick management practices.

You'll see that much of what has been shared in this book feeds into one of these motivational factors. Involvement and participation in setting objectives and self-monitoring progress leads to people having a sense of achievement. People want to feel in control of their work and lives. Catching people doing things well and feeding back promptly and regularly is motivating. Helping people see the bigger picture and how their role contributes to the whole is motivating. Encouraging people to come up with their own solutions and ideas boosts motivation. Giving people the opportunity to stetch themselves is motivating. And having review mechanisms in place to recognise progress also helps.

Paradoxically, the absence of these things doesn't cause people to become demotivated. Their absence just doesn't increase motivation. Similarly, when you address the things that demotivate people, you don't get motivated people.

Factors that demotivate people
Five things that demotivate people and cause job dissatisfaction:
1. Bureaucratic rules, policies and administration.
2. Poor supervision.
3. Poor work conditions.
4. Salary below current market rates.
5. Poor relationships with colleagues.

As you might expect, excessive bureaucracy, rules and regulations are likely to create a working atmosphere where people feel disinclined to give their best. Similarly, if the standard of your supervision is inadequate, and you have a poor relationship with your supervisor, you are unlikely to feel motivated.

Research has shown that your relationship with your immediate supervisor or manager is extremely powerful, both positively and negatively. You can work for a fabulous organisation with brilliant leaders, but if you have a terrible relationship with your supervisor, life is miserable and you're likely to leave. Conversely, if you work for a terrible organisation, but have a great boss who you respect, who takes a keen interest in you, who encourages you and who looks after you, you're likely to stay, work hard and give your best. This highlights the importance of hiring, training and developing great team leaders, supervisors and managers.

It's not a black and white picture. If managed well, these potentially demotivating factors can be brought to neutral and may even have a motivational impact – but only a small one.

Exercise: Creating an environment where people feel motivated

- How can you organise your people's work to give them the opportunity to gain a sense of achievement when they've completed it? Or as they're making progress with the work?
- When and how can you recognise when your people are doing good work?
- How can you make the work interesting and challenging?
- How can you give people more responsibility?
- How can you help them grow and advance?

The answers will be the opposite to the old-fashioned management view of people as cogs in a machine: don't think, don't deviate, do as you're told, follow the rules.

Similarly, with the demotivational factors, you need to ask how you create an environment that avoids these elements. In particular, focus on making sure that your policies and procedures are as simple as possible. Ideally, you want to operate with a handful of guiding principles and minimise the need for rules.

Whilst it's often strongly denied, there's a direct correlation between the number of rules a company has and the degree to which the company – the senior management – trust their people. If you trusted everyone to do the right thing, you wouldn't need any rules. Again, regardless of whether you agree or not, asking the question, 'To what degree do I trust the people who work for me?' opens up a helpful perspective on what sort of culture you have. Every organisation has a culture. It's either a working environment that you've deliberately and carefully nurtured and cultivated, or one that's morphed from the powerful undercurrents that you've allowed to flow unchecked.

A clear vision, a meaningful purpose and uncompromising values will all act to give an organisation a strong set of guiding principles to operate by, negating the need for many rules.

You can indirectly impact the motivation levels of your team by creating a working environment where they get the chance to take on challenging work, to contribute to something bigger than themselves, to get a real sense of achievement, and to play to their strengths. You may not get there with every role all the time, but it's a worthy aspiration and merits the effort.

How engaged are your people?

As well as motivated people, you want people who are fully engaged in what they're doing and in what you're trying to achieve as an organisation. You therefore want to measure engagement levels. It's particularly valuable because engagement is a headlight measure – it tells you something about the future. There's a tendency to focus on rear-view mirror measures, like sales and profit. If sales and profits fall, the cause usually occurred some time ago – hence the terminology, rear-view mirror measure. For example, it might be that customer service has deteriorated over the past six months and that's now manifested in a fall in sales. And perhaps service standards waned because there was a change in supervisors 12 months ago and, because you were so busy, the weekly briefings dropped off. If a routine engagement survey had been carried out it would have picked up on a change of mood within the team. During the follow-up workshops – which should always accompany any engagement survey – the issues could have been addressed and an improvement plan put in place.

Bear in mind, as with any survey or questionnaire, carrying out an engagement survey creates expectations. People expect feedback, action and improvement, whether its customers or staff. The key thing is that everyone gets to be involved in the all-important follow-up workshops. And it's the resulting actions where the real value is created.

The survey itself is easy to carry out and takes very little time – five to ten minutes. To get a high response rate, explain that the purpose of the survey is to help create an even more effective and enjoyable workplace. It will allow each person to discuss how their workplace could be improved; to identify specific ways in which individually and collectively you can improve the culture and working environment; and it will help to identify the specific support individuals and teams need. Demonstrating a genuine desire to improve the working environment will ensure a high response rate. The response rate for subsequent engagement surveys will very much depend on what happened after the first one. Did you follow up and make the agreed changes?

Various engagement surveys are available online. The best and most well-known is Gallup's Q12. Gallup distilled many years of research down to 12 key questions that measure employee engagement. They have run their survey across thousands of organisations all around the world. You can adapt some of the wording and add a few more questions if you wish. But only a few. Resist the urge to change too much. Whatever you might think, your business isn't that unique.

Here is the complete list of questions that Gallup discovered measured the degree of engagement of a workforce: [6]

1. I know what is expected of me at work.
2. I have the materials and equipment I need to do my work right.
3. At work, I have the opportunity to do what I do best every day.
4. In the last seven days, I have received recognition or praise for doing good work.
5. My supervisor, or someone at work, seems to care about me as a person.
6. There is someone at work who encourages my development.
7. At work, my opinions seem to count.
8. The mission or purpose of my company makes me feel my job is important.
9. My associates or fellow employees are committed to doing quality work.
10. I have a best friend at work.
11. In the last six months, someone at work has talked to me about my progress.
12. This last year, I have had opportunities at work to learn and grow.

---

6 https://www.gallup.com/access/323333/q12-employee-engagement-survey.aspx

To each question there are four response options: strongly agree, agree, disagree and strongly disagree. There isn't a sit-on-the-fence 'neither agree nor disagree'.

The key is to carry out a survey. It doesn't really matter which survey you go for. And the vital part is the follow up. Having an external facilitator can help the process run more smoothly and ensure meaningful, practical outcomes are captured. It also introduces confidentiality that can help people be open and honest. The survey does not require people to identify themselves.

Gallup's questions are hierarchical, meaning that question one is more important than question two, two more important than three, etc. Scoring high marks on questions 10, 11 and 12 isn't as good as scoring high on question one.

Getting high scores on the first four questions will have a greater impact on the future success of your business than getting high scores on the other eight questions and low scores on the first four.

Celebrate and have some fun along the way

Business and work are a tough gig, especially if you're a team with lofty aspirations and high expectations. Much will go wrong; often things that are out of your control.

It's therefore important – vital – to take a little time out to celebrate. And not just when you achieve a goal or smash a target. It's more important to recognise, celebrate and reward effort.

If one individual has a great success, it's rarely their genius that's responsible. It's usually a team effort. Often the foundations will have been laid by others who came before. And a large chunk of their success will have only been possible because of favourable conditions. Yes, recognise and celebrate success. But more importantly, recognise and celebrate effort. Celebrate effort and you'll get determined people who persevere.

If you can engender an atmosphere that's safe and fun – even playful – you'll also get more ideas and more improvements. You want to encourage people's natural curiosity and inventiveness. There's enough in life that's serious. Inject some fun and light-heartedness into business.

Pizza nights

Grabbing pizza and going bowling doesn't make work fun. Quite the reverse. It subtly says that it's not possible to have fun at work. We have to go elsewhere and do other things to have some fun. By all means go out for a team pizza, but don't kid yourself that you've just made work fun.

Competitions

And don't have competitions with one winner, e.g. the person who achieves the highest level of sales this month gets an all-expenses long weekend trip to Paris. It can destroy the motivation of others and potentially drive suboptimal behaviour as everyone (on the same team) tries to beat their colleagues. Set a bar that everyone has the opportunity to clear. Everyone who exceeds sales of £20,000 this month gets an all-expenses long weekend trip to Paris. (You'd obviously make sure such competitions are self-funding.) For a similar reason, don't have an employee of the month scheme as these can demotivate everyone apart from the nominee – and after a while everyone realises the well-meaning scheme is being awarded on a rota basis.

You could have a scheme where team members could nominate other team members for recognition because they've gone above and beyond, or they've done something special. The day when your team members start observing and recognising each other for doing good work is a great day.

Suggestion schemes offering monetary rewards usually don't work either. The best way to kill a suggestion scheme is to launch it with great fanfare, spend a long time debating the ideas, overanalyse them, only justify one or two, with management taking responsibility for implementation. The way to make a suggestion scheme work is to encourage small, every day improvement ideas; quickly give a response to every idea; implement most of them; and involve the idea nominator in the implementation.

Exercise: Plan in your celebrations

- What occasions or milestones will you celebrate this quarter?
- How do your team want to celebrate?

Summary

Look after your team, and your team will look after your customers, your customers will look after your business (by paying on time, reordering, making referrals, etc.), and your business will look after you (in return for the communal wealth your entrepreneurial venture creates).

Your direct reports are the most important people in your life. Spend most of your time with your best people.

Pay people decently and fairly. Respect them and appreciate what they do. Become observant. Notice when your team does their job well, or goes out of their way to help, or improves something, and thank them. Sending the occasional appreciative note to someone's home will have a disproportionately positive impact on their morale.

Money's power to motivate is limited. However, and ironically, get money wrong and its power to demotivate is high.

Motivation is an inside job. Therefore, you can't motivate people directly. But you can create a working environment where employee engagement and motivation is more likely. Excessive rules and bureaucracy will result in a demotivating environment. Adopt a handful of guiding principles.

The great motivators are a sense of achievement, interesting and purposeful work, and recognition for doing good work.

If you do nothing else, ensure that everyone knows why they're on the payroll. Clarify the specific results you want them to deliver.

Make sure people have the right tools and equipment to do an excellent job.

Explain to people how their work fits into the bigger picture. The meaning and purpose in each role needs to be linked to the overall purpose of the organisation.

Play to people's strengths and deploy them where they'll flourish.

Over and above doing their jobs excellently, expect your people to learn and grow, to contribute over and above what's expected. Share your belief that they have the potential to excel. Set high standards for them.

Do not tolerate less-than-acceptable performance. Deal with poor performance immediately. Don't assume the person is at fault. Initially check that expectations are understood, that the right tools are available to do the job, and training has been adequate. Be calm, objective, positive and constructive. Encourage the individual to generate their own improvement plan. Provide any support required. Agree a reasonable time period to make progress.

Let go of people who can't or won't perform. Your business can't afford to carry passengers. It's unfair to jeopardise everyone else's future by having underperformers on the team.

When it comes to recruitment, have a process to follow. Involve your team in the process. They usually know better than you if someone is going to fit in and excel in a role.

When you're recruiting, attitude and skills are both important – but attitude is more important. Skills can be taught. Generally, attitude was fixed a long time ago. As much as possible, make the selection process mirror what the job entails day-to-day.

Communication isn't about what's said or not said, it's about what's heard and understood. Regular, purposeful and well-run meetings are your primary means of communicating.

Celebrate along the way. Reinforce and reward effort, the right behaviours and actions, not just the successes and high points. You and your team spend most of your waking hours at work. Make it an enjoyable and rewarding place to be.

If you're investing in a business education, you may want to study finance, marketing, selling, operations, innovation, technology, etc. What is equally important – possibly more important – is to study behavioural psychology, motivation and emotional intelligence.

There's nowt so queer as folk.
OLD NORTHERN ENGLISH SAYING

Checklist Exercise: Team

The following checklist exercise will be helpful in identifying the progress you've made and in selecting the areas you want to focus on next. It will be useful to review this checklist once a quarter as part of your quarterly planning process.

- Put a tick in the 'DONE' column for those items you already do or are happy with.
- Make a second pass through the checklist and highlight those things that you'd 'LIKE TO' work on next.
- For each 'LIKE TO' item that you've highlighted:

  » What benefits will come from completing it (or what consequences will be avoided)? Jot down the benefits (in your planning notebook).

  » How excited do you feel about cracking on with this activity? Score your level of excitement out of 10 and put your score in the third column of the checklist.

  » Prioritise your 'LIKE TO' activities based on their beneficial impact and how excited you feel about taking action now.

  » Pick the one or two items from the top of your prioritised list and commit to making them a reality.

  » What's the simplest action you can take right now to get moving?

- Put this book down and make a start (or if impractical at the moment, schedule the activity in your calendar).

Some of the items on the list are relatively straightforward and self-explanatory. Others will need a plan behind them and assistance from other people. The purpose of this exercise is to identify which improvement initiatives you feel motivated to commit to, and to encourage you to find a first, small, simple action step to get you going.

	TEAM	DONE	LIKE TO	EXCITED
	RECRUITMENT	✓	✓	Out of 10
1	We're constantly & actively on the lookout for great people to join our team.			
2	Before recruiting we see if we can automate or process engineer the work to be done.			
3	We have a list of specific characteristics & attitudes that team members ideally have.			
4	We have a recruitment process. It's efficient & screens out unsuitable applicants.			
5	The team is involved in the recruitment process, especially our best performers.			
6	Job adverts ask people to explain why they want the role & why they'd be good at it.			
7	We always speak to applicants on the phone before committing to meet them.			
8	Our selection process exercises mirror what the role entails as closely as possible.			
9	We recruit for attitude & potential more than skills (though they may be important).			
10	Applicants complete a strengths assessment & psychometric profiling.			
11	We run a group assessment of short-listed people to introduce some competition.			
12	We share with applicants where we are & why we're excited about our future.			
13	We always take up references.			
14	We have an onboarding process that quickly assimilates our new team member.			

	ORGANISATION	DONE	LIKE TO	EXCITED
15	We have a chart that shows the relationship between different roles in the business.			
16	We have an organisational chart that shows the required structure in 12-months' time.			
17	We accept that people's names may appear against several roles (in the early days).			
18	We have an emergency plan & succession plan should any individual leave.			
19	We have selected an external team of professionals to support us. (advisors, etc)			

	PERFORMANCE MANAGEMENT	DONE	LIKE TO	EXCITED
20	We understand the different developmental stages of a high performing team.			
21	Everybody has a written explanation of their responsibilities & deliverables.			
22	Owners, directors and senior managers know their responsibilities & deliverables.			
23	Every person understands what results they're paid to deliver.			
24	Team members are given the right tools & equipment to do their job well.			
25	Team members are given prompt feedback for doing things well.			
26	Performance below expectations is addressed in private as quickly as possible.			
27	A performance improvement plan is agreed where performance issues exist.			
28	All role descriptions include a requirement to identify & share improvement ideas.			
29	Team members are encouraged to take risks in their area to make improvements.			
30	We identify people's strengths, play to those strengths & develop those strengths.			
31	We help people manage any weaknesses that impact their performance.			

	COMMUNICATION	DONE	LIKE TO	EXCITED
32	We have a series of meetings that are the communication rhythm of our business.			
33	Every meeting has a stated aim. We always ask, "What's our aim here?"			
34	We have established 'ground rules' to ensure meetings are productive & disciplined.			
35	We have a fixed agenda for our meetings and keep to time.			
36	We make a point of recognising what's going well & progress.			
37	We capture specific actions at the end of meetings – and complete those actions.			
38	We continuously refine & improve the effectiveness of our meetings.			
39	We regularly share our business vision, purpose and values with the team.			

		DONE	LIKE TO	EXCITED
40	We have quarterly planning meetings.			
41	We share progress and plans with the wider team via a quarterly address.			
42	We hold weekly progress & issue/problem solving meetings.			
43	We hold short daily "what's happening" meetings to share progress & priorities.			
44	All staff have periodic performance review & development planning meetings.			
45	Periodically we review all meetings to ensure they're still relevant.			

	MOTIVATION	DONE	LIKE TO	EXCITED
46	We know what aspects of a job and work environment motivate people.			
47	We design work roles so people get a sense of achievement from what they do.			
48	We regularly recognise the good work that people do and thank them.			
49	We bring out the meaning in a role & how it contributes to our overall purpose.			
50	We mould jobs so that they play to people's strengths and the work they enjoy.			
51	We allow people to take responsibility for how they complete their work.			
52	We know what aspects of a job and work environment demotivate people.			
53	We minimise rules, bureaucracy and policies, relying more on guiding principles.			
54	We know that a direct supervisor has greatest influence on someone's motivation.			
55	Team members are paid promptly, fairly and commensurate with their contribution.			
56	We carry out an annual engagement survey & work on identified improvement areas.			
57	We regularly recognise & celebrate progress and have some fun along the way.			

CHAPTER 5
Systems

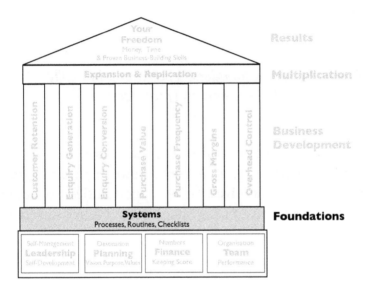

Systems feature in every chapter and are a common theme throughout this book. Your collection of systems is the key foundation block to the stability of your business and serves as the platform on which your business is built.

A system is a step-by-step process that, if followed, produces a particular outcome.

The benefits of systems are:
- Predictable and consistent results.
- Reduced chaos and greater order, meaning less stress and smoother progress.
- Reduced time taken and skill required for the person using the system, therefore easier training and delegation.

- Fewer choices and decisions to make so less energy depletion.
- Frees you up from doing the task yourself – and ultimately, from having to run your business.

The aim is for your business to become one big, open system, built of integrated, smaller systems. Your systems will be open systems rather than closed systems (they never change) because they'll need to adapt and change in response to a changing world. Critically, a systems-driven business that isn't dependent on you increases the sale value of your business.

> *At its core, a fully functioning business is basically a set of systems and processes.*
> JOHN JANTSH

Systems will take care of around 80% of your routine business tasks, leaving you with more time, energy and brain power to invest in problem solving, improvement initiatives, new opportunities, relationship building with your team, customers, suppliers and other stakeholders, personal development, etc.

Once you've established a system you can either:
- delegate it to a team member
- outsource the function
- automate it through the use of technology.

The improvement ideas you embrace and implement from this book can (and should) be systemised.

For example, looking from the outside in, if you've ever dealt with a company and received excellent customer service every time you've dealt with them, that will be because they have systems behind that service. Ironically, the more personalised the service, the more likely it is that a well-tuned system lies behind it.

That company will have separate systems for:
- recruiting the right people to the right roles
- training those people

- monitoring the performance and development of those people
- capturing your order
- communicating with order processing
- dispatching your order
- having the right amount of stock available
- stock replenishment
- communicating with you.

...and a host of other systems besides.

Personal Systems

Much of what you do on a daily basis is routine, which in effect is a personal system. Life would be too hard if you didn't operate by routine. So, as well as thinking of systemising your business, think of systemising what you do personally. This will allow you to dedicate more time and energy to higher value and more interesting activities and adventures.

Example: Personal systems

- Start of day routine.
- End of work-day close down routine.
- Weekly weight training routine.
- Daily exercise routine.
- End of day routine.
- Professional development book reading system.
- End of week review and planning routine.
- Start of month routine.
- Weekly day-off routine.
- Monthly financial review and plan routine.
- "Everything with a home and everything in its home" system.

What to systemise?

Answering a couple of basic questions will determine if an activity needs systemising or not.

- Do you repeat this task regularly?
- Does this task take longer than fifteen minutes?

If the answer to these questions is yes, then you need a system.

If you're doing this exercise to reduce the number of tasks that you carry out, then additional questions would be:

- To what degree do I dislike doing this activity?
- How much time does this task absorb?

For those activities that you dislike doing and that absorb a significant portion of your time, you want to create a system for doing it, train someone else to do it, monitor them for a period to ensure they can do it adequately, and let them get on with it. (Delegation process.)

The first step in systemising your business is the relatively straightforward task of listing all the repeating activities that you want to systemise. Divide your business into its main functions:

- Leadership and management
- Finance and administration
- Team (recruitment, training, performance management, etc.)
- Marketing (generating enquiries)
- Sales (converting enquiries)
- Operations (customer order fulfilment)

What to systemise first?

It can be a little daunting and potentially paralysing when you think of systemising the whole business. From your long list of activities to systemise, the next step is to prioritise them into the order you're going to tackle them.

Exercise: Where to start systemising?

For each activity, ask these questions and give a score out of three for each. (One is low negative impact and three is a high negative impact.)

- How much pain, aggravation or stress is this activity causing?
- How much time is this activity absorbing?
- How much negative impact is this activity having on customers?
- How much negative financial impact is this activity causing?

Add up the scores for each activity and rank your list with the highest scoring activities at the top – your priorities.

Given that there's potentially great benefit from systemising anything near the top of your list, you can ask your team which one they'd like to tackle first. This helps get buy in and engagement to the improvement process. Remember to position this initiative positively. The aim isn't to eradicate anyone's role, the aim is to make their life easier and less stressful, freeing up their time to do more interesting and valuable things.

You might encourage your team to pick something they think could be fixed relatively quickly. A quick win is a great confidence booster and creates some momentum for your overall business systemisation initiative.

Whatever activity you decide to work on first, there will be some kind of existing system in place, even if it's not documented. It's important to understand what it is. You want to know where you're starting from. Think of what's being done today as your 'factory reset' system – what you revert to if your new, improved system doesn't work.

A bad system will beat a good person every time.
EDWARDS DEMING

System mapping

Understanding the current steps taken is discovered through observation and questioning. For example, perhaps you want to understand the current process for collecting overdue payments. Here are the questions you might ask:

- When do you decide to do something about an overdue payment? What's the trigger for taking some action?
- What's the first thing you do?
- Why do you do that?
- What do you do next? Why do you do that?
- Is there anything you do in between those steps?
- What do you do if that happens? And what do you do if this happens? etc.

The questions aren't sophisticated or difficult to answer. As people answer, you need to be sketching out the process they're describing as a flowchart on a large piece of paper. Sticky notes can be useful as you can move them around and easily add in extra notes. Flip chart paper or a roll of decorators' lining paper (£5 from a DIY shop) is useful.

One thing to be aware of is that people may not be totally honest when answering your questions. People may believe there's an official or prescribed way of doing things. They might think they'll be in trouble or that you'll consider them stupid if they tell you how they really do it. (Obviously they won't be in trouble and you won't think they're stupid.) Observation can therefore sometimes be more illuminating than questions. Becoming a good observer of people is a vital skill to develop. This possibility of misinformation highlights the need to position your systems improvement initiative as something that's going to make life easier and better for the people involved.

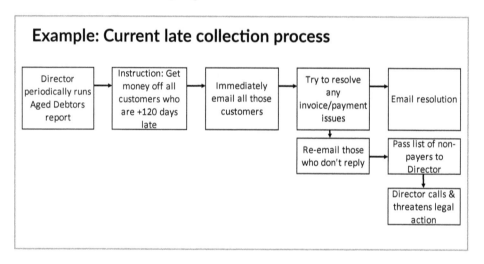

Example: Current late collection process

Director periodically runs Aged Debtors report → Instruction: Get money off all customers who are +120 days late → Immediately email all those customers → Try to resolve any invoice/payment issues → Email resolution

Try to resolve any invoice/payment issues → Re-email those who don't reply → Pass list of non-payers to Director → Director calls & threatens legal action

System improvement

The best and most practical course of action is to propose a few, simple improvements to a system.
- Gain agreement on your initial improvement plan from all involved.
- Implement those new steps.
- Monitor what happens.
- Reconvene after a period of time and analyse and discuss what the impact has been.

Don't be tempted to create and implement the perfect system. If you scored your current system a two out of ten, initially aim to make it a three or four. Going from a two to a ten out of ten is unlikely – and your 'failure' may put you off trying again. Build your business step by step.

If someone takes a shortcut in producing the outcome you want, pay attention – they've just made an improvement to the system. As long as it doesn't compromise the outcome or negatively impact other parts of the business, those shortcuts are in effect system improvements.

Using the previous example, your team might decide to initially:
- Issue all invoices on a Monday afternoon.
- Telephone all customers with invoices exceeding £1,000 on a Tuesday morning, checking that they've received the invoice, that they're happy with the service provided, checking that the invoice is correct, and ascertaining when the invoice will be paid.
- Run the aged debtors report once every two weeks on a Friday. Rank overdue payments (+30 days) by value to create a priority list.
- On a Tuesday and Thursday between 10am and 11am, telephone customers whose payments are late (+30 days) and ascertain when payment will be made, and if there's an issue, capture the details and resolve as a priority.
- Follow up with an email, thanking customers for confirming payment or outlining action that will be taken to resolve issue.
- Monitor the total value of all late payments every two weeks.

For the moment, all the other process steps remain the same.

In this example, the team are tackling two things. Firstly, aiming to avoid late payments occurring by calling clients as soon as an invoice is raised. Secondly, tackling the backlog of late payments.

You'll see how you'd want to improve this system as the late payment situation improves and ultimately create a system that eradiates any late payments.

It's likely that other systems – or lack of them – will come into play. In this example, perhaps there's will be a need to look at the sign-off system for services carried out for a customer to ensure invoices are accurate and will be approved without issue.

A list of business procedures to systemise

Whilst this is not a definitive list, here are systems that are common to many businesses. You will be able to add more to the list given your particular circumstances.

Finance & Accounting Systems
Raising invoices & collecting payment
Overdue payment resolution & collection
Purchasing system
Month-end close down
Accruals
Financial performance tracking & reporting
Business forecasting & budgeting
Cashflow forecasting
Bank reconciliation
Payroll & pensions
HMRC returns & payments
Record management

Operations & Office Management Systems
Start of day
End of day
Order capture
Order fulfilment
Order tracking
Order follow up
Quality assurance
Customer guarantee
Return order
Customer satisfaction assessment
Stock ordering
Stock control
Office supplies management
Staff rostering
Staff communication
Phone answering
Email
Data backup & archiving
Computer & software maintenance & upgrade
Equipment maintenance & replacement
Vehicle maintenance
Vehicle standards
Security
Insurance

Marketing & Sales Management Systems
Marketing & sales planning
Customer retention
Customer referrals
Customer reviews
Customer case studies
Enquiry generation
Enquiry conversion
Pricing
Proposals & quotation
Prospect diagnostic assessment
Customer additional needs assessment
Product & service development
Prospect & customer database management
Keeping in touch
Website management
Tracking of key numbers & ratios

Team Management Systems
Communication
Alignment (with vision, purpose, values, objectives)
Succession & contingency planning
Recruitment & selection
Onboarding
Expectation & objective setting
Performance management
Strengths assessment
Training & development
Team building & engagement
Remuneration & reward
Conflict resolution
Disciplinary

Business Planning Systems
Annual planning & budgeting
Quarterly action planning
Weekly progress meetings
Market research
Product & service development
Business forecasting
Business improvement

Summary

Systemising the routine and repetitive elements of your business will make life easier for you and your team. Systems, if followed, guarantee consistently good outcomes. Ultimately, they're the thing that will allow your business to work without you.

Virtually every element of your business and every idea shared in this book can and should be systemised. When you implement an idea and it works, always ask, "Now, how can we systemise this?"

Organise around business functions, not people. Build systems within each business function. Let systems run the business and people run the systems. People come and go but the systems remain constant.

MICHAEL GERBER

Checklist Exercise: Systems

The following checklist exercise will be helpful in identifying the progress you've made and in selecting the areas you want to focus on next. It will be useful to review this checklist once a quarter as part of your quarterly planning process.

- Put a tick in the 'DONE' column for those items you already do or are happy with.
- Make a second pass through the checklist and highlight those things that you'd 'LIKE TO' work on next.
- For each 'LIKE TO' item that you've highlighted:
  - » What benefits will come from completing it (or what consequences will be avoided)? Jot down the benefits (in your planning notebook).
  - » How excited do you feel about cracking on with this activity? Score your level of excitement out of 10 and put your score in the third column of the checklist.
  - » Prioritise your 'LIKE TO' activities based on their beneficial impact and how excited you feel about taking action now.
  - » Pick the one or two items from the top of your prioritised list and commit to making them a reality.
  - » What's the simplest action you can take right now to get moving?
- Put this book down and make a start (or if impractical at the moment, schedule the activity in your calendar).

Some of the items on the list are relatively straightforward and self-explanatory. Others will need a plan behind them and assistance from other people. The purpose of this exercise is to identify which improvement initiatives you feel motivated to commit to, and to encourage you to find a first, small, simple action step to get you going.

	SYSTEMS	DONE	LIKE TO	EXCITED
	PRINCIPLES	✓	✓	Out of 10
1	We recognise that a business is in essence an income-generating system.			
2	We recognise our business needs to be made up of multiple, connecting sub-systems.			
3	We recognise that systems deliver consistently good results with less effort.			
4	We recognise that systems free our people to create, improve & develop our business.			
5	I know systems will reduce reliance on me & ultimately free me from the business.			

	PERSONAL SYSTEMS	DONE	LIKE TO	EXCITED
6	I've identified routines to improve my effectiveness & conserve energy.			
7	I have a start-of-the-day routine.			
8	I have a routine when I'm going to concentrate & focus on my most important work.			
9	I have a work close-down routine.			
10	I have a regular exercise routine.			
11	I have an end-of-the-day routine.			

	BUSINESS SYSTEMS	DONE	LIKE TO	EXCITED
12	We have a list of all the systems that we would like to establish in the business.			
13	We have prioritised those systems based on their positive operational impact.			
14	We are creating or improving 1 or 2 systems all the time (part of our quarterly plan).			

15	We are involving the team in developing & refining those systems.			
16	We are capturing systems in a manual – in writing, with screenshots, photos, video.			
17	We are using process maps to pictorially show how systems work.			
18	We periodically review all systems to check they're still relevant & working well.			

CHAPTER 6

Business Development

Marketing is so basic that it cannot be considered a separate
function. It is the whole business seen from the point of view
of its final result, that is, from the customer's point of view.

PETER DRUCKER.

Putting your business foundations in place will give you a solid
base on which to build. Ironically, putting the foundations in place will
also increase your profits and cash. Business development is where you
will significantly improve your business profits. This section is split
into two chapters. The first runs through some business development
fundamentals and the second dives into the nitty gritty of practical
business development initiatives. As with other parts of this book, you
may wish to dive into the nitty gritty and find a quick, easy, profitable win

that you can implement straight away. That's great. But please come back and work through the fundamentals. There's gold in these pages too!

The aim of business development is to increase your profits in a sustainable way. There are two main themes:
- Keeping the customers you've got by fulfilling their needs on a consistent basis and ensuring those customers are profitable.
- Building on that base in seven specific business development areas:
    1. Customer Retention
    2. Enquiry Generation
    3. Enquiry Conversion
    4. Purchase Value
    5. Purchase Frequency
    6. Gross Margins
    7. Overhead Control

These two themes can be broken down further into five progressive stages:
1. Ensuring that all current customers are profitable.
2. Retaining current profitable customers.
3. Determining the segment of ideal customers you wish to serve, and with which distinctive products and services.
4. Developing business with current customers.
5. Attracting and securing new customers that fit your ideal.

This business development fundamentals chapter covers:
- **Servicing:** Assessing how you're currently performing in terms of customer service.
- **Profiting:** Determining whether your customers and products are sufficiently profitable.
- **Differentiating:** Understanding what it means to be different and to stand out from alternative suppliers in a way that's meaningful to customers.
- **Communicating:** Positioning your business in the marketplace and communicating with your chosen customer audience.
- **Actioning:** How the seven business development improvement areas combine to generate significantly more customers, sales and profits.

The next chapter will then share practical, proven strategies and tactics for developing your business in a systematic way.

- **Tactics:** A wide selection of proven, real-life ideas in each of the seven key activity areas.

Customer delivery and service performance

Before embarking on any exciting new business development adventures, addressing the basics can be a lucrative exercise. Start by determining if you're keeping your hard-won customers. There's no point in bringing new customers through the front door if your existing customers are leaving through the back door.

Analyse your records to determine how long you've traded with your current and former customers. For example, look back two years and identify all those customers who started trading with you in the first 12 months of that two-year period. How many of those companies are still trading with you today (current customers) and how many aren't (former customers)?

For example, 60 new companies started trading with you in that first 12 months. 20 of them are still trading with you. Your (crude) retention rate is 20/60=33%. This might be sufficient analysis to tell you that you need to do something about retaining existing customers before you focus on finding new ones.

You may wish to dig a little deeper. You might look at how long those former customers traded with you. Of the 40 who've left, 30 made only one purchase whilst 10 made four purchases over a six-month period. You'd want to investigate what's happening when you first interact with a new customer. You could observe or ask your frontline customer service team. Or you could speak to those former customers. Or you could get some friends or mystery shoppers to pose as new customers.

As well as looking at why customers might be leaving, explore why customers are staying. Speak to those 20 current customers to discover what they like about your service. Understanding why people stay is more valuable than why they leave. Often, it's about being more consistent in delivering the 'stay' factors with all customers.

Collecting and analysing data is time consuming. Have a clear reason for doing it. Don't do it just for the sake of it. In the previous example, the compelling reason is to improve customer retention and increase your profits. Keep digging until you discover where the improvement opportunity is. And then stop and make the improvement!

Evaluating customer service performance

In addition to analysing historic information, you want to set up a system for monitoring customer service on an ongoing basis. Customer surveys are particularly useful and one of the simplest and most effective is the Ultimate Question and Net Promoter Score.

The Ultimate Question is: On a scale of 1 to 10 (1 being very unlikely and 10 being very likely), how likely are you to recommend us to family or friends/colleagues or associates?
- People scoring a 9 or 10 are classed as promoters and are marked as +1.
- People scoring a 7 or 8 are passives and are marked as 0.
- People scoring a 6 or less are detractors and are marked as -1.
- Net Promoter Score (NPS) = % Promoters *less* % Detractors

These two examples show how NPS works:

Survey 1

Customer	Score		Mark
A	9	Promoter	1
B	8	Passive	0
C	9	Promoter	1
D	5	Detractor	-1
E	6	Detractor	-1
F	10	Promoter	1
G	9	Promoter	1
H	9	Promoter	1
I	8	Passive	0
J	8	Passive	0
10	81	Total	3
Avg.	8.1	**NPS**	30%

Survey 2

Customer	Score		Mark
A	10	Promoter	1
B	9	Promoter	1
C	9	Promoter	1
D	7	Passive	0
E	6	Detractor	-1
F	10	Promoter	1
G	9	Promoter	1
H	9	Promoter	1
I	9	Promoter	1
J	8	Passive	0
10	86	Total	6
Avg.	8.6	**NPS**	60%

NPS is a harsh scoring mechanism as these two examples demonstrate. The average scores in both surveys are between 8 and 9. However, one NPS result is twice as high as the other – and neither is close to 100%.

It doesn't particularly matter what your initial score is – it is what it is. The important things are:
- you keep measuring it.
- you take action and your score starts to improve.

Ironically, you might view 30% as a good score in the sense that it represents a great improvement opportunity. The average scores of 8.1 and 8.6 may lull you into a dangerous sense of complacency. The key is to establish a baseline – and start improving from there.

Expect measurable progress in reasonable time.
JIM ROHN

The ultimate question only takes your customers 20 seconds to complete so you should get a high response rate. You might then ask one of these useful follow-up questions:
- **Promoters:** What would you say to someone about dealing with our company? This will provide insights into how you might communicate with prospective customers.
- **Passives:** What would we have to improve for you to rate us a 9 or a 10?
- **Detractors:** What are the reasons for your score? Again, the responses will give you clear pointers for where you need to improve. You will also want to see if you can address the issues raised for that particular customer.

Customer and product profitability

Along with determining how well you're retaining your customers, you need to know how profitable your customers and products/services are. Your business may be profitable overall, but you want to dig down and see how profitable your different customer groups and product groups or services are. You don't want to be working your socks off to retain unprofitable customers!

If working out customer profitability is a challenge, ask your finance manager, your accountant, your business coach or an analytical specialist to help with the analysis. However, here is an overview of an approach you can take.

First determine what period of time you're going to investigate. The last full calendar year or your last full financial year would work well.

As an example, a specialist furniture company that wholesales to the retail sector had 12 customers. Their accounts showed that they made sales of £150,000 and gross profits of £64,650 (equivalent to an overall gross margin of 43%.)

When they dug into the detail, their customer sales analysis showed their biggest customer (A) had sales of £40,000 and represented 27% of total sales. Their top 3 customers (A, B & C) had combined sales of £95,000 and represented 63% of their sales. They loved those guys! Having one large customer is a double-edged sword. The profit from one large customer can cover many of your overhead costs and give you breathing space to develop your business. However, one large customer may become very demanding, and your business is vulnerable should they leave – or worse still, they absorb all your time and energy.

Sales analysis (for specialist furniture wholesale business)

Customer	A	B	C	D	E	F	G	H	I	J	K	L	TOTAL
Sales	£40,000	£30,000	£25,000	£16,000	£13,000	£8,000	£5,000	£4,000	£3,000	£2,000	£2,000	£2,000	£150,000
Share of Total Sales	27%	20%	17%	11%	9%	5%	3%	3%	2%	1%	1%	1%	100%

Share of Sales		
Customers A, B & C	£95,000	63%
Other customers	£55,000	37%
Total	£150,000	100%

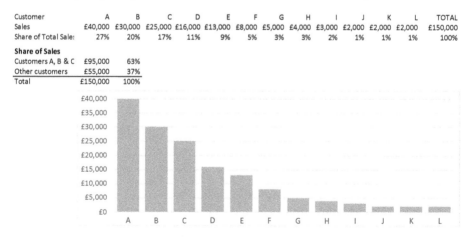

When management dug further into the numbers to determine how profitable those customers were, another picture emerged.

Gross profit analysis

Customer	A	B	C	D	E	F	G	H	I	J	K	L	TOTAL
Sales	£40,000	£30,000	£25,000	£16,000	£13,000	£8,000	£5,000	£4,000	£3,000	£2,000	£2,000	£2,000	£150,000
Cost of Goods	£34,000	£15,000	£11,250	£8,000	£6,500	£4,000	£2,000	£1,600	£1,200	£600	£600	£600	£85,350
Gross Profit	£6,000	£15,000	£13,750	£8,000	£6,500	£4,000	£3,000	£2,400	£1,800	£1,400	£1,400	£1,400	£64,650
Gross Profit Margin	15%	50%	55%	50%	50%	50%	60%	60%	60%	70%	70%	70%	43%

Share of Gross Profit

Customers B & C	£28,750	44%
Others customers	£35,900	56%
Total	£64,650	100%

Their biggest sales customer (A) wasn't their most profitable customer – far from it. Customers B and C generated 44% of gross profits. Customer B generated more than twice the profit of customer A, the largest customer from a sales perspective.

Looking at percentages can be misleading. In this example, there are three customers with gross profit margins of 70%. However, they generate a very modest level of profits in absolute money terms.

Customer A isn't as profitable as their level of sales suggests. However, at least they're profitable. If you discover unprofitable customers, you need to do something about the situation. There are 2 options: make them profitable or let them go. Both options are covered later.

This analysis starts to show where you could be focusing your efforts. In the example, you'd want to spend time developing more business with customers B and C. You'd also want to think about how you renegotiate terms with customer A.

You can do a similar exercise with the different products or services you supply. For instance, in the previous example, the specialist furniture company supplied hand-crafted tables, sofas and picture frames to those 12 retail customers.

Product Type	Tables	Sofas	Frames	TOTAL
Sales (units)	200	50	600	
Price per Unit	£350	£1,000	£50	
Sales	£70,000	£50,000	£30,000	£150,000
% of Total	47%	33%	20%	100%
Costs of Goods Sold				
Materials	£15,000	£25,000	£2,000	£42,000
Labour	£10,000	£25,000	£1,000	£36,000
Packaging	£4,000	£2,350	£1,000	£7,350
Total Costs	£29,000	£52,350	£4,000	£85,350
Gross Profit	£41,000	-£2,350	£26,000	£64,650
% of Sales	59%	-5%	87%	43%
% of Total	63%	-4%	40%	100%

As you already know, the business is profitable, generating gross profits in the last full year of £64,650. However, an analysis by the major product groups reveals that while sofas represent 33% of sales, they're actually losing money. Picture frames represent 20% of sales and are generating 40% of gross profits. Two thirds of gross profits are coming from the sale of tables. As a priority, you'd want to look at the costs associated with producing sofas and their pricing, which would involve negotiations with your customers.

A third level of analysis would involve looking at the three product groups and the twelve customers combined. These examples are sufficient to give you a flavour of the benefit and necessity of digging into your customer and product numbers.

Building capacity for growth

If you want to serve more customers, you need to have sufficient capacity to serve them well. Carrying out the analysis and then acting on the resulting improvement initiatives will not only increase the profits in your business but will free up capacity, e.g. by parting with unprofitable customers or dropping unprofitable products and services. Implementing systems to deliver a better and more consistent service will also release capacity.

The first step to increase capacity is to understand where the bottleneck is in your production and delivery process. Finding and expanding bottlenecks will depend on what type of business you operate. For a manufacturing business it would involve mapping out your production processes, studying flow rates, etc. You may even need external specialised process management help. If you're an accountancy practice, it may be as simple as realising you need another accountant. If you produce picture frames, it may mean a second assembly machine – or perhaps an evening production shift in addition to a day shift.

Positioning your business in the market

The previous exercises have been concerned with assessing and improving what you already have – ensuring your service meets customers' expectations; retaining your customers for longer; making sure your customers and your portfolio of products and services are sufficiently profitable; ensuring there is capacity to take on new clients.

Before embarking on any new marketing campaigns, you need to clarify the market segment you wish to serve and what an ideal client looks like.

When a new business starts trading, even if it sets off with a clear idea of who it's going to serve, those ideals are often compromised along the way. Financial pressures, a belief that you can help everyone, a natural reluctance to say no, and the distraction of operational overwhelm often result in a real mixture of customers – big and small; near and far; business and consumer; lovely and pain-in-the-backside; payers and non-payers, etc.

Now is the time to reassess that. Your ideal is to occupy a market space where you're the only supplier. That may be difficult but it's not impossible. It has more to do with defining the market space you wish to serve than it does with creating a unique product or service. A more realistic aim is to become the 'supplier of first resort' for your target customers.

Exercise: Market Positioning

The following questions will help determine your market positioning:
- Who are your ideal customers? Who would you love to be doing business with?
- Geography: Where are your ideal customers?
- Demography: What sorts of companies are they? What sorts of people are they?
- Psychology: Who are they? How do they think? How do they behave? What are their aspirations?
- What are their needs? What do they worry about? What do they want?
- In a few sentences, how would you define this group of ideal customers? Can you even produce a 'target list' of companies or individuals?

Being different in a meaningful way that your customers appreciate and value.
- What are the things that make you different in a way that is meaningful to your ideal customers?
- What are you truly excellent at – better than anyone else? (Products? People? Services? Company?)
- What do customers and former customers think of you and your service?
- What's your compelling 'Why?' Why do you do what you do? And why do your customers care?

Commitments and guarantees.
- What are the major objections or risks for prospective customers?
- What commitments can you make, or guarantees can you offer?

Your list of ideal customers

If you're a business-to-business company, then it's feasible to come up with an actual list that includes company name, location and address, contact names, phone number, size of business, etc. Desk research would give you other helpful information such as growth over recent years, ambitions for the future, current suppliers, changes in personnel, competitive threats, etc.

If you're a consumer business, an actual list of names would be harder, but you'd be able to generate a handful of avatars that represent your ideal customers.

For example, if you're selling a high-priced piece of legal software that only large law firms can afford, then your list might be the top 100 law companies in the UK. As well as researching who those companies are, you'll be able to find out who the Managing Partners are, who the Finance Directors are and who's responsible for IT. Your marketing effort and budget suddenly becomes more focused and laser-like when you only have a handful of companies in your sights.

Another example: if you're specialists in repairing and refurbishing fans, motors, pumps and gearboxes within five days for Facility Management companies based within a 60-minute drive time of Manchester, it's possible for you to create a definitive list of specific companies you wish to serve.

A list of current and former customers is also highly valuable. Inexpensive technology allows you to keep accurate and up-to-date records on a customer relationship management (CRM) system. Used in a disciplined way, this allows you to track and manage customers so as to serve them better. An accurate and well managed CRM also becomes something that adds financial value to your business when you come to sell it.

Example: Wedding photographer

A generalist photographer not only decided to focus just on weddings, but decided to be very selective and work with fewer wedding customers – but for a longer time, ideally a lifetime. They'd decided that it was hard work constantly selling one-off purchases. Once they'd completed a wedding assignment, that customer was on their CRM system. They were then able to interact with their clients throughout their lives and capture all those special moments – anniversaries, birthdays, baby arrivals, graduations, special family occasions, family pet portraits. What a service and what a privilege to follow and pictorially document a family's life!

One way to determine what an ideal customer looks like is to identify those customers you consider to be your best customers. For each, write down why you've classified them as one of your 'best' clients.

You'll notice that there's a pattern of overlapping characteristics. You can now pick the characteristics that constitute an 'ideal customer'. Perhaps you have to add in a characteristic 'ideal' that none of your current best customers has. Once you've built this picture of your ideal client, you'll be clear about what you're looking for and can think about where you might find them. You're unlikely to find an ideal customer. However, if you know what you're looking for, you're more likely to find customers that are a close match.

Example: Ideal customer exercise carried out by an engineering company.

The customers we classify as "best" customers

Brights' Fans & Rotors	Local	Regular weekly jobs	Pay on time	No bother	Have referred customers to us	Guys like working with them
Brannigan Manufacturing	Really nice guys to deal with	Never mention charge rates	Interesting, varied work	Some really big jobs	Tolerant if things not quite to plan	Smooth payment & paperwork
Peel & Peel Solutions	Big, profitable jobs	Guys like working on their jobs	Stayed loyal	Grown over the years	Great potential for more work	
Fuller Lifts & Escalators	Biggest client	Pain to get paid properly	Can be aloof at times			
East Line Bakery	Local	Regular steady work	Tolerant if things not quite to plan	Have referred customers to us	Great potential for more work	
Roberts Industrial Showers	Local	Really nice guys to deal with	Guys like working with them	Always pay on time	Stayed loyal	

From this simple analysis, here's the defined characteristics of their ideal client:

- Regular work, ideally jobs coming in every week. Ideally, periodic large refurbishment jobs too.
- Interesting and varied work that the engineers enjoy working on.
- Local. Ideally within a 30-minute drive-time of the workshop.
- Potential for growth. Ideally, a customer that is growing and expanding.
- Nice people to deal with. Get on with their job and let us get on with ours. Respectful of our expertise and advice.
- Good administrative system.
- Pay promptly every time. Ideally, willing to pay within 30 days.
- Refer other customers to us.
- Tolerant. Flexible and accommodating when needed.

The analysis of best customers gave a base of ideal characteristics. A few of those characteristics have been enhanced to create an 'ideal customer' profile. You'll notice that their biggest client was initially classified as one of their best clients. On reflection, it appears that their biggest client doesn't have many attractive characteristics – apart from being the largest customer from a sales perspective. That's fine – it's just good to realise that they may be the biggest but not necessarily the best or the ideal.

Exercise: Defining the ideal customers you'd like to do business with

- List your 'best' customers (or types of customer).
- What characteristics make them a 'best' customer?
- What are the common characteristics that you'd like all ideal customers to have?
- Are there other characteristics you would add to your list (that current customers don't have)?
- Create an avatar (or several) of your ideal customer(s).
- Work out how you'd determine if a prospective customer was close to your ideal.
- Ensure that your marketing and sales people are clear about what your ideal customers look like.
- Think about where you might find those ideal customers.

Standing out from the crowd

You can now start thinking about how you'll position yourself in the eyes of those potential new customers on your ideal client list.

Think about your business from two perspectives:
- **Inner reality:** How good you are at practically meeting you customers' product and service expectations.
- **Outer perception:** How well you're perceived by those potential customers. In effect, how well you communicate that inner reality to your potential customers.

Does the outer perception of your business do justice to its inner reality?

You may outscore all alternative suppliers on every parameter that's important to a potential customer. However, if those potential customers perceive that you're no different to all other potential suppliers, then that perception is their reality. For example, if your website looks like everyone else's, those potential customers will assume that all aspects of your business are just like everyone else's.

Firstly, you need to determine how good your inner reality is and whether you need to make improvements. In the majority of cases, a business's inner reality is better than how it's projected to the outside world. As discussed previously, gaining feedback from customers will start to build an objective picture of how good your products and services are.

Standing out in a crowded marketplace is often not as hard as you might think. Most companies aren't good at it and fill their marketing brochures, websites, adverts and the like with generalities, platitudes and hard-to-understand jargon.

Exercise: Standing out in a meaningful way to searching customers

- Test this out by putting yourself in the shoes of a customer. Look at your website and alternative supplier websites. Or better still, because you know your sector too well to do this exercise objectively, find a friend who doesn't know your business and ask them to help by carrying out the exercise.
- Do you know what differentiates one supplier from another?
- Would you know which supplier truly understood your needs?
- Do you feel they're speaking right into the heart of your needs?
- Could you easily see which supplier promised a credible solution?
- Can you see the evidence that substantiates their claims?
- Do they use language that you understand?
- Does their tone resonate with you?
- Do you feel compelled to take the next step and get in touch?
- Do they make getting in touch easy?

The key is to put yourself in your potential customers' shoes, start thinking about what they think about, and then communicate with them (in their language) about the things they care about.

Using customer-centred communication as a point of difference

Most businesses just talk about themselves in their marketing literature, starting by telling you when they were established and how many years they've been trading.

The blunt truth is that most potential customers don't care about you and your business. They care about themselves – and how you might be able to solve their problems or make their life better.

There are two elements to marketing communications:
- **Strategic:** This is the core message – the vital "what".
- **Tactical:** This is the "where" and the "how" (websites, brochures, direct mail, magazine adverts, etc.).

When you're thinking about your strategic marketing, there's a neat equation you can apply to all your tactical marketing channels (your website, brochures, etc.)

The equation has four parts:
- **Interrupt:** Grab the attention of your audience with a compelling headline that speaks to their concerns or issues. Your research (observing and listening to customers) will tell you what keeps them awake at night. And it's not always the obvious things. You might think that they're interested in how fabulous your software is. They might be concerned about making a bad investment recommendation to their boss and losing their job. Don't make assumptions. Find out. And then speak to the thoughts and concerns that are swirling around your potential customer's head.

- **Engage:** Tell them that there is a solution to their problem. Give them hope!

- **Educate:** Give them sufficient relevant information to help them make a sound decision or move to the next step. It's untrue that people have short attention spans. If you're speaking about a real issue or opportunity, and sharing relevant, interesting and compelling information, people will remain engaged. Everyone wants to be educated about things that promise to solve their problem or make a positive impact on their lives.

- **Offer:** Help people take the next step. Make it simple, low risk, and easy to take. The best offer is usually providing the customer with more relevant, valuable information that's going to help them make a good decision when the time's right. If they're not ready to buy, ask for their contact details in exchange for that information. That will allow you to continue the relationship-building process by sharing other pertinent information with them.

Example: A children's play centre wants local parents of infant-aged children to book one of their themed play and tea parties for their child's birthday.

In the early years of school, all a child's classmates will get invited to their birthday party. This can be daunting in terms of space and crowd control if parents have the party at home, and expensive if they take the whole class to an external venue.

Interrupt: Concerned about the cost of inviting the whole class to your child's birthday party? (Other interrupting headlines are available!)

Engage: There's an exciting and affordable solution that will ensure every child has a great time – and you can relax knowing it's all within budget.

Educate:
- We provide food, drink, birthday cake, balloons and a party bag for each child. There's a wide selection of food options for you to choose from.
- Parties are hosted by a qualified and trained party host, ensuring that the children are looked after, they're entertained with fun games, and they play safely on all the play equipment.
- There will be themed characters in costume on hand to meet and greet the children.
- You and any other parents attending will be looked after by our customer service team and you'll have access to our 5-star café.

> • Depending on numbers, parties cost between £125 and £195.
>
> **Offer:** Simply click the link and reserve your spot now. We'll then call you to discuss the details to create your special and memorable party.

When it comes to crafting powerful and engaging words, invest in the professional services of a copywriter with advertising and marketing experience. Yes, it'll cost more than if you do it yourself, but you'll get a far more effective result (more qualified enquiries). Your job is to do your research and draft a good brief for the copywriter.

If your product and service – your inner reality – is better than the competition, you can be distinctive in a real and tangible way. However, you can also differentiate your business by simply communicating in a more powerful and customer-centred way. Your communication becomes the differentiator, often because other suppliers' marketing is self-centred and full of generalities.

Another differentiation strategy is to focus on a tightly defined market segment – a *niche*. This might be a certain type of customer. Or a particular age group. Or a specific geographic area. Completing the ideal customer exercise will help develop your *niche*. It's easier to sidestep all the generalists and tailor your services and communication to a particular audience, enhancing your specialist expertise and reputation in the process. Being all things to all people is usually not a good strategy.

If you're specific, you'll miss 95% of all the opportunities out there; if you're general, you'll miss 100% of them.

For example, as a heating and plumbing business, you'd be attracted towards an accountant who specialises in serving heating and plumbing businesses, in preference to a generalist accountancy practice. Behind the scenes, it might not matter for the accountancy practice what type of business you are. The accountancy practice might have separate website landing pages: one for heating businesses, one for kitchen businesses and one for landscape gardening businesses!

Being undifferentiated is not the ideal place to be. You're thrown into an arena where the only real differentiator is price! And you don't want to be competing on price.

Finding your ideal customers

One of the best marketing questions to ask is:

Where will I find my ideal customers in the greatest concentration?

The answer will help you decide where to deploy your marketing content tactically to have the greatest chance of generating new enquiries.

For example:

- A physiotherapy practice posted leaflets advertising their services on the notice boards of all the local sports clubs.
- A commercial cleaning business joined their local chambers of commerce because they knew they'd meet good clients there – and the sorts of influential clients who'd introduce them to other potential clients.
- A garage specialising in high-end German cars decided to erect an advertising banner close to the exit of an upmarket supermarket. They also paid a small team of people to walk the streets of their local town, posting a leaflet through the door of every house who had certain makes of German cars parked on their drive.
- A kitchen design company accessed the list of people applying for planning permission from their local authority. They identified ground floor extensions above a certain size in particular areas and wrote to those people.

Exercise: Finding your ideal customers in greatest concentration

- Sketch out what a great or ideal customer looks like.
- With this person in mind, think of at least three places where you might find lots of these sorts of people.
- Which place will have the most?
- What mechanism can you use to communicate with these people in that place?

The numbers side of business development

Think of business development as a chemical reaction. You put money into an initiative, there's a reaction and, after a period of time, customers, sales and profits are produced. For the reaction to be deemed a success you'd want more money (profits) to be generated than the money you put in. Ideally, you'd want:

- the money generated to be far greater than the money invested.
- the reaction to happen quickly and the money generated to be in your bank account as fast as possible.
- to invest as little as you could to get your return to make the investment affordable and low risk.
- the reaction to work every time you invested your money.

This section looks at important business development numbers and how you can use them to understand what makes a successful 'reaction'.

The financial value of a customer

Determining how much a customer is worth is one of the most significant numbers you will ever calculate. And when it comes to understanding how much to invest in your marketing, it's a number that you'll find invaluable.

Building on the customer retention and customer profitability exercises at the beginning of the chapter, you can calculate how much gross profit each customer generates over their lifetime. You can work this out on a customer-by-customer basis, calculate an average, look at the high and low values, or compare one type of customer to another.

Here's how it works:
- Purchase value per transaction: £A
- Purchases per year: B
- Years as a customer: C
- Gross margin: D% (gross profit as a % of sales)
- Lifetime value (LTV) = A x B x C x D

Example: A specialist garage

The garage carried out the exercise and arrived at the following numbers (they estimated some of the numbers as they had incomplete data):

- Purchase value per transaction: £287
- Purchases per year: 1.4
- Years as a customer: 6 (estimate)
- Gross margin: 55% (estimate over that period)
- LTV = £287 x 1.4 purchases per year x 6 years x 55% gross margin = £1,326

And the result for their most valuable customer was:

- Purchase value: £328
- Purchases per year: 3.5
- Years as a customer: 11
- Gross margin: 55% (estimate over that period)
- LTV = £328 x 3.5 x 11 x 55% = £6,945

The calculation doesn't take into account the fact that customers may well introduce other customers to you. Technically, some of that value should be credited to them, making them even more valuable.

Exercise: Calculating the lifetime value (LTV) of a customer

Even if you have to estimate or guess your numbers, work out the LTV of a customer.

A   A customer's average purchase value is? £
B   On average, how many times a year do they do business with you?
C   How many years are they a customer for?
D   What's your gross profit margin? %

Lifetime value = A x B x C x D =

How to calculate your marketing budget

Think of marketing as the process of buying or acquiring customers. To be profitable and earn a return on your investment, a customer needs to generate more profit than it costs you to acquire them.

Say you decide you want your new customers to cover the marketing cost of acquiring them by the end of the first year. Using the previous garage example, a new customer (on average) generates gross profits in year 1 of: £287 x 1.4 x 55% = £221. To payback in the first 12 months, your customer acquisition cost (your marketing cost) needs to be less than £221 – hopefully far less.

Another critical marketing number to know is how many of your enquiries turn into customers – your enquiry conversion ratio. If you know that you convert one in every four enquiries, you have a conversion ratio of 25%.

For example, a marketing agency is going to run a marketing campaign for you, and you agree to pay £25 for each enquiry generated.

- Cost per enquiry = £25
- Conversion rate = 25% (4 enquiries = 1 customer)
- To acquire 1 customer, you need to pay for 4 enquiries = £25 x 4 = £100. Your customer acquisition cost is therefore £100.
- New customer gross profit in year 1 = £287 x 1.44 x 55% = £221
- Gross profit less acquisition cost = £221 - £100 = £121 in the first year.
- Customer's full lifetime value = £287 x 1.4 x 55% x 6 years = £1,326
- Overall gross profit contribution = £1,326 - £100 acquisition cost = £1,226

A pretty good deal. On that basis, you wouldn't have a fixed marketing budget, you'd buy all the enquiries you could afford. (Assuming you had the capacity to serve all those customers.)

Knowing these numbers opens up other interesting questions, such as:

- If a new customer generates £221 gross profit in year one, how much would you be prepared to reward a team member who introduced a new customer? £50? £100? £200? (Do your company's role descriptions include an expectation that your team members will endeavour to introduce new customers to the business? They should.)
- If a customer stays with you for six years on average, what would you be prepared to invest in a retention strategy that resulted in them

remaining for an extra year? If you have 100 customers and you could extend the average lifetime to seven years, that extra year is worth £22,099 in additional gross profit (100 customers x £287 x 1.4 x 55%).

Start tracking and analysing these critical numbers:
- Number of enquiries
- Conversion rate from enquiry to customer
- Marketing cost per enquiry
- Customer lifetime value

Initially you may have to use estimates, but it'll help you in making more informed marketing decisions.

There will be a time lag between the point when you invest in a marketing campaign and the cash from any customer purchase. The time lag will vary depending on your type of business. For example, with an online consumer business, you may place a Facebook advert and within 24 hours, customers are paying for orders. By contrast, perhaps you own an accountancy practice. Signing up clients might take a couple of months as they deliberate whether or not to switch accountants. The first piece of chargeable work is their year-end accounts. Year-end is seven months away. And it then takes three months for them to get all their information together. Once you've completed the accounts, it then takes them another two months to pay you – a long time! In determining your marketing budget, affordability and cash flow are factors to consider. Be aware of when your marketing investment will translate into cash in the bank.

The factors to take into account when determining what to invest in marketing:
- Your available capacity to service new customers. Creating demand that you can't supply will damage your reputation and result in lost customers.
- The time lag between paying for a marketing campaign and the cash from new customer sales hitting your bank account.
- Your key numbers: number of enquiries; enquiry conversion rate; cost per enquiry; customer lifetime value.

7 ways to improve your profits

Every businessperson wants more customers, more sales and more profit. However, you can't directly get more of those things. Customers, sales and profit are all results of preceding activities.

The four results you want more of are:

A. Customers
B. Sales
C. Gross profits
D. Net profits.

The seven activities that give you those results:

1. Retaining customers.
2. Generating customer enquiries.
3. Converting enquiring customers into purchasing customers.
4. Increasing customers' purchase values.
5. Increasing customers' purchase frequency.
6. Increasing gross profit margins.
7. Reducing overhead costs.

A. Customers = 1. Retained customers + (2. Customer enquiries x 3. Enquiry conversion)
B. Sales = A. Customers x 4. Purchase value x 5. Purchase frequency
C. Gross profits = B. Sales x 6. Gross profit margins
D. Net profits = C. Gross profits – 7. Overhead costs

This example shows how these seven activities combine to generate the four key results.

Example: Seven activities base numbers

		CURRENT	
	Existing Customers	200	
	X	X	
Activity 1	RETENTION RATE	67%	
	Retained Customers	133	
Activity 2	ENQUIRIES GENERATED	200	
	X	X	
Activity 3	CONVERSION RATE	33%	
	New Customers	67	
	Total Customers	200	Result 1
	X	X	
Activity 4	PURCHASE VALUE	£200	
	X	X	
Activity 5	PURCHASES per YEAR	4.0	
	Total Sales	£160,000	Result 2
	X	X	
Activity 6	GROSS MARGIN %	50.0%	
	Gross Profit	£80,000	Result 3
	less	-	
Activity 7	OVERHEADS	£10,000	
	Net Profit	£70,000	Result 4

Your business development efforts need to focus on those seven key activities. Using the starting numbers in this example, here's what happens if a 10% increase is achieved in each area:

Example: Seven activities 10% improvement

	CURRENT	GROWTH			YEAR 1	
Existing Customers	200				200	
x	x				x	
1 RETENTION RATE	67%	+	10%	=	73%	
Retained Customers	133				147	
2 ENQUIRIES GENERATED	200	+	10%	=	220	
x	x				x	
3 CONVERSION RATE	33%	+	10%	=	37%	
New Customers	67				81	
Total Customers	200				227	Result 1
x	x				x	
4 PURCHASE VALUE	£200	+	10%	=	£220	
x	x				x	
5 PURCHASES per YEAR	4.0	+	10%	=	4.4	
Total Sales	£160,000				£220,059	Result 2
x	x				x	
6 GROSS MARGIN %	50.0%	+	10%	=	55.0%	
Gross Profit	£80,000				£121,032	Result 3
less	-					
7 OVERHEADS	£10,000		-10%	=	£9,000	
Net Profit	£70,000				£112,032	Result 4
			Increase:		**£42,032**	
					60%	

- Customers increase from 200 to 227 (+27%).
- Sales increase from £160,000 to £220,000 (+38%).
- Gross profit increases from £80,000 to £121,000 (+51%).
- Net profit increases from £70,000 to £112,000 (+60%).

A 10% improvement is modest. A retention rate increasing from 67% to just 73% is achievable, as is increasing a conversion rate from 33% to just 37%.

Perhaps you believe you can significantly improve your conversion rate. Rather than converting one in three enquiries (33%), you embark on a sales training programme and start converting two out of every three enquiries (67%). Your sales training programme costs £6,000, increasing your overheads from £10,000 to £16,000. This is how your numbers would look for the next year.

Example: Six activities 10% + 1 Activity 100% improvement

		CURRENT	GROWTH		YEAR 1	
	Existing Customers	200			200	
	x	x			x	
1	RETENTION RATE	67%	+ 10%	=	73%	
	Retained Customers	133			147	
2	ENQUIRIES GENERATED	200	+ 10%	=	220	
	x	x			x	
3	CONVERSION RATE	33%	+ 100%	=	67%	
	New Customers	67			147	
	Total Customers	200			293	Result 1
	x	x			x	
4	PURCHASE VALUE	£200	+ 10%	=	£220	
	x	x			x	
5	PURCHASES per YEAR	4.0	+ 10%	=	4.4	
	Total Sales	£160,000			£283,947	Result 2
	x	x			x	
6	GROSS MARGIN %	50.0%	+ 10%	=	55.0%	
	Gross Profit	£80,000			£156,171	Result 3
	less	-				
7	OVERHEADS	£10,000	+ 60%	=	£16,000	
	Net Profit	£70,000			£140,171	Result 4
			Increase:		£70,171	
					100%	

You've just doubled your net profits.

Imagine the results if you achieved a 10% improvement in each of the seven areas for the next five years. In the next example, there's been no increase in gross margin in any of the five years and overheads have actually increased by 10% each year. The other five activities have increase by just 10% each year – the conversion rate has only increased from one in three to just over one in two (54%). You will see that net profits have increased nearly seven-fold from £70,000 to £683,648!

Example: Seven activities 10% improvement over 5 years

	CURRENT	GROWTH	YEAR 1	GROWTH	YEAR 2	GROWTH	YEAR 3	GROWTH	YEAR 4	GROWTH	YEAR 5
Existing Customers	200		200		227		281		367		502
	x		x		x		x		x		x
1 RETENTION RATE	67%	10%	73%	10%	81%	10%	89%	10%	98%	10%	100%
Retained Customers	133		147		183		249		359		502
2 ENQUIRIES GENERATED	200	10%	220	10%	242	10%	266	10%	293	10%	322
	x		x		x						x
3 CONVERSION RATE	33%	10%	37%	10%	40%	10%	44%	10%	49%	10%	54%
New Customers	67		81		98		118		143		173
Total Customers	200		227		281		367		502		674
	x		x		x		x		x		x
4 PURCHASE VALUE	£200	10%	£220	10%	£242	10%	£266	10%	£293	10%	£322
	x		x		x		x		x		x
5 PURCHASES per YEAR	4.0	10%	4.4	10%	4.8	10%	5.3	10%	5.9	10%	6.4
Total Sales	£160,000		£220,059		£329,117		£520,747		£860,088		£1,399,507
	x		x		x		x		x		x
6 GROSS MARGIN %	50.0%	0%	50.0%	0%	50.0%	0%	50.0%	0%	50.0%	0%	50.0%
Gross Profit	£80,000		£110,029		£164,558		£260,373		£430,044		£699,753
less	-										
7 OVERHEADS	£10,000	10%	£11,000	10%	£12,100	10%	£13,310	10%	£14,641	10%	£16,105
Net Profit	**£70,000**		£99,029		£152,458		£247,063		£415,403		**£683,648**

Achieving modest year-on-year improvements in seven key areas will transform the profits in your business.

Even if you don't know all your numbers at the moment (most people don't know them all), use some estimates and see what the potential impact on your business could be:

Example: Your seven activities ??% improvement

	CURRENT	GROWTH	YEAR 1	
Existing Customers	☐		☐	
X	X		X	
1 RETENTION RATE	☐	+ ☐ =	☐	
Retained Customers	☐		☐	
2 ENQUIRIES GENERATED	☐	+ ☐ =	☐	
X	X		X	
3 CONVERSION RATE	☐	+ ☐ =	☐	
New Customers	☐		☐	
Total Customers	☐		☐	Result 1
X	X		X	
4 PURCHASE VALUE	☐	+ ☐ =	☐	
X	X		X	
5 PURCHASES per YEAR	☐	+ ☐ =	☐	
Total Sales	☐		☐	Result 2
X	X		X	
6 GROSS MARGIN %	☐	+ ☐ =	☐	
Gross Profit	☐		☐	Result 3
less	-		-	
7 OVERHEADS	☐	☐ =	☐	
Net Profit	☐		☐	Result 4
		Increase:	☐	

Testing your marketing improvement ideas

As detailed in the Finance chapter, before going full tilt with a new marketing initiative, it's important to test out the initiative on a small scale.

Measuring is the only way to discover whether your marketing investment is delivering you a decent return – or whether it's just an avoidable expense! (Stopping marketing campaigns that aren't working is a great way of saving money and increasing your profits.) It's possible to rank different marketing initiatives by building in good measuring and monitoring systems.

When your monitoring and analysis reveal that you have a successful trial initiative, you can roll out the campaign. Resist the temptation to stop or change a marketing initiative that continues to work. You might think the campaign has become boring or stale, but if the numbers are telling you it's still working, stick with it.

Summary

Before contemplating the search for new customers, make sure you have a system for excellently serving the customers you already have, that you're retaining them, and that all those customers are adequately profitable.

Calculate the Lifetime Profit Value (£) of your customers (purchase value x purchase frequency per year x gross margin x years as a customer). Keep this powerful number front-of-mind when devising your business development campaigns.

Understand what you do from the perspective of the issues you resolve for your customers. How do you make their lives better? Or less bad? Understand the combination of relevant factors that make you stand out in the minds of your chosen customers. And understand the characteristics of you ideal customers.

How well you meet the needs and wants of your customers is the 'inner reality' of your business. How well potential customers perceive your inner reality is the 'outer perception' of your business. Your marketing communication (the outer perception) should faithfully mirror the inner reality.

Business development is about improvement and growth. It's therefore about numbers. It's about knowing whether you get more out than you put in. It's about measuring and tracking everything.

Understand the combined power of making marginal improvements in the seven key business development areas. Work on one or two improvement strategies in each of those seven areas every quarter.

Compound interest is the eighth wonder of the world. The person who understands it, earns it; the person who doesn't, pays it.

ALBERT EINSTEIN

Checklist Exercise: Business Development Fundamentals

The following checklist exercise will be helpful in identifying the progress you've made and in selecting the areas you want to focus on next. It will be useful to review this checklist once a quarter as part of your quarterly planning process.

- Put a tick in the 'DONE' column for those items you already do or are happy with.
- Make a second pass through the checklist and highlight those things that you'd 'LIKE TO' work on next.
- For each 'LIKE TO' item that you've highlighted:

  » What benefits will come from completing it (or what consequences will be avoided)? Jot down the benefits (in your planning notebook).

  » How excited do you feel about cracking on with this activity? Score your level of excitement out of 10 and put your score in the third column of the checklist.

  » Prioritise your 'LIKE TO' activities based on their beneficial impact and how excited you feel about taking action now.

  » Pick the one or two items from the top of your prioritised list and commit to making them a reality.

  » What's the simplest action you can take right now to get moving?
- Put this book down and make a start (or if impractical at the moment, schedule the activity in your calendar).

Some of the items on the list are relatively straightforward and self-explanatory. Others will need a plan behind them and assistance from other people. The purpose of this exercise is to identify which improvement initiatives you feel motivated to commit to, and to encourage you to find a first, small, simple action step to get you going.

BUSINESS DEVELOPMENT FUNDAMENTALS	DONE	LIKE TO	EXCITED
KEEPING WHAT WE'VE GOT THAT'S PROFITABLE	✓	✓	Out of 10
1 We track customer retention & have a minimum retention rate target.			
2 We have a retention strategy & have exceeded our acceptable retention rate.			
3 We track customer profitability & have a minimum acceptable profitability target.			
4 We follow a system for addressing low profit or unprofitable customers.			
5 We have a system for monitoring how well customer expectations are met.			
6 We track individual product & service profit contribution.			
7 We follow a system for addressing low profit or unprofitable products & services.			

PREPARING FOR GROWTH	DONE	LIKE TO	EXCITED
8 We have a business development plan.			
9 We have the capacity to serve more customers (or a capacity expansion plan).			
10 We have defined the segment of the market that we wish to serve.			
11 We have defined our ideal customers & created avatars of them.			
12 We have a combination of service factors that differentiates us in our chosen market.			
13 We stand out in way that is valued & appreciated by our ideal customers.			
14 We understand what issues, problems or opportunities our potential customers have.			
15 We understand the difference between our 'inner reality' & the 'outer perception'.			
16 We have a guarantee that neutralises customers' purchasing concerns.			
17 We understand & have calculated the Lifetime Profit Value of our customers.			
18 We understand & track the Acquisition Cost of new customers.			
19 We know the combined power of small increases in the 7 development activities.			
20 We have modelled our increase in profits by improving the 7 development activities.			

CHAPTER 7

Business Development Strategies & Tactics

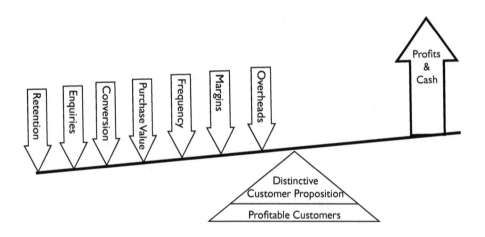

An alternative way of looking at the seven business development pillars is to think of each of them as applying a downwards force to a lever, that lifts the profits of your business (as illustrated in the diagram).

You want to increase the force of each area, and ultimately have all seven areas acting on the lever.

The lever rests on a pivot point made of two business development fundamentals:

- **Profitable customers**: A stable system for serving customers, where all those customers are profitable.
- **A distinctive customer proposition**: A stand-out business offering that's meaningful to your prospective customers.

As you progressively implement your business development strategies and tactics, the lever is forced down on the left-hand side, and your profits and cash are raised on the right-hand side.

Everyone lives by selling something.
ROBERT LOUIS STEVENSON

This chapter shares practical and proven ideas for improving each of the seven activity areas. At the end of each section, you're asked to consider which one or two ideas you believe could have an immediate impact – and that you feel excited about cracking on with. Remember that you're already busy. To start doing something new, you'll have to stop doing something else. It's best to pick one or two things that will be relatively easy to implement and give you a quick win. This will also build your confidence. You can then come back and scan the ideas a second and third time.

Here's a reminder of the seven activity areas:
- **Retention:** Keeping hold of your hard-won and profitable customers.
- **Enquiries:** Engaging with the people and businesses you can help and making the phone ring.
- **Conversion:** Helping people make a sound purchasing decision and come on board as a customer.
- **Purchase value:** Ensuring you're fully meeting your customers' needs and increasing how much they spend in the process.
- **Purchase frequency:** Doing business with your customers more often.
- **Gross margins:** Maximising the value you add and making sure your pricing reflects that.
- **Overheads:** Regardless of the prevailing economic conditions, keeping tight control of your overheads.

1: Retaining your good customers

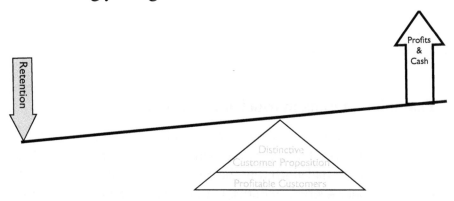

When customers leave, the biggest cause of their defection is what's termed 'perceived indifference' – they didn't think you cared. Great customers don't always get the attention they deserve because they're unassuming and don't cause you any hassle – they just keep ordering and keep paying the invoices. They don't necessarily register on your radar until one of the team casually mentions that they haven't placed an order for the last three months or they haven't seen them recently. When it comes to customers, your time is often taken up dealing with those noisy customers who seem to complain about everything and who are difficult to please; the ones who constantly ask for discounts and always settle their invoices late.

It's always easier to keep a customer than find a new one.

Don't be seduced into chasing new customers and allow existing customers to fall away. First, keep what you've got. Second, develop what you've got. And then thirdly, you can think about finding new customers.

Here is a selection of practical and proven ideas for improving customer retention:

Keep in touch (KIT) with your customer

If you do nothing else, simply pick up the phone and speak to your customers. Ask them how they're doing. Thank them for being such a good customer to work with. You'll probably make their day! Keeping in touch doesn't mean hitting customers with a constant stream of sales messages. Keeping in touch can be done by phone, postcard, letter, email, a personal visit, coffee, or lunch. Make life easier for yourself by creating a KIT reminder system. And it doesn't always have to be you; this could become a company-wide system.

Example: Keeping in touch with your customers

A wholesaling business with over a thousand customers identified that they had 16 customers who accounted for 36% of their sales. The general manager had lunch with the owners of each of those 16 retail businesses once every six months. At the end of each lunch, they took out their diaries and simply booked in their next lunch appointment. The general manager also had a simple system of noting down little personal details about his customers. You don't have to keep everything in your head. Those 16 customers are still customers.

Know your customer (KYC)

The better you know your customer – their likes, dislikes, preferences, family, hobbies, communication style, aspirations, pressures, etc. The more appropriately you can interact with them, the better you can serve them, and the stronger the relationship grows. Stronger relationships equal longer relationships – that can withstand the occasional stumble. You can combine customer knowledge with your KIT strategy. Knowing that your customer enjoys reading and is about to go on a fishing holiday, sending them a small book on fishing takes 'keeping in touch' to a whole different level. Everyone enjoys being on the receiving end of little acts of kindness. You might come across an article about an amazing fishing trip and forward it onto them. All these little touches demonstrate that you're thinking about them. Don't try and keep every customer's personal details in your head. Have a system for capturing and recording them.

Take customers to business events

There can be a tendency to serve customers but do nothing else to develop the relationship. A relevant business event (seminar, conference, exhibition, talk, etc.) can give you and your customer new ideas and insights. More importantly, it's a shared experience – something you can talk about and discuss afterwards. (This activity works well with members of your team too.)

Survey your customers

This is an opportunity for customers to quantify and qualify how well you're performing. It's also an opportunity to identify how you can make things even better. Bear in mind that asking for feedback always creates an expectation that things will improve! Excellent feedback is also an opportunity to ask for a review and a referral.

Pass referrals to customers

Everyone loves a referral. Look for opportunities to introduce potential customers to them. Understand from your customer what makes a good customer for them. Your customer may also be in need of alternative or better suppliers, so they can be good referrals too. Have your customer in mind and keep your eyes and ears open for opportunities to help them.

Post reviews for customers

You enjoy reading a good review about your business – so leave one for your customer. You don't have to be a customer to leave a review. You have a unique insight into their values and ethos that would be pertinent reading for one of their potential customers. It's also appropriate to update a review on an annual basis.

Build a community of customers

You're stronger and more committed when you're part of a club or a community. Bringing your customers together can be a great tactic for building loyalty. They will all have something in common and it's surprising how often they form friendships or do business with each other. It could be a lunch, a seminar, a workshop, a trip to a sporting event, etc. As with most of these strategies and tactics, keep in mind how valuable a customer is by referring to their lifetime value (LTV). This will help you set the budget for your community building initiatives.

Transform customers into VIPs

Everyone likes to feel special. If you have particularly good customers (who buy regularly, take your advice, let you do your job, pay on time, refer other customers to you, and are a joy to work with) then create a VIP membership for them where they get special privileges. You can create an actual VIP Membership – or if it's more appropriate, just keep them on your internal VIP list and treat them accordingly. Keep in mind how much they contribute each year. The special privileges don't have to be related to your business. You can negotiate with other businesses to provide discounted or free products or services which you can pass on to your VIP customers. Those other businesses will see value in giving offers to your customers in the hope they'll become long-term customers of theirs too. Use your imagination and take the initiative so you can stand out from the crowd.

Joint planning sessions with customers

Schedule in time to understand your customer's future aspirations and plans. The more you know in advance, the better you can plan and prepare to help with their future development and growth.

Example: Planning ahead with customers

The first time an engineering company did this with one of their clients, they secured a large project management contract for a factory move. The client was initially resistant to the meeting, believing that there wasn't anything coming up that the engineering services company could help them with. They didn't realise that project management was a service the engineering company offered – they thought that they just did emergency repairs and machine refurbishments. They jumped at the chance of using the engineering company because they knew through experience that they were thorough, reliable and great communicators. They also wouldn't have to go through the aggravation and risk of finding an untested project management company.

Exceed your customers' expectations

The old adage holds true – under promise and over deliver. Deliver it in less time and at a lower cost than you said. Keep your customer surprised on the upside. Look for little ways to deliver additional, unexpected value.

Give the best deals to your best customers

Your best customers should get the best deals. Period. If you ever run an incentive for prospective new customers, at the same time make sure you give your best customers the same deal or better. Keep in mind the lifetime value of your best customers.

Reward your best customers

The principle of the loyalty card that all coffee shops have is a good one. It can be scaled up to larger businesses.

Exercise: Retaining your good customers

- From the ideas shared in this section, which one or two capture your imagination?
- How could you get them going?
- Which team members could you get involved?

2: Generating new customer enquiries

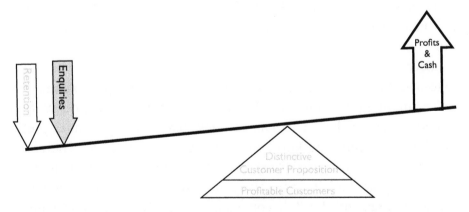

Generating more customer enquiries is often the first – and sometimes only – area where businesspeople focus their attention. There can be a lengthy time lag between investing money on a marketing campaign and the point when the cash from a new customer sale lands in your bank account. Of the seven key activity areas, generating new enquiries ranks number seven. The other six are primarily concerned with improving what you already have and will impact your profits more quickly. You don't have to start with enquiry generation. Analyse each area of the seven activity areas to determine where you'll get the best return for your time, effort and money.

Here is a selection of practical and proven ideas for generating new customer enquiries:

Create a customer referral strategy

Referrals are your number one strategy in terms of generating enquiries. Whilst many businesses receive referrals, they often come about in a passive way. Create a system for actively stimulating referrals. The ideal is to have a business that can live and grow on referrals alone. Imagine not having to invest any time or money in marketing! Building a referral-based business merits your thought and consideration.

> *In sales, a referral is the key to the door of resistance.*
>
> ROBERT FOSTER BENNETT

Firstly, it's about taking your existing good customers on a journey to becoming 'raving fans'. Implementing the ideas in the customer retention section will help. By definition, raving fans rave about you and can't help themselves from recommending you. In effect, they become your sales force.

Secondly, when you first enter into a trading relationship with a new customer, there needs to be a conversation about referrals. Explain why you're building a referral-based business. You don't like the distraction of spending so much time looking for new customers – you much prefer spending that time working with your great customers. Therefore, it's in your new customer's best interests to minimise your marketing efforts! You can explain about the community of great customers that you're building, and they'll become a part of it. This has to be genuine – not just a hollow sales script. Tell them not to start thinking about who to refer yet; they should do that only when they're delighted with the service they've received. (Most people can't help themselves and do start thinking about who to refer!) Get their agreement: "Does that make sense? Is that okay?"

The very best time to ask for a referral is when your customer is on an emotional high – when they're delighted with your service or when they're bowled over because you've gone an extra mile or two for them. For example, when they've seen the new machine you've installed ahead of schedule humming along at full capacity.

Remember that people typically refer people like themselves. Great customers refer other great customers. Less than good customers refer less than good customers. Be careful who you ask for a referral – until all your customers are great customers and raving fans!

Referrals are a long-term strategy, not a short-term tactic. Building a community of raving fans takes time and effort.

And get your team asking for referrals too. Looking for and introducing new customers should be part of every team member's job description. They should be able to talk knowledgeably and positively about the business. Remind your team that you're here to serve and help others and the more of that you do the better. As well as inserting a clause about referrals and business development ideas in everyone's job description, provide training and teach people what to look for and how to talk appropriately about introducing a potential customer to the business.

Contacting former prospects and customers

Sometimes when prospects say no, what they really mean is "no, not at the moment". Establish a reminder system to check in with former prospects. On other occasions, you may have lost out to a competitor. It's always worth a follow-up call a couple of months later. The person may have made a decision they're now regretting but feel too embarrassed to call you back. People typically don't like admitting they've been wrong. Hopefully you'll find that things are going well for the person but it's surprising how often you'll hear the words: "Funny you should call, but I was wondering if we could get back together again."

Always part on good terms with a customer and leave the door open. Similarly, don't assume that former customers won't be customers again. Often customers leave because of a change in circumstances, rather than because you've done anything wrong. Have a system for keeping in touch with former good customers. And if they don't need your services, always ask who they know who may need your services. If you feel it's a little pushy doing all this asking, think of yourself as a doctor with a cure for a terrible disease. It's your duty of care to find the sick people you can cure! It's unprofessional not to.

Give your customers stories to share

Giving a customer a story to share is a powerful way of generating referred enquiries. Everyone loves stories.

Example: A kitchen design business making use of a story

As well as installing great kitchens, the business had a process that made the job go smoothly and ensured a fabulous end-of-the-journey experience for their customer. The installers always arrived on time. They always tidied up. They explained where they were up to and what the plan was for the next day. At the end of the job, as well as clearing up and cleaning as best they could, they had a professional cleaning company come in to ensure the new kitchen was gleaming. A local florist provided a large bouquet of flowers to co-ordinate with the kitchen. All pretty good stuff, and enough to delight the homeowners. However, next to the flowers was a package that really had wow impact.

At the initial meeting three months earlier, it came out that the lady of the house was a big Cliff Richard fan. This nugget of information was tucked away. What the company had bought and wrapped up was a large, coffee-table book on the life and career of Cliff Richard! The customer was astonished! Yes, she loved her kitchen – and the flowers. But what she was bowled over by was her book, and the fact that the company had remembered this little personal detail.

No doubt her family and friends loved her kitchen. But when she was out and about, the story she enthusiastically shared was about her Cliff Richard book and how amazing the company were.

The book cost £12. The kitchen cost the best part of £27,000. People love stories. Give your customers stories to share.

Google My Business

You will have come across businesses who've promised to get you on the first page of Google – often in exchange for large sums of cash. However, there is a free, do-it-yourself way to achieve that: Google My Business. When you type into Google 'financial planners near me' or 'conveyancing solicitors in Warrington', the map with the red pins that appears on the first page of search results is Google My Business. There are always the paid adverts at the top of the page (with the little 'AD' to the left of the company name), then comes the Google My Business map, and then the organic business listings (the ones that are most relevant and searched for most often). Google My Business registration is simple, and Google's guidance is easy to follow. And as for most things in life, there's plenty of short explanatory videos on YouTube.

Before spending a penny on online marketing, make sure you're on the front page of Google by registering your company with Google My Business.

In addition to Google, there are many free, online directories. It's worth spending an evening registering with the more important ones. Simply search for 'the three best free online directories to register my business with'. Read a couple of the articles that your search generates and decide which will be the best ones for your type of business. Get at least a handful of customer reviews on each – see next section.

Customer reviews

To make your Google My Business listing stand out, collect some good customer reviews. Many businesses have no reviews. Some have one or two 1-star reviews from disgruntled customers who've taken umbrage and shared their displeasure with the rest of the world – you don't want any of those. (Remedy for bad reviews coming up.) A few more businesses will have a handful of 4 and 5-star reviews. But virtually no one will have 10s, even 100s, of 4 and 5-star reviews. If you're on Google My Business with 65 reviews averaging 4.8, all other things being equal, people are going to get in touch – guaranteed. And all for free.

If I say I'm great, you're sceptical. If enough of my customers say I'm great, you'll get in touch.

The very best time to ask for a review is when your customer is on an emotional high. If you're a nutritionist's practice, perhaps when a client arrives at their session and tells you that last month has been the first month they haven't been troubled by their digestive disorder for four years.

Position reviews at the start of a customer relationship. "When we've worked together for a couple of months and you've benefited from the programme, to help other potential clients, would you be kind enough to share your experiences via an online review?" Everybody says yes. When it comes to asking for a review a couple of months later, you already have their agreement, so they'll say yes again.

Whilst 65 reviews with comments like "awesome", "really great guys", or "good buying experience", may get the phone to ring, a more detailed review can also do the selling job for you. Good reviews can be an enquiry generator and an enquiry converter.

Firstly, you want a mechanism for asking how happy your customer is with your service (see net promoter score in the Business Development Fundamentals chapter). Assuming they're happy, you want to ask them to leave a review. Make the process as easy as possible. Send them the review link and a couple of questions. Have a templated email set up so that you can send it whilst you're talking. Ask them to check the email has arrived and they can open the link. Having got them that far, it's likely that they'll do the review straight away. Many people will sincerely promise to leave you a review, but don't – their busy lives take over and they forget.

When someone leaves a review, thank them and leave a reply: "Great to hear that your mother loved her flowers. I hope she had a really special day. Please give us a call if we can help out on another occasion."

The people who read reviews are looking for help with something. Their search may have left them confused and overwhelmed by all the online information. You want your review to speak right into the conversation that's swirling around their head.

Here's a set of simple questions a nutritionist practice could send to a customer:
- **Question 1:** What were you thinking about when you were looking for someone to help with your digestive disorder?
- **Question 2:** Why did you choose to contact us?

- **Question 3:** What have you found since we've been working with you?
- **Question 4:** What would you say to someone else who's considering using our services?

So, the full review might look like:

"When I was looking for help with my IBS condition, I felt confused and overwhelmed by all the information out there. I downloaded a really helpful document from Natural Nutrition. It was written in plain English and shared some useful guidance on how to read food labels. When I called for an appointment, they were friendly and professional. After just three sessions, the pain from my digestive disorder has eased significantly. You've got nothing to lose by getting in touch with Natural Nutrition. Great outcome. Lovely people."

Far more powerful than: "Really great guys. Awesome service."

If punctuality is a real differentiator in your sector, ask them a question about how they found your punctuality (assuming it's excellent!). If payment options are often a sticking point in your sector and you offer a great solution, ask them about payment options. Steer the review towards things that are important to your prospective customer and are a differentiator for you.

Some customers say they struggle with what to write. You can always suggest you write a draft for them, which they can then amend. Anything that helps them post that review.

And what to do about bad reviews?
- Take the complaint seriously.
- Look to rectify the situation.
- Thank the customer for bringing it to your attention. (It would have been preferable if they'd brought it to your attention before posting their review, but hey, that's life.)
- If you're at fault, admit it.
- Apologise.
- Put things right as fast as possible.
- Compensate the customer in some way.
- Improve your process.
- Tell the customer how you've improved your process as a result of them bringing it to your attention.
- Thank them again.

They'll possibly change their review to a positive one – perhaps even a glowing one. And if they don't change their review, chalk it up to experience.

If they don't change their review, capture what you did to put things right in the 'Review Reply' section. You can dilute a bad review and your overall rating by getting far, far more positive reviews. Other visiting customers will then see that this one poor review is an exception, and you'll come across as reasonable and keen to put things right. If the reviewer was extremely unreasonable, it'll reflect poorly on them rather than you.

Never argue online. And be prepared to be wrong, even when you're right! The trait of having to be right all the time means someone else must be wrong, which creates an enemy who then hurts you. Being right all the time can be an expensive business!

Good reviews may make you and your team feel good, but their real value is in their ability to get the phone to ring and to generate enquiries – and to improve your enquiry conversion rate. Make them an integral part of your marketing. Create a process for capturing them. Set yourself a target of securing a certain number each month. Other businesses are often ignorant or lazy when it comes to reviews, so make them a real differentiator for your business.

Create a question-answering website

You can guarantee that if you searched online for a hairdresser in Harrogate, then every hairdresser's website will look the same. Slightly different words, pictures and colours, but in essence, the same. Most websites focus on how brilliant the company is. Few companies consider what customers need from a website. Once you do, you can provide information that helps answer their questions, provide reassurance and educate people on how to make a good buying decision. It's what people want. And only a few businesses do it.

It's worth remembering that what Google (other search engines are available!) want is relevant content that satisfies customers' search questions. Yes, there are tactics and tricks to get you noticed, but the place to start is with genuinely helpful, relevant, and regularly updated information. Before producing any copy (the words you write) for your website, you need to understand your potential customers. That means doing some research, observing what they do and say, asking them questions and listening to their answers.

You might be fantastic at cutting hair or designing greenhouses, but you're not an expert at writing copy. Engage a copywriter to produce the copy. Yes, it'll cost you a little money, but you'll get a more powerful and compelling result in far less time. Bear in mind that your copywriter will need something to work with, so you'll still need to do your customer research.

Include informative videos on your website (and other places online)

Not all people like reading and a video can get a great deal of information across in a short period. Unlike the written word, it is also more effective at getting across authenticity and passion through tone and body language. It involves a little more time, effort and money but it's worth the investment.

Either get your videos professionally produced or do them yourself in an amateurish way. You're an amateur so don't try and make a professional video – they look naff. If you're not comfortable speaking to camera, ask someone to interview you. This will distract you from the camera: "So, Bob, tell us what customers should expect when they commission you to build a greenhouse for them?"

If you're the business owner, it's good to have you featured, explaining what drives you to produce such excellent greenhouses, and how you want to enhance the gardening experiences of your customers. It's also powerful to feature other colleagues from your business, talking passionately about their part in the process and how it adds to the product and the customer experience. The process should be an emotional one, building up the personal relationship between your team and the customer. People buy from people and buying decisions are emotional ones (justified with logic). Once you're on a video roll, capturing customer reviews and testimonials on camera adds even more weight to your website.

It's worth remembering that you're not selling greenhouses, you're selling the dream of what a greenhouse allows a gardener to do. Whilst a customer will be excited when they order their greenhouse, more excited when the installation project is complete, they'll be utterly joyous when it's full of vibrantly coloured plants, fruits and vegetables next summer. This is when they're on their emotional high. This is the time to capture your video testimonial. A series of customer videos showcasing and talking about all the plants they've grown in their greenhouses is powerful and inspiring.

Whilst websites are classified as an enquiry generation activity, they also have the ability to convert enquiries too. Even with high ticket items like top-end greenhouses, you can move your prospect close to the point of purchase.

Blog regularly

A great way of keeping your website up-to-date and relevant is to continuously add valuable content in the form of blogs. You don't have to write them all personally. You can engage your team and make use of guest bloggers too. Remember that each of these articles is a marketing piece and should be written with the customer in mind. They should also have an offer and a call to action: "For more information on how to grow prize winning dahlias, email our flower expert Beverly@greenhousesRus.com."

Network where potential customers hang-out

Having defined your ideal customers, the next question is: "Where will I find those ideal customers in the greatest concentration?" Whilst there are many formal business networking events, there are also other occasions and locations where certain groups of people meet. It could be conferences, conventions, training events, golf days, exhibitions, etc. These gatherings are often overlooked but are great networking and prospecting events. People tend to be more relaxed and open and it can be easier to establish new relationships.

Speaking at networking events is a powerful way to establish your credibility and open the door to more potential customers. You may be a natural public speaker. Most people aren't. Invest in some training, rehearse, and keep practising. The more you do it, the better you'll get. Watch what other people do and absorb the best bits. Like anything in life, with training and deliberate practice you'll get better. Remember though, your aim as a speaker isn't audience ovations, it's people saying, "Can we talk?"

Video your talks. Whilst watching them may make you cringe, it's the most powerful way of improving. You can also load the video onto your YouTube channel and forward the link to anyone who wanted to come along to the event but couldn't make it.

Host a bring-a-friend business event

Events make customers feel special. And it's good if they can bring a plus-one business associate – perhaps one of their suppliers or customers or a fellow business owner. This helps them forge a deeper relationship with a key business associate. For you, in addition to cementing your relationship with your customer, it introduces you to a prospective new customer in a very low key, pleasant environment. Events take time, effort and money, and you'll need your team involved. The cost has to be considered in the context of your customer lifetime value. This is not the occasion to pitch your services. It can be an occasion to share a good news story about one of your customers. Ideally, one of your customers sharing the story is even more powerful. Make sure you have a mechanism for following up with everyone. A simple thank you card or posting a memento of the occasion a few days later will suffice. Again, don't send them a sales brochure. Keep in touch with them and wait for a buying signal – "Could we get together for a coffee?" or "Please could you send us one of your brochures?"

Alliances, other people's lists (OPLs), and host beneficiaries

Consider joining forces with another business who want to serve the same customers as you. You'll need to get on well with the other business. You could draw up a simple joint plan and agree to run a trial for six months. Two minds, two sets of complementary skills, and two marketing budgets combined may have a disproportionate impact for both businesses.

Alternatively, is there a business with customers you'd like to be serving? If you can tap into their list of customers (whilst conforming with those customers' communication preferences and to GDPR regulations), OPLs are a fabulous shortcut to a concentration of ideal customers. Your excellent service will enhance the reputation of the list owner, so feel confident to approach the business about using their list.

The host beneficiary concept takes OPLs one step further. It works like a joint promotion. You approach the list owner with an attractive offer for their customers. The owner contacts their customers, positioning the offer as something they've sourced and negotiated for their most important customers. The owner benefits by enhancing the relationship with their customers, and you benefit because you get people taking up your offer.

Bear in mind that you have to make the running and do all the work. Despite the benefits and logic of how well this can work for the host beneficiary company, it's surprising how many companies just don't see it or can't be bothered. Finding an open-minded partner who can see the potential might take some time – but it's worth it. Whatever campaign and offer you come up with for your partner's customers, trial it first so you can refine it and iron out any issues. Quite rightly, your partner's list is precious, and they need to be certain that you and your attractive offer will enhance their relationship with their customers.

For the people who take up your offer, have a second offer for them to come back a second time. For new customers, the drop off between first and second transaction is relatively high. The drop off rate between the second and third transaction is far lower, so incentivise customers to come back that second time. You may get a few people who take your offer and run but don't worry about that. Keep in mind the lifetime value of the people who stay.

When it comes to offers, look for something of high perceived value to the customer and low cost to you. Straight discounts are costly. A £50 discount is worth £50 to the customer and costs you £50. And it's not exactly very exciting – and can devalue your product or service. If you're offering a free treatment that normally costs £75, that's great value for a customer. If you've got an underutilised member of staff who will be delivering that service, it doesn't cost you anything on the basis that you're paying their salary anyway.

Example: A host beneficiary offer between an optician and a dentist

An optician's practice was opening a third branch in a new town. There is an established, dental practice a little further down the high street. It was a well-to-do town and the dentist's clientele would make superb customers for the optician. The optician knew that once someone become a customer, they remained loyal to the practice for ten years plus. But getting them through the door in the first place was a challenge, as they'd experienced when they opened their second branch. They introduced themselves to the dental practice owner and offered them and their staff a complimentary eye test and an optical coherence tomography scan. The dental staff liked the layout of the optician's practice and really liked the optician and her staff. The optician shared the idea of extending the complimentary offer to the dentist's customers. The dentist was receptive and said they'd give it a go. The optician drafted the letter which the dentist then tweaked. The optician printed and organised the letters in batches, bought all the stamps and the dentist signed the letters and posted them. Over a three-month period, 28 people took up the offer and most became customers of the opticians.

Whatever your business, introduce yourself and get to know the other business nearby. If you're able to let them experience your service on a complimentary basis, it's likely they'll speak well of you and refer people to you. You could even host a little social event for local businesses after you move in. Yes, it'll take a little money, time and effort, but it's great to establish a local sales force!

Building lists of potential customers

If you run an advert offering free guitar pics, the people who'll take up your offer are guitar players. If you're in the business of selling hand-made guitars, you've just inexpensively created a list of people (guitar players) who may be interested in your guitars. Your marketing now becomes far more targeted and cost efficient.

For example, offer a downloadable report on '25 Simple Ways to Sell Your Home More Easily' if you're an estate agent looking for people who are considering selling their home.

Using competitions to list build

Tailored competitions are another effective way of creating a list of potential customers. Competitions can be run offline (via a local or national magazine or newspaper, at an event or show, etc.) or online (Facebook, etc.). You can have one winner, and countless runners up, allowing you to get back in touch with everyone who enters. A couple of important points. Make the competition something that will attract the sort of people you want to do business with; or run your competition at a specialist event or in a specialist magazine where you're guaranteed an interested audience.

For example, if you're selling greenhouses, you might run your competition whilst exhibiting at a Royal Horticultural Society show or in a specialist gardening magazine. The winning prize might be a greenhouse, the (countless) runners-up prizes might be a book: 'Landscaping Projects for Beginners'. Even if your competition is run in a generalist magazine or paper, this competition will only attract people with gardens, who are interested in gardening and who would like a new greenhouse. Make the competition easy to enter. It's good to have a tie-breaker question: "In one sentence, tell us what you'd most like to grow in a greenhouse and why." (This could also be a good source of marketing copy!)

If people have given you their address on the competition entry form, it also allows you to tailor your follow-up in a more appropriate way. Small greenhouses to people with small gardens, large greenhouses to people with large gardens in more affluent areas.

Direct mail, postcards and lumpy mail

Even in this electronic age, direct mail still works. Large, successful companies wouldn't use it if it didn't. Personally, you may consider it as junk mail and chuck it in the recycling, but companies who use direct mail extensively are the masters of data analysis and know what works and what doesn't. These companies track their campaigns and once they find the formula that works, they keep running with it. They know their numbers and they know they get a return on their investment. You can do the same, albeit on a smaller scale. As with most of these strategies, the key is to be specific about your audience and where you'll find them in greatest concentration. Your prospective customer list is key.

The most important aspect in direct mail is writing to the right person. The world's most beautifully crafted letter is worthless if it goes to the wrong person. Who's your 'right person'?

Close behind it is the content of your letter. You need to focus on what's going to make their life better – solve a problem or satisfy a desire. (See the four elements to the marketing equation in the Business Development Fundamentals chapter – interrupt, engage, educate and offer). Understanding customer issues comes from your research, which is often as straightforward as listening to existing customers: "What were you thinking about before your first contacted us?"

One piece of direct mail is rarely sufficient. Rather than a single mail shot, it's best to think of a multi-touch direct mail campaign.

Postcards are particularly effective. They can't carry as much information as a letter, but they stand out better. They're also more likely to be kept, perhaps being stuck to a notice board or fridge.

Lumpy mail is a variant of direct mail, where you include a physical item in your mailing. Lumpy mail will stand out and be remembered far better, although the ingredients for crafting a well-written letter still apply. For example, if you're a holiday cottage company, you could attach an enveloped tea bag to the top of your letter with the headline: "Make yourself a brew and think about a relaxing stay in the Yorkshire Dales." Or if you sell holiday homes in the Yorkshire Dales, you could attach a key to the top of your letter with the headline: "Could this be the key to your dream holiday home in the Yorkshire Dales?"

A coloured, handwritten envelope with a Royal Mail souvenir first class stamp also helps your letter stand out. It's unlikely to clinch the sale, but they will remember your letter – with a smile! – when you make your follow-up phone call. Your direct mail piece is unlikely to precipitate an instant sale, especially if you're selling holiday homes in the Yorkshire Dales. Its only purpose is to 'sell' the next step in your process, which might be returning a form or answering a phone call. If you want someone to return a form, make it easy for them by including a stamped addressed envelope.

You can be imaginative and bold when it comes to lumpy mail. For example, the company who sent a mannequin's arm to people with a label attached saying: "I'd give my right arm for a meeting with you." Or sending a single shoe with the message: "Now that I've got my foot in the door, let's sit down for a chat." Another example is a financial planning company who sent a bottle of champagne to prospective customers with a request for a 20-minute phone conversation.

You couldn't send a mannequin's arm to 1,000 people – but you could send one to 20 well-chosen potential customers. The key is finding the ideal people you want to do business with. The key is your list.

And it's important to know your numbers and to do the maths. A £25 bottle of Champagne plus £6 postage to 20 people will cost you £620. If 20 bottles of Champagne turn into 15 calls, and they turn into 5 meetings, and they turn into 1 customer who's worth £1,800 profit in their first year and £567 a year for the following 14 years, that's a pretty good deal. But you must know your numbers!

Write a book, a white paper, or a report

Being able to give someone a book written by yourself, rather than a business card, is impressive. It establishes your credibility and makes you stand out from the crowd. And your own book makes great lumpy mail.

A book might be too big for a first step. A short, interesting blog might be the place to start. The key is to offer something of value and relevance to your audience. You might not think of yourself as an expert, but relative to your potential customers you are. You have valuable information that they'll be interested in. Have a go.

Expert reports and white papers act as great lead magnets to attract prospective customers. The low-risk, no-cost, easy-next-step offer in your direct mail piece might be to send a report on the current state of the holiday home market in the Yorkshire Dales in exchange for simply returning a form or making a phone call. Perhaps you want to make it a free download on a landing page or on your website in return for someone filling in their contact details.

Put your team in uniforms

A smart, clean uniform creates a great first impression. As the name implies, uniforms ensure a uniform standard across your whole team. Uniforms attract attention, and sometimes enquiries, when your team are out and about. Train your team on how to handle enquiries that come their way. Give them all business cards. Business cards are useful and make your team members feel proud and important. Staff like wearing uniform – assuming it's comfortable, practical and well-designed. They don't have to think about what to wear each day, they avoid wear and tear of their own clothes, and it helps make them feel part of a serious business. Agree with the team how it should be worn and standards of cleanliness. It will need replacing periodically. Shabby, worn out uniform won't enhance your reputation – quite the opposite. Putting you web address and phone number on your uniforms can be useful too.

Livery your vehicles

Your vehicles can become free mobile advertising. Make sure what you do and your phone number are big and bold and can be photographed easily. Ironically, your business name isn't critical. Anthony Atkins & Sons is less important than the fact that you're 'cellar conversion specialists'. As with uniforms, keep your vehicle clean and tidy. If someone peers through the window and sees empty coffee cups, papers strewn everywhere, and an overflowing ashtray, they assume those standards reflect how you do business.

Parking your vehicle in high traffic locations can also be a winner. For example, a couple of hours parked in a supermarket carpark on a Saturday morning, close to the entrance, can work wonders if you're a decorating business, or a domestic heating business, or a landscaping business. Think about the ideal customers you're looking for before picking your supermarket!

If fully liveried vehicles are a stretch, magnetic door panels are a simple and inexpensive alternative.

Advertising leaflets and knocking on

If you're a business who provides services in the home, ensure your team members drop leaflets through the front doors of the six houses to the left, the six to the right and the twelve opposite the house you're working at. Better still, train your team to knock on those doors, explain that they've just completed a job for Mr. Evans at number seven, and hand them a leaflet. It might be appropriate to knock on and leaflet the properties ahead of carrying out the work. For example, two or three boiler services on the same road on the same day is very efficient. The installation cost per house is far lower if you can install solar panels along a whole row of houses rather than just one.

You can reduce the likelihood of your leaflet being filed in the bin by putting useful information on it. As well as what you do and your contact details, perhaps put some useful local phone numbers – local council, local police, Citizens Advice, etc. Perhaps you can team up with some complementary businesses or trades from your local chambers of commerce or business network group and produce a joint leaflet of key phone numbers – heating, plumbing, electrician, florist, decorator, aerials, drive cleaning, etc. As well as increasing the likelihood of the leaflet being put on the fridge, the cost is also shared.

If you provide a recurring service, before you leave, remember to schedule the next service, even if it's 12 months away. If you are a heating engineer (or similar), leave a sticker with your contact details on the boiler or a magnetic business card on the fridge – plus a few business cards for the homeowner to pass onto their friends. People are always on the lookout for reliable plumbers. Make it easy for them to call you and refer you.

Put A-boards in prominent positions

A-boards are another marketing basic that are often overlooked. Again, make what you do and your phone number big and bold. If you're working on a side road, leave the board close to the main road.

It will be helpful to get a professional to advise on colours and design and to ensure that all your marketing materials tie together. Check out that colours and designs work well on different surfaces. Does your logo work on a van, a tee shirt and a letter head? Don't let an indulgent designer put design ahead of your key marketing message – what you do and how people can get in touch. Keep things simple.

Train your team on how to use marketing material (leaflets, A-boards, business cards, magnetic door panels, etc.) and how to handle enquiries. Practise and role play different enquiry interactions with them. Most businesses don't do this. You'll steal a march on your competitors if you do.

Employ a salesperson

You might currently be the most effective salesperson in your company. However, you can't do it all by yourself and you have other important things to be doing too. Don't underestimate the role your team can play in actively looking out for and introducing potential clients. However, taking on a professional salesperson can be a transforming step. Recruit an experienced salesperson with a track record. Of all the people you'll employ, a good salesperson is probably the hardest to find. Consider making the role highly commission-based – and be generous with the commission. Have an effective monitoring and review process in place from the outset. A good salesperson should expect to be managed in this way. Ensure the individual has the marketing tools to do their job well. Be clear about what you expect. Is this a person to convert enquiries generated by your marketing campaigns or are you expecting them to generate customer enquiries too?

Exercise: Generating new customer enquiries

- From the ideas shared in this section, which one or two capture your imagination?
- How could you get them going?
- Which team members could you get involved?

3: Converting enquiring prospects into purchasing customers

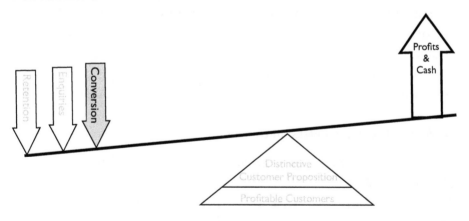

This is one of the first places to go when you're looking to make fast improvements to profits. Whilst you're looking to make incremental improvements in many other parts of your business, this is one area where you can realistically think about doubling or trebling profits within 12 months. Currently, every four enquires might be turning into one piece of business. If you can turn every four enquires into to two pieces of business, all other things being equal, you've just doubled your

BUILDING A SUCCESSFUL BUSINESS

sales and gross profits. Enquiry conversion really is an exciting area to focus on!

Here is a selection of proven ideas for converting enquiries into more business:

Start measuring conversion rate

Most business don't track enquiries and therefore don't know their conversion rate. When they do start tracking, they're often shocked that it's less than they thought. Ironically, a low conversion rate is a good thing. It means that you've got bags of room for improvement. If your conversion rate is 90%, there's not much you can improve. If your conversion rate is 20%, you've got the opportunity to double, treble or even quadruple your conversion rate and your gross profits.

If your conversion rate turns out to be 100% then your prices are too low. Keep nudging up your prices until your conversion rate drops to at least 90%. Your higher cash margins will more than make up for your lower conversion rate.

Start tracking each enquiry that comes into the business. A simple spreadsheet is sufficient to get you going. Note what happens to each enquiry: Does it turn into business or not? After a short time, a pattern will emerge. If you can, estimate the value of each enquiry so that you can measure conversion rate in absolute terms and in value terms.

Simple enquiry and conversion tracker

Date	Enquiry	Won/Lost	Value	Won/Lost
01-Jan	Ann	Lost	£100	£0
02-Jan	Bob	Lost	£100	£0
03-Jan	Celia	Lost	£100	£0
04-Jan	Derek	Won	£200	£200
Total	4	1	£500	£200
Conversion		25%		40%

You may wish to define what a 'qualified enquiry' is before it's entered into your enquiry and conversion tracker. If you're getting a high number of enquiries that you immediately disqualify, you'll want to look at your marketing – it's not doing its job well enough.

If you've got a long sales cycle because you're selling a high-cost product or service, it'll take longer for your baseline conversion rate to emerge. Don't find an excuse not to measure your conversion rate, even if it's difficult to do. You need that baseline measure so that you can see what impact your improvement initiatives have.

There's something magical about measuring the conversion rate ahead of making any improvements – it increases just because you start measuring it. To make it improve a little bit more, share the measure with your team or ask one of the team to post it on a communal notice board.

Here's a more detailed example of an enquiry tracker for a photography business. You'll notice that they're also capturing other information such as how much the customer spends, and whether the customer subsequently leaves them a review or refers another potential customer.

Example: Enquiry tracker for a photography business

No.	Enquiry Date	Source	Sub-Source	Prospect Name	Type	Booking Date	Shoot Date	Viewing Date	Spend	Review	Referral	Comment
143	01-Feb	Internet		Amy	Wedding	20-Feb	12-Sep					
144	01-Feb	Referral	Beverly	Brian	Studio	01-Feb	14-Feb	21-Feb	£1,245	✔	✔	His sister Ali
145	03-Feb	Call	Former client	Cathy	Studio	03-Feb	05-Mar					
146	04-Feb	Leaflet		Donald	Studio	10-Feb	01-Mar					
147	04-Feb	Leaflet		Eric	Studio							Out of his budget

The enquiry tracker information can then be collated, analysed and presented on a monthly tracker.

Monthly enquiry conversion summary for a photography business

	Month	Jan	Feb	Mar	Apr	May	Jun
1	No. of Enquiries	35	65	45	48	52	60
2	Est Enquiry Value £	£22,750	£29,250	£24,750	£31,200	£34,840	£36,000
3	No. of Photo Shoots	12	20	18	20	24	35
4	Photos Purchased £	£11,640	£14,600	£11,700	£13,000	£12,960	£15,750
5	Avg. Enquiry Value (2/1)	£650	£450	£550	£650	£670	£600
6	Avg. Shoot Value (4/3)	£970	£730	£650	£650	£540	£450
	Conversion Rates						
7	Shoots/Enquiries (3/1)	34%	31%	40%	42%	46%	58%
8	Photo £/Enquiry £ (4/2)	51%	50%	47%	42%	37%	44%

CONTINUED

In this example, the monthly analysis shows some interesting trends:
- **Line 1:** The number of enquiries is increasing each month – good news. (February's high number is probably because of Valentine's Day.)
- **Line 6:** The average value of photographic shoots is dropping month on month (from a high of £970 to £450) – a worrying trend and one to investigate.
- **Line 5:** The average enquiry value is variable but seems stable.
  Line 7: As well as enquiries increasing each month, the number of enquiries that are converted into photographic shoots is also increasing (from 34% to 58%) – good news.
- **Line 8:** However, the conversion rate on a value basis is dropping each month (51% to 44%) – not good. It seems that lower value enquiries are converting well but the higher value enquiries aren't.

You can see how this information and analysis will direct your questioning and your subsequent investigation, allowing you to focus your improvement efforts.

Qualify prospects before engaging

When the phone rings, you're delighted that someone's interested in your service. The last thing you want to do is tell them you can't help. You keep the enquiry alive. When eventually it doesn't turn into business, you remember that you knew in your gut it wouldn't convert into business. Or worse still, it turns into a piece of business that becomes difficult to handle and might even be unprofitable.

Whilst your intuition is often a good judge, it's helpful to have some logical criteria for determining whether a prospect is going to be a good fit for your business. If the answer is "No", then the earlier you end the relationship the better. To satisfy your need to help everyone, have the names of a couple of decent alternative suppliers for the enquirer. (If you're really cute, you could negotiate a referral commission.) Always position a referral in a positive way. Don't tell the person their business is too small for you, just tell them that there's someone who can do a far better job for them and give them the other company's phone number – or better still, arrange for the other supplier to give them a call.

Determining your qualification criteria goes back to the work you've done on determining your ideal customers.

Create a sales process

Whilst other tactics may give you a bigger one-off improvement in conversion rate, this is the most important long-term activity to work on. A sales process will give you better and more consistent results with less effort. Whilst it's called a sales process, a better way to think of it is as a customer purchasing decision-making process. It's something that helps your potential customer make a decision that's in their best interests. It's therefore appropriate to share the process with your enquiring customer and outline to them the benefits of following the process.

However, the key word is process – a step-by-step path along which you help a customer move as they gain information, have their questions answered, consider their options, have any objections allayed, and arrive at a point where they can make a 'buy or don't buy' decision. If you've done your job correctly, when someone arrives at the end of the process, they should be making a buy decision. If they're going to be a 'don't buy' they should be filtered out at one of the intermediate steps.

The length of your process will depend on the importance and value of the purchase. Deciding whether to purchase a £20 bag of coffee beans will be a short process. Whether to buy a £20,000 coffee machine will be longer process with more steps.

A coffee machine purchasing decision-making process (sales process) might look like this:

There needs to be enough steps to ensure people feel confident to make a decision – but not too many. Sometimes you'll get people who want to buy immediately. Don't hinder them – don't force them through your beautifully crafted sales process just for the sake of it – but do make sure it's the right thing for them to do.

A sales process improves your conversion rate in two ways. Its primary function is to guide people to where they can make a decision. However, the fact that you have a meaningful process to help people speaks volumes about how you do business. It says a great deal about what kind of a supply partner you're going to be. It gives people confidence in you and your business.

Some team members kick back against getting out a questionnaire when they're in front of a prospective customer. They feel it makes them look unprofessional – as if they don't know their job. Invariably those people who don't have a questionnaire arrive back at the office with a missing piece of vital information. Most potential customers see a questionnaire as a good thing – it makes you look thorough, well-prepared and professional. It gives you structure. You can fully listen to what the potential customer is saying, verbally and non-verbally, as you're not distracted by trying to remember your next question. You don't miss anything vital. Most importantly, people following a process have better results than those who carry everything around in their heads.

Initially it doesn't matter what your process looks like. You'll get better results with a process than without one. If you keep monitoring, measuring and making refinements, your process and your results will improve.

Remember to ask for the sale

The last step in the sales process is when your potential customer becomes a real customer. A simple thing that can be overlooked is asking for the business. Even after taking a customer through the whole process, some people feel slightly awkward and a little embarrassed to ask the critical question. Or you let them go away to think about it. Find a form of words that you feel comfortable with that in essence asks for the business: "So, are we going to give this a go?" or "If you let me know your purchase order number, you can have your machine installed before the weekend."

For example, a company who supplied replacement chain for forklift trucks took most of their enquiries over the phone. They added one simple sentence to the end of enquiry calls that increased their conversion rate from 55% to 73%. "And your purchase order number is?"

Regular sales training

Many business owners claim they're not salespeople. If you help people make buying decisions, you're a salesperson. You may never have had the title 'Salesperson' or had any formal training, but you are in the business of sales. Believing you're not a salesperson is unhelpful. It closes your mind to learning and improving your sales skills. Change your mind. Accept that you are a salesperson. If you want to help people and make your business more profitable, start working on your sales skills on a regular basis.

Progress is impossible without change. And those who cannot change their minds cannot change anything.
GEORGE BERNARD SHAW

As with all skills, it doesn't matter where you're starting from. And it doesn't matter how good everyone else is. What matters is that your skills are better this week than they were last week. Simply picking up a sales book, any sales book, and applying some of the techniques that appeal to you is a great place to start. If you don't get the opportunity to read, download an audio you can listen to in the car. A £10 investment in a book might just transform your business. (A list of recommended sales books can be found in Appendix B.) And what's good for you is also good for your team. Get them improving their sales skill too. Listen to the same books and then compare notes.

Prepare, practise and rehearse

Top performers in every field of life dedicate themselves to getting ready. You should do the same. Whether it's a phone call or a seminar, practising will help you perform better when it comes to the real thing. It may be embarrassing and it may be time consuming, but it will pay dividends in terms of better results. If a potential customer's lifetime value is £25,000, how long would you rehearse for if it resulted in you winning that business?

Record, review & improve

Top performers also dedicate themselves to getting better. You should be the same. Probably the most powerful way to do that is to make audio or video recordings when you're performing (and when you're rehearsing). Schedule time to listen to or watch those recordings with a notebook and pen. Time consuming and potentially embarrassing, but an investment that will return great improvements and better results.

Genuinely listen and understand.

Firstly, you need to ask diagnostic-type questions to understand a prospect's issues, frustrations or concerns and how they impact on their business and on them personally. Accurate diagnosis is half the solution. A doctor can only prescribe once they've done a thorough diagnosis – and you should do the same. People may consider your solution once they feel you've understood them. And you can only offer the right solution after you've listened and understood.

> *Seek first to understand; then to be understood.*
> STEPHEN COVEY

Businesses are made up of people, and people are emotional characters who make emotional decisions. If you're responsible for making a £100,000 investment decision for a corporation, you have to ensure there's a logical, financial justification for making that decision. But you've got emotions invested in that decision: pressures from your boss; the stress of it going wrong – the last incumbent was sacked for a bad decision; another department is vying for the company's limited budget; it's a career-defining decision. As a salesperson, get to know the person in front of you and what's happening in their life.

Turn quotations into proposals

A quotation tends to focus on one thing – cost. In a buying decision, there are other factors that are important. Make sure that people are giving appropriate weight to all those other factors. The place to start in a proposal is to restate the problem or opportunity that needs addressing. Demonstrate your understanding of how this is impacting your customer and highlight how life is going to be better once the project is complete.

Give your customer a number of options:
- A budget version.
- The one they asked for.
- An improved and enhanced version.

It's surprising how often they'll go for your enhanced (and more expensive) option. Focus on the elements that are important to them.

If timescales are important, stress how you'll manage the project to complete it in a certain period of time. If avoiding business interruption is important, explain how you'll manage the project accordingly. Include relevant case studies and testimonials.

Assume the sale

Think of your prospect as already your customer. Use language that intimates that you've already started working together. Rather than "If you go ahead, at stage two I'll give you some options for tiling the workshop extension", use inclusive language: "At stage two we'll go through the tiling options."

Turn cost and price into an investment

When people think of cost, they think of themselves being worse off. When they think of investment, they think of what they're going to get back. Always use the word 'investment' because the truth is your customer is always going to get back more than they paid. This might be intangible. What value might they put on peace of mind or being able to sleep at night? You can't truly put a value on what your customer gets. (Which is one of the reasons why so many businesses under-price their services – they underestimate what their customer actually gets.) Sometimes the customer gets an actual, demonstrable return on their investment. On other occasions, the customer's return may take the form of avoiding a potential negative consequence. Not investing £2,000 in a timely machine refurbishment may result in a production line breakdown at a later date that costs £20,000. If your customer talks cost, you talk investment. Identify and ideally quantify the beneficial outcomes for your customer.

Present proposals in person and get all the decision makers in one room

If you're asked to submit a proposal, go to the effort of presenting it in person. Your success rate will be higher than if you just email or post it. In person, you can talk it through and answer any questions or queries. You can also ask for the business at the end of the process.

By being there in person, you have the opportunity to flush out any doubts the person is having and reassure them by addressing their queries. It's hard to do that by email. If a prospect says they need to think about it, always ask them what they need to think about. "I need to think about it" is usually just an ingrained, automatic response. If you challenge it, you'll often get "You're right. I don't need to think about it. Let's go ahead." Alternatively, "I need to think about it" may mean that there's something you've not covered. Ask what they need to think about and deal with it whilst you're there. Occasionally, they do need to think about it. If that's the case, make sure you arrange a follow up meeting as soon as possible – don't allow them to "get back to you". Stay in control of the process.

If you can, in a competitive situation where other companies' proposals are being considered, always submit or present your proposal last. You'll be top-of-mind and your chances of being successful will be higher.

When there are multiple decision makers, get them all in the same room. Don't allow someone to share your proposal to a joint decision maker without you there. The absent person will only focus on one thing: "How much!?" If someone tells you they make all the decisions, be sceptical to the point of not believing them. If you're in the business of selling expensive items to householders, always get both partners involved in the process.

Always stay in control

Never let anyone "get back to you". You've spent fruitless and frustrating hours trying to get hold of people after you've presented your proposal. At the end of each process step – at the end of every conversation – always agree on the next step and when it's going to happen. Confirm this in your follow up note. Send them a calendar invite – even if it's for a five-minute phone call. They're busy people so you appreciate how important scheduling their time is. You're doing it for their benefit. Indirectly, your thoroughness and how you manage the process reflects how good a supplier you'll be and will help you convert more business.

Always follow up

People work extremely hard to generate enquiries – and then don't get back to people. Despite their good intentions, daily life takes over.

They do all the pressing, urgent stuff, forgetting just how valuable (lifetime value again) a new customer is. Exhibitions are a classic. You spend a small fortune in attending the event and invest a huge amount of effort capturing enquiries and are then "too busy catching-up" when you get back to the office. The key is to schedule follow-up time into your diary following any enquiry-generating activity (exhibition, seminar, network event). If you go to a two-day exhibition, schedule two days (or four half days) for follow-ups; if you go to a two-hour network meeting, schedule (block the time in your calendar) two hours for follow-ups.

Case studies and 5-star reviews

Reviews are covered in detail in the previous Generating New Customer Enquiries section. In essence, if you say your business is the best around, people will be sceptical. If customers say you're fabulous and you've transformed their lives, they'll be believed. Third party endorsements are powerful.

Case studies offer potential customers a more detailed account of how the process or project has worked for other customers like them. The higher the investment level, the greater the need for case studies. As with virtually everything else in this book, creating a process and standard format for capturing and presenting case studies will give you better and more consistent results with less effort. Talk about case studies at the beginning of the relationship and gain your customer's agreement to create one when the project is complete. Customers like providing case studies because it makes them look and feel important.

Use accreditations and awards

Accreditations and awards will enhance your reputation and credibility and boost your conversion rate. Detail how the accreditation benefits your customer. All other things being equal, an 'Award-Winning Design Agency' is better than a 'Design Agency'. An 'Accredited Gold-Standard Training Company' is better than a 'Training Company'. It may also be that you need certain accreditations before you can tender for projects, particularly for large companies and public sector organisations. Awards and accreditations can also be used as a mechanism for creating and maintaining high standards and robust processes within your businesses. However, beware of being distracted by chasing awards.

Make sure you've got the basics in place and have the time and energy to enter – these things are always more involved than you imagine.

Make it easy to buy, easy to pay for, and make your customers lazy

Make your forms as simple as possible and ask for as little information as is necessary. If something is going to be difficult (perhaps due to regulatory requirements) then tell customers it's going to be a little complex but you're going to make it as easy as possible for them – and you'll hold their hand each step of the way. It's illuminating to buy something from your own company to determine how easy or difficult it is.

Do as much as possible for your customer so they do as little as possible. Eradicate all the opportunities for them to get fed up and go elsewhere. Book their next appointment. Send them timely reminders. Always give them the best deal. Make recommendations to them. Exceed their expectations. Make them feel special. Keep in touch. Make them lazy.

Amazon are the masters of these techniques. Often, it's a 'one click' purchase so you're not tempted to go anywhere else. And if you do look for an alternative, the other supplier's checkout process is never as slick, and you flick back to Amazon. It can be educational to study companies like Amazon and mimic some of the things they do.

Offer a guarantee around a customer concern or frustration

Take away as much risk as possible from the customer. Your customer may have doubts because they've not bought before. Or your sector may have a reputation for always being over budget and behind schedule. Focus on the one thing that customers are most concerned about and take away that concern with a guarantee. As much as possible, have no conditions attached to your guarantee: "Our no-questions-asked money-back guarantee gives you peace of mind and allows you to purchase with confidence."

The key is to make sure your customer never activates the guarantee. That's achieved by having sound processes that consistently deliver the desired results. If your sector has a reputation for never returning customer calls, develop a system for ensuring that you do. "If we can't answer first time because we're with another customer, we'll call you back within 30-mintues – and if we don't, we'll send you a £100 M&S voucher."

For example, you may not perceive returning customer calls as a deal-breaker – because you're the world's best solicitor. However, it might be a deal-breaker for your customers. A decent solicitor who promptly returns calls might do more and better business than the world's best solicitor who is neglectful of returning calls. And it's much easier to work out how to return phone calls than it is to become the world's best solicitor. From a marketing perspective, "Fed up with solicitors who don't return your calls? We return all customer calls within 30-minutes – guaranteed!" stands a good chance of generating more enquiries than "Want the world's very best solicitors fighting your corner? Simply give us a call now."

Be attractive

Are you attractive? Are people drawn to you, your business and your service offering? Think about how you can be attractive to the people you want to do business with. Perhaps it's how enthusiastic your team are on the phone. Perhaps it's how exceptional your packaging is. Perhaps it's your reputation for being early for every meeting. Perhaps it's how much you smile. Perhaps it's how clean and shiny your shoes are! Perhaps your 'reassuringly expensive' offer attracts people who truly appreciate the value of what you deliver and repels those late-paying, constantly complaining, discount-hunting price-shoppers. Don't hide your light under a bushel. Be attractive.

Offer samples and make try-before-you-buy offers

The classic is the old puppy-dog close. "Take the puppy home free for a month. If you're not totally in love with him at the end of month then just bring him back!" (Not that I'm advocating you take on the responsibility of a dog without prior serious consideration.) If you're confident that your product and service will exceed people's expectations, samples, demonstrations and trial periods are a great way of convincing people. They're all great risk-reduction tactics.

Critical non-essentials

The essentials of a business are its core products and services. The essentials are what customers pay you to provide and deliver. Quite rightly, you need to create, maintain and develop your products and services so that they're fit for purpose, conform to requirements, and ideally, exceed your customer's expectations. However, customers often don't focus on the technicalities of what you do when they're deciding whether to do business with you. That's not because they think the technicalities are unimportant, but because they often don't understand them. For example, they can't differentiate between the services of one accountancy practice and the next. So, when a customer is scouting the market for a firm of accountants, how do they know which one is the best?

A prospective customer will draw conclusions about the essential technical competence of an accountancy firm based on all the non-essential, non-technical aspects of the practice. For example, if you're punctual; if your reception is clean, tidy and has fresh flowers; if your receptionist uses their name; if every person they pass in a corridor says hello; if you've researched your potential customer; if you use a diagnostic questionnaire to ascertain the customer's needs; if you send a prompt follow-up letter. The potential customer will assume that you're a good technical accountancy practice because every interaction and experience has been positive and of a high standard. However, if you're late, if you're disorganised, if everyone's rushing around, if the customer can't find somewhere to park in the carpark, if there's no soap in the loo, they'll assume that when it comes to the actual accountancy services, you're not as good as the first company. The assumption has been driven by all those non-essentials. When it comes to influencing customer decisions – and your conversion rate – focus on the quality of your non-essentials.

Non-essentials are critical!

The term critical non-essentials was coined by Paddi Lund, a celebrated Australian dentist, although the use of critical non-essentials has been around forever. Paddi had exceptional standards when he carried out dental work for his clients. However, his practice only started to take off when he employed a highly personable receptionist. Initially, he was rather peeved that people were coming to his practice because of his gregarious receptionist rather than for his superb dental work. Until he realised that people weren't able to truly understand or appreciate the technicalities of his dental work but did understand and appreciate a well-run and friendly reception area. The penny dropped! He carried on doing exceptional dental work, put poured energy and imagination into all those non-essential things that people did understand and appreciate.

When you realise how important all your prospect touch points are, you can be deliberate about making each one excellent. In fact, it's easier to make everything excellent, whether it's a customer touchpoint or not. And the key to that, again, is systems and processes.

How you do anything is how you do everything.

If you're selling a £5,000 service, look at every touchpoint and ask yourself if that's a £5,000 touchpoint. Are you serving instant coffee or do you have an espresso machine – or at least one of those pod machines? And a wide selection of teas? Have you got a large vase of fresh flowers in your reception? And a wide range of interesting, up-to-date magazines? Is your receptionist expecting your visitor and do they greet them by name? When you realise how valuable a customer is (lifetime value) and understand how people make decisions, you'll look at all aspects of your customer interactions with fresh eyes.

To be done well, critical non-essentials have to be a team effort. This is another opportunity to engage your people in a vital aspect of the business. Not everyone can impact the technicalities of what you do, but everyone can identify and create memorable, critical non-essential touchpoints. You'll be pleasantly surprised by how imaginative and proactive your team is. For not much money, you'll have a more engaged team and will turn more prospects into customers.

Exercise: Converting enquiring prospects into purchasing customers

- From the ideas shared in this section, which one or two capture your imagination?
- How could you get them going?
- Which team members could you get involved?

4: Increasing the value of customer purchases

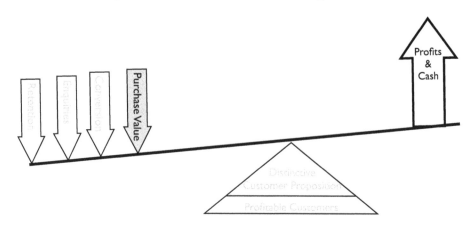

When a customer makes a purchase, they may not have thought through or aren't aware of other things they may need or want. It's your responsibility to prompt them and present them with those other options.

As you understand your customers better, you may also wish to expand your range of products and services in response to any additional unmet needs. It makes life easier for customers, and your average customer purchase value and your profits increase as a result.

Here is a selection of proven ideas for increasing customer purchase values.

Checklists and tell & sell matrices

Businesses often assume that customers are aware of all the products and services they offer. In reality, most customers aren't – or have forgotten. A simple way of overcoming this is to create a matrix with customers down the side and products and services along the top. Each box in the grid is split along the diagonal. The upper left triangle is ticked if you've 'told' the customer about that service. The lower right triangle is ticked if you've 'sold' that service to that customer. This is a great visual aid for seeing where the opportunities are within your customer base.

Example: A Tell & Sell matrix for an accountancy practice

Here's an example for an accountancy practice, where they've included the date when they introduced their client to a particular service. On the basis that a client's requirements is likely to change over time, this allows them to re-mention their services at appropriate intervals.

Tell & Sell Matrix	Year-end Accounts	Management Accounts	Bookkeeping	Payroll	Tax Advice	Pension Advice
Client A	✔ ✔	03-Feb-20 ✔	03-Feb-20 ✔	03-Feb-20 ✔	09-Jun-20 ✗	09-Jun-20 ✗
Client B	✔ ✔					
Client C	✔ ✔	02-Mar-20 ✗	02-Mar-20 ✗	03-Oct-20 ✔		
Client D	✔ ✔	08-Apr-20 ✗	08-Apr-20 ✗	07-Jul-20 ✗		
Client E	✔ ✔	27-Jun-20 ✔	27-Jun-20 ✔	01-Sep-20 ✔	01-Sep-20 ✔	
Client F	✔ ✔	03-Aug-20 ✗	03-Aug-20 ✔	03-Aug-20 ✗	27-Oct-20 ✗	
Client G	✔ ✔					

A similar idea is to have a checklist of all the things that a customer may need to purchase. For example, a customer comes into your retail outlet to buy a bike. Not only do they come out with their new bike, but they also purchase a helmet, lights, a padded seat cover, a pump, a lock and mudguards. They decline the poncho as they apparently have no intention of cycling in the rain. They spend £850 on the bike. The extras – some essential, some not – are £235, and you sell those extra products at good margins. All your sales assistants have a checklist on a clipboard. Your sales assistants also have a safety checklist that they work through with customers before allowing them to leave your store with their bike.

Up-sell & cross-sell

Offer your customers choices and options – your platinum, gold and silver packages. By highlighting the additional features and benefits and overall better value of your superior products and services, the customer can receive better value, and you can increase your average value sale. When making a proposal to a customer, in addition to offering what's asked for, create a budget option and a higher-priced, enhanced option. People rarely want to go for the budget option and will often choose the higher-priced, better value option.

If you're making a house purchase through a conveyancing solicitor, occasionally they will ask when you last updated your will and check whether you have Powers of Attorney in place. All solicitors should ask these questions – not to do so is tantamount to professional negligence. The customer is then aware of the benefits of having these things in place, and more critically, the consequences of not having them in place. The customer can then make an informed buying decision.

It won't boost a customer's average purchase value, but make sure you've got a down-sell option for customers too – that 'budget' option. On occasions, a customer may decide that they can't afford the product or service they'd like, even with an easy-payment plan. For example, if attending your full-time course isn't an option for them at the time, your excellent eLearning programme may meet their needs and fit their budget.

New products, range extensions, and added value services

Over time, the world changes and your customers' needs change, so be on the look-out for introducing new products and services. The danger of not keeping things fresh and updated is that you may be overtaken by competitors or one day just become irrelevant. As you get to know your customers better, you'll see more opportunities to make their businesses or lives easier and better with new products and services. As customer relationships grow, so does trust, and you'll find it easier to introduce new products and services and grow your sales in the process.

Selling in bulk and bundled offers

You don't want to promote excessive consumption or encourage purchases that may be wasted or not used. However, there can be genuine cost savings in providing products in bulk. Therefore, it's appropriate to share those savings with high-usage customers. Similarly, bundling related products together can be good for your customer. In the previous example, the bike-purchasing customer could have purchased a bike with the mudguards, stand, rack, lights, lock and helmet, plus a first month bike check and a 12-month service as a bundled offer. This 'unique' bundled offer also becomes difficult to price compare.

Availability and impulse purchases

Many businesses apply pressure on their buyers (sourcing team) to minimise stock holding. In the days of high interest rates, avoiding tying up cash in stock was more important. (In principle, it's good to avoid tying cash up in stock if you can – see Finance chapter.) However, the biggest customer gripe isn't prices, it's when the products they want to buy aren't available. Running stockholding too tightly can easily result in out-of-stocks. And not only do you lose the sale on the missing item, but you might also lose the customer, especially if you're often out of stock. Measuring stockholding is relatively easy, whereas measuring lost sales through out-of-stocks isn't easy to measure. Therefore, be careful of prioritising low stockholding over good product availability. It's better to carry a little extra stock and have superb product availability than risk being out of stock.

Bear in mind, if a customer can't find a product, as far as they're concerned, it's out of stock and you lose the sale. Make sure whatever products or services you sell, they're available and people can find them. And availability doesn't just apply to retail outlets. If you're a solicitor's practice, perhaps you need to have a list of available services on the wall outside your premises. Don't be lazy or arrogant and assume people know what services solicitors provide.

Give people the opportunity to make impulse purchases. If you're a dentist, give customers the opportunity to buy their toothbrushes, toothpaste, mouthwash, floss, etc. whilst they're paying for their treatment. Remember to book in their next check-up whilst they're in front of you too. And if you're a dentist or optician or similar, you'll also want your customers on a monthly treatment plan.

Gift cards can make excellent impulse purchases – although you'd have to know someone very well to buy them a gift card for a trip to the dentist! They are an excellent way to allow customers to purchase products and services for their family and friends. Best of all, you are virtually guaranteed a new customer. Gift card sales also mean you get paid in advance. And there's a reasonably high percentage of gift cards that never get redeemed. You're paid in full without the expense of providing the product or service. However, a new customer is far more valuable than a one-off 100% margin sale, so think how you might increase the use of any gift cards sold.

Train your team

Having ideas on how to boost your customers' average purchase value is a great start. The successful implementation of those ideas will come down to two things: firstly, creating a system for doing it; and secondly, training your team on how to operate that system. If you offer a monthly plan (e.g. a dental plan), you'll benefit from training your team on how to introduce the plan to your customers. You may well have marketing literature available, but it's more powerful if your team can speak to your customers in an appropriate way and at an appropriate time about the benefits of the plan and how they can come on board. It's good to rehearse and practise so that everyone feels comfortable and confident.

Limited availability, scarcity and deadlines

Introducing a limited quantity of specially sourced product for a short time period can drive up average purchase value. When it's gone, it's gone! Cut price supermarkets and their infamous middle aisle are experts at this. If you have a database of customers, let your regular, best customers know about any special deals you've sourced and negotiated. You could even run a special, closed-door event just for them – and perhaps a few of their friends.

Introducing a minimum spend and letting go of low spending customers

When you crunch your numbers, you may discover that it costs more to serve certain customers than they generate in gross profit. In effect, your high-spending customers are subsidising your low-spending customers, and your profits are being supressed.

Example: Setting a minimum spend at a design agency

A design agency discovers that their small customers are only marginally profitable and absorb a disproportionate amount of time to service. This also compromises the service they're able to offer their larger clients. Their team don't particularly enjoy working on the smaller accounts, as the work isn't as varied, interesting or challenging

---

– and the smaller clients often don't have the internal resources to fully implement the campaigns the team create. Management decides that when they receive new enquiries from smaller businesses, they'll refer them to another agency who are focused on those types of clients. They also explain to their existing smaller clients that in three months they'll be increasing charge rates and introducing a minimum quarterly spend. If those clients feel they want to move on, they'll help them find an agency that better fits their needs and help them migrate smoothly over to their new agency. They're now able to put more time and energy into helping their larger clients develop their businesses. The creative team are happier too.

Payment terms and making things easy to buy

Affordability can sometimes be an issue for customers. If your cashflow allows, and with proper credit checks, you may want to help customers buy your products and services by offering payment terms or extended credit. Perhaps a monthly subscription model might work better than a one-off sale. As an alternative to asking customers to purchase a £2,000 software package, you charge them £25 per user per month.

If you're an e-commerce business, you'll have the frustration of abandoned baskets at checkout. Understanding where and why people abandon purchases, and then making improvements to your checkout process, is time and money well invested. Conversion rate optimisation can be a complex business so you may want to invest in specialist services.

Consultancy services

Many businesses, ahead of making an actual sale, give away a huge amount of value in the form of free consultancy services – without realising it.

A potential customer makes an enquiry. During the resultant conversation, it becomes apparent to the enquiring customer that there's many more aspects to their purchase than they first realised. They need to know more before they can ask other potential suppliers to quote. However, they don't have to pump you for information; you willingly share everything you know, doing their job for them by, in essence, giving them the brief. Yes, they may look on you favourably and you do get a shot at pitching for the business, but it's not guaranteed you'll get it. In other sectors, there are service providers who earn their living from creating those project briefs. Don't give away your expertise. Either charge for it directly or get agreement that the project is yours. If you wish, you can always offer to deduct the consultancy charge from the project implementation fee if you're the chosen supplier. You may even establish a consultancy arm to your business. You probably take your expertise for granted as you've lived and breathed it for the whole of your professional life. Take some time to work out how valuable your expertise is to clients and start charging accordingly.

Exercise: Increasing the value of customer purchases

- From the ideas shared in this section, which one or two capture your imagination?
- How could you get them going?
- Which team members could you get involved?

5: Increasing customer purchase frequency

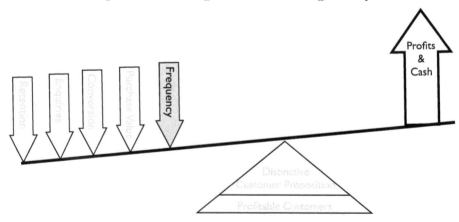

In eagerness, you can sometimes find yourself racing on to the next potential customer and inadvertently forgetting about the ones you've already got. By not investing time and effort in exploring how to serve current customers more fully, you may be missing out on more frequent customer purchases.

Here is a selection of practical and proven ideas for increasing customer purchase frequency.

Next visit, reminder systems, keeping control and follow-ups

Before a customer leaves, always schedule their next appointment or review. Even if they're not keen, pencil in a date, explaining that you'll get in touch four weeks before the appointment to check whether it's still convenient. Even if it's a routine eye test that is 24 months away, book it in the diary. This makes life easier for your customer. You could even send them a calendar invite with a 4-week reminder. You'll also want to have some genuine reasons to keep in touch with your customer during that 24-month period – perhaps when this season's range of sunglasses comes in. Whether it's a dental check, a haircut, a car's MOT or a pension review, most businesses can find a customer-centred reason for booking a next appointment.

Three of the principles that run throughout this book come into play again:

- **Systems:** Create a system for booking in next visits and next points of contact.
- **The Last Word:** Always get agreement on when you'll next be in contact.
- **Follow-up:** When your customer has had an appointment and you've booked their next appointment, follow-up and send a confirmation.

Attention to detail will help you: stand out from competitors, increase purchase frequency, improve customer retention, and increase the likelihood of referrals. Your customer will have no reason to consider alternative suppliers.

Service visits and maintenance programmes

It's a fact of life that everything wears out and breaks down. When a customer has made a purchase, it's a great time to build in a servicing and maintenance programme (to ensure they get on-going good use out of their purchase or investment). Prevention is better than cure.

If you're selling infrequently purchased capital items, think what on-going or periodic service you can provide for your customer. It's likely you've put in huge effort to win that customer, so consider how you can further leverage the trust that you've built up during the process.

If you're a distress purchase (e.g. the car's broken down), then think about a related positive sale that you could make to increase purchase frequency. Perhaps book the car in to have the air conditioning coolant checked and topped up in April. Or perhaps you offer a monthly valeting service. Now there's a good idea! You could even sell valeting gift cards!

Loyalty cards and annual rebates

Customer loyalty is something to be engendered, recognised and rewarded. Whether it's a simple coffee card stamp or frequent flyers club, loyalty schemes work. Continuous exceptional customer service is the most effective way to build loyalty. One of the keys is to understand how many months or years transpire between purchases or how long on average a customer remains a customer. Recognise and reward customers who have traded with you for a longer period than average. For example, if the average time someone is a customer is nine months, introduce a bonus or reward at the 12-month point. This is another area where your thoughtfulness and imagination can surprise customers and help differentiate your business.

Similar to loyalty cards, an annual rebate scheme can increase how frequently and how much a customer purchases. It's also a way of rewarding your bigger customers without disrupting your regular pricing or tariffs. Rebates work best when you've done your research to understand the potential of a customer. For example, if you represent 20% of a customer's purchases, and two or three other suppliers fulfil the rest, then that customer is likely to fall into your high potential development category. A rebate may be appropriate to incentivise more frequent and higher purchase volumes. (Although obviously, it's better to increase purchase frequency and volumes without having to offer a rebate.)

Help your customer grow

If you're a business-to-business company, then the better your customer does, the better you do. Understanding your customer's business – their aspirations, their development plans, etc. – can help you help them. Most suppliers won't even think about doing this. As well as growing your own sales, you'll be deepening and strengthening that all-important customer relationship to the point where it becomes a partnership.

Offer a broad, relevant product range

Again, related to understanding your customers, offering more of what they buy will increase purchase frequency and sales. It'll also make life easier for them if they have to deal with fewer suppliers. You'll find that they are relatively price insensitive on certain items, forsaking a slightly better deal somewhere else for the convenience of buying from you. As well as offering a broad range of products and services, make sure your customers know that you offer all those products and services. You never want to hear "I didn't know you did that" after they've bought that item somewhere else.

Right first time, every time, and make yourself indispensable

The easier you make doing business, the less reason your customer has for going elsewhere. Make your core product and service delivery absolutely excellent. And make every other customer touchpoint excellent too. Everybody in the organisation needs to have an attitude that everything within their sphere of responsibility needs to be done excellently, even the inconsequential things that no one else sees.

Seasonal promotions, special occasion offers, competitions and themed events

Tying-in offers to particular times of year or special events can be another good reason for engaging with customers. There's spring, summer, autumn and winter. There're sporting events such as Wimbledon, the Olympics, World Championships, etc. There are events like Easter, General Elections, Royal Weddings, American Independence Day, etc. And there's constantly an 'appreciation week' or 'awareness day'. Firstly, establish a 12-month rolling calendar of events. Are any of those events an opportunity to engage with your customers? Such opportunities will take planning and effort so it's best to make your plans at least three months in advance.

Most people love competitions. This is a good mechanism for encouraging customers to engage. Competitions can be built around new, improved or seasonal products and services. They can be very helpful at traditionally slow times of year. The best types of competition are ones where everyone can win something – one winner and everyone else a runner-up.

You could go one step further than a special occasion offer and host your own event. This will be another investment of time and effort, but the return comes in extra sales and another opportunity to stand out from your competition. It can be fun and is also a good way of engaging your team, both in the imaginative creation of the event and in its execution.

Implement a keep-in-touch schedule

Even without a plan to introduce new offers or to share additional service opportunities, keep in touch with customers on a regular basis. Typically, customers aren't interested in monthly newsletters that tell them about your company's summer outing or how well you've done this year. They're interested in one thing – themselves, and anything that might benefit them. Have a genuine reason for getting in touch and make it something that benefits your customers. Getting in touch on an ad hoc basis is better than not getting in touch at all, but it's far better to have a systemised and scheduled procedure for how and when you get in touch. Fill your newsletters with helpful information (e.g. how to keep your air conditioning in tip-top condition), special offers (free refills of screen wash during June), and customer stories (servicing Anthony's racing green 1962 E-type Jaguar; a bit of history about the E-type; a nice photo of Anthony, your servicing team and the car – and if it's an e-newsletter, a 10-second video of Anthony revving the engine).

Exercise: Increase customer purchase frequency

- From the ideas shared in this section, which one or two capture your imagination?
- How could you get them going?
- Which team members could you get involved?

6: Increasing gross profit margins

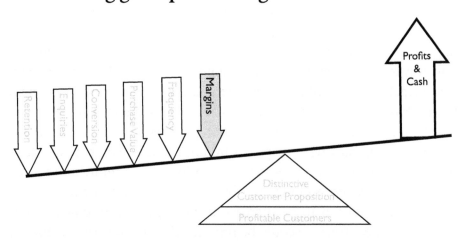

This is an area where you can have a quick and sizeable impact on your profits. Many businesses undervalue the services they provide so it's an area with plenty of potential for improvement.

Here is a selection of proven ideas for increasing your gross margins.

Put your prices up

Most businesses rarely put their prices up. And if they do, it's usually because their costs have risen rather than because they've improved and are now adding more value to their customers.

The big fear of putting prices up is that customers will leave. All of them. They don't. Usually none of them leave. And if any of them do leave, it's the ones who are buying on price and would leave anyway if they got a slightly better deal somewhere else.

The people who have the biggest issue with prices going up is the seller – you. Usually, the biggest hurdle to putting prices up is a mental one rather than an economic or competitive one. Many psychological barriers can be erected: "Customers will leave"; "We've traded with them for a long time – we don't want to fall out"; "We don't want to rip people off"; "We don't want to be one of those expensive companies"; "We've always been known as great value for money and we don't want to lose that reputation"; "We're not good enough to charge more"; "We don't want to be the most expensive".

Often the only way to overcome that mental block is to actually put prices up and see what happens. Perhaps you put a toe in the water and increase prices for a segment of customers (if that's feasible in your type of business). Or perhaps put up prices for new customers. Or next time you submit a proposal to a potential new customer, you add 10% more than you normally would. You can hypothesise indefinitely. The only way to know what the impact is going to be is to take action and put prices up. If it turns out to be the wrong thing to have done, you can put them down again. There's unlikely to be any permanent damage.

If you're not losing any business on price, you're probably charging too little. Keep putting your prices up until at least some people leave or don't buy. Fewer customers at higher prices can generate more profit, can be less time consuming, and business overall often becomes less stressful. In addition to an increase in profit, the time that servicing fewer customers frees up could be reinvested with your best customers, or in developing your team, or planning the future of your business, or reading, or thinking, or with your family – or all of the above.

If you're putting your prices up for the first time in a long time, there's unlikely to be any adverse reaction. It's good to fully understand how your product and service benefits your customers and to focus your customers' attention on that. What customers should be focusing on is the value they receive rather than the price they pay. But often they don't – and sometimes you collude with them by making price the most important factor.

Price is what you pay. Value is what you get.
WARREN BUFFETT

You could do worse than using this quote and then explaining how your customer gets value from the service you provide.

*The cynic knows the price of everything
and the value of nothing.*
OSCAR WILDE

It's also worth remembering that you were brought up to believe that "you get what you pay for". People typically equate price with quality. Something that's cheap isn't as good as something that's expensive. Most customers don't really want cheap. They want value for money.

"Reassuringly expensive" was Stella Artois's advertising slogan for 25 years.

MasterCard's "Priceless" campaign successfully focused peoples' attention on the noble aim behind their purchase rather than the cost of it. For example, people bought a television on credit so that the whole family could watch television together. "There are some things money can't buy. For everything else, there's MasterCard." Remember that people buy emotionally and justify their purchase logically – even businesses buying industrial products. Focus your customers on value.

So, if you're delivering the best value, why not charge the highest prices? Somebody has to be the most expensive. Why not you?

Depending on your margins, a modest increase in price can have a disproportionate impact on your gross profits. If you're buying at £60 and selling at £100, a 10% price increase to £110 improves your gross profits from £40 to £50 per unit, a 25% increase.

Avoid giving discounts

Have confidence in the value you deliver and the (new, higher) price you charge. During the buying process, educate prospective customers on the quality and benefits to them of your product and service. Whatever you may think and however much they might grumble, a customer always gets more value from your service than the money they give you – or otherwise they wouldn't make the purchase.

However, as a negotiating tactic, there's nothing wrong for your customer to ask for a discount. Be prepared to give an answer. Think what you'll say in advance rather than trying to think on your feet. Rather than giving an outright no, you might say that you've worked hard at making sure customers pay a competitive and fair price that reflects the value you're delivering. If you often get asked for discounts, you might even mention during your sales process about how you make sure that customers are paying a keen price and that discounts aren't offered.

If you wish to seal or sweeten the deal with a discount, avoid making a monetary discount. During the buying process, your customer may have revealed something that would be of value to them, something you can easily accommodate. If normal installation is two weeks, but the customer needs the project starting as soon as possible, you can offer to bring forward installation to this Monday. If the customer has asked for a discount on £2,000 worth of garden furniture, you could offer them £200 worth of plants.

As a general rule, if you are going to include something for free, include something of high perceived value to your customer but low cost to you. £200 worth of plants might only cost you £50, whereas a 10% discount on the garden furniture would cost you £200 out of a profit margin of £800.

As a second general rule, as part of the negotiation get a concession in return for your offer. For example, if they also buy the seat cushions they were considering, you can give them £200 worth of plants for free. Or perhaps in return for a fast turnaround weekend installation, you can ask for a testimonial or case study.

By the way, if you're selling garden furniture and cushions, sell the most expensive item first. A £60 cushion might seem expensive. However, it seems less expensive if you've just spent £2,000 on furniture.

If you've charged someone a lesser amount in return for something that benefits you, make sure your invoice highlights the full amount. If you're a marketing agency and decide to offer a pro bono service for a local charity, clearly show the full commercial rate, and then the 100% discount applied. At least your charity customer will see the normal cost of the work you've done for them. And you'll realise the value of the work you've done for them too and will be less likely to overservice them.

Don't be afraid to lose the sale. Find the customers who truly value what you do, rather than pandering to price shoppers and discount seekers.

If you win business on price, you'll lose it on price.

Buy better and ask for better terms

At least once a year write to all your suppliers giving them an overview of how your year has progressed. Share your plans for the coming year. Ask them for better prices, especially if you're buying more products or services from them. If that proves fruitless, ask them for better payment terms. Or ask them for some marketing support. That might come in the form of marketing materials or a contribution to your marketing budget. Ask them to support a promotion you're planning with some free stock. Perhaps ask them for an end-of-year bonus for hitting a target. Be imaginative, persistent and don't take no for an answer. If you persist, they'll say yes to something.

Ask, and you will receive.
MATTHEW 7:7

Improve your negotiation skills

If you feel that you lack experience and confidence, go on a negotiation course. Or at least buy a book on negotiation. (See recommended books in Appendix B. *Never Split The Difference* by Chris Voss is excellent.)

One of the fundamental keys to good negotiation is to be prepared. Know your supplier well. Check their accounts and see how well they're doing financially. Read their literature and press releases. Find something you could offer them that they'd appreciate and value – perhaps a review or an introduction to a potential new customer. Periodically send them a thank you card. The more they like you, the more likely they are to treat you well.

Practise. Look for opportunities to have little negotiations with people every day, even if you don't need to. Test out the negotiation tactics you learn to see how they work in practice.

Join or create a buying group

When it comes to buying, high volume purchases are a strong lever. Banding together with other businesses who buy the same product can be helpful. As well as having greater leverage to negotiate a keener buying price, you can send the best negotiator in to bat on your behalf. The whole process can be less time consuming too. In business, you don't have to do everything yourself. Collaborating with others is a good strategy and can benefit all.

Effectiveness and efficiency improvements

Products and services that don't perform as expected is probably the fastest way to see profits disappear through refunds and replacements. Lost customers and negative word-of-mouth can do unseen but even greater damage. It's also demoralising for team members to see returned products and have to listen to and appease cross and frustrated customers. Right first time has to be so much more than a slogan on a poster. It has to become part of your organisation's DNA. Each process and procedure must be looked at, monitored, improved, and refined – constantly.

Blame and punishment for errors has to be replaced with an atmosphere where finding mistakes is recognised as an opportunity to learn and improve. You can't fix things that are hidden away. Documented systems, team training and on-going monitoring are the key to producing consistently good products and services. Eradicating rework costs, or re-delivery costs, will boost your gross profit margins. Firstly, focus on effectiveness (right first time), and then focus on productivity and efficiency. Don't compromise on quality.

Change your mix of customers and products

If you have any unprofitable customers, dropping them will automatically improve your gross profits. Many businesses don't know how profitable – or unprofitable – each customer is. Carrying out that analysis is one of the most powerful profit improvement pieces of work you can do. If you have any unprofitable customers, make them profitable or ease them out of the business.

It can be particularly tough if you discover that your biggest customer from a sales perspective is also your worst customer from a profit perspective. That's more common than you might imagine. Immediately sacking off your biggest customer might have an impact beyond your gross profit margins, leaving you with excess overhead capacity that you can't immediately cover. Increasing prices and reducing the costs of serving that customer is the first place to go. If that proves difficult, you may need to play a longer game by building up your other, more profitable customers and attracting new customers, to manoeuvre yourself into a stronger negotiating or sacking position. Or you may decide that a smaller but more profitable business is preferable and let your big but unprofitable customer go.

A similar profit analysis exercise can be done across your product and service range. Encouraging sales of higher margin items will improve overall gross profits. We can all be seduced by sales, but it's profits that really count (and cash that really, really counts).

Other options may exist for improving product margins. Introducing complementary products and services with higher margins may be beneficial for your customers and profit improving for you. Perhaps sourcing and negotiating exclusive products and services for your customers. Or perhaps going down the own label route. If your supplier has excess capacity, they may be willing to sell to you under your own label at a lower price. This protects the reputation and prices of their branded products and generates additional incremental profit for them.

Re-design products

If you're in a position to redesign a product, you may be able to achieve the same performance with less input of material or energy or time. Doing more with less (ephemeralisation) and continuous, never-ending incremental improvement (Kaizan) can be a practical organisational ethos that results in a product or service that is constantly improving and constantly reducing in cost. Good for your customers and good for your profits. It is also likely to keep you one step ahead of your competition. Create the right working environment and culture where you and your team are constantly looking for better ways of doing things.

If you try and stand still, you'll go backwards. Keep improving, keep growing, keep moving forwards.

Vertical integration with companies above or below you in your supply chain

Buying or merging with your suppliers or customers may make good commercial and logistical sense and result in improved margins and profits. Possibly beyond the scope for most smaller businesses, but something to consider.

As with so many of these strategies and tactics, it's having the time to consider and explore alternative ways of doing things and having the courage to give them a go.

Eliminate theft

Most people don't set out to steal but may do so if the opportunity arises. Identify and eradicate those opportunities. Perhaps make this a team effort – your staff may well see what you can't. If theft is going to happen, it isn't usually committed by customers, it's committed by staff or staff colluding with family members. Be aware of this and be realistic, even if you trust every member of your team.

Trust everyone but tie up your camels.

ANCIENT ARABIC SAYING

Think about what may tempt people and take those temptations away. Pay people decently and fairly. Carry out perpetual or regular stock-takes. Take sensible precautions if you have high-value items. Have clear rules around theft and stick to them. Involve staff in determining what the deterrents should be and what the consequences of theft should be. Live by a consistent set of principles and values. Treat everyone the same, whether they're manual warehouse workers or senior executives and directors.

Exercise: Increasing your gross margins

- From the ideas shared in this section, which one or two capture your imagination?
- How could you get them going?
- Which team members could you get involved?

7: Controlling overheads

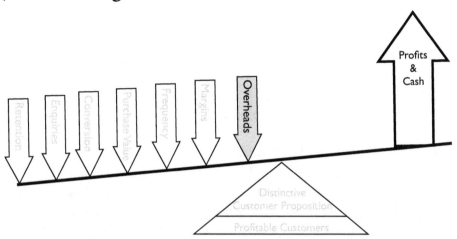

Whether the economy is in recession or in expansion, always keep your overhead costs as keen and tight as possible. Whilst growing top-line sales and margins is the way to create a financially successful business, reducing overheads should always be on your agenda. The general trend is that products and services keep improving in performance but the cost of them keeps falling. Look at what happens to the cost of your mobile phone contract each time you renew it. So, keep looking to see where you can get better value.

Here is a selection of practical ideas for reducing your overheads.

Targeted cost cutting

Identify every single area of cost. Allocate one of the team as the responsible owner of each cost area. Set them the challenge of reducing that cost over the next quarter (with no negative impact on the business) by, say, 10%. To avoid any unforeseen negative business impacts, have them present their proposals before they take any action. They'll rise to the challenge, your overheads will reduce, and your net profits will increase.

On a broader point, engaging your team in finding new and better ways of doing business is good for them and good for you. You don't have the preserve and responsibility for all ideas.

Maintenance programme

It's more cost effective in the long term to maintain things rather than to fix them when they break. A planned maintenance programme will keep things running better and for longer. It will also reduce the likelihood of breakdowns and interruptions at critical times. It also engenders a sense of pride in team members if the organisation cares about looking after things properly.

Prevention is better than cure.

DESIDERIUS ERASMUS

Engage freelancers and outsource

If the flow of work is variable, then it may be more cost effective to cope with the peaks by using freelancers working on an hourly or day rate. Whilst the rate may be higher than that which you'd pay internally, the short duration means that overall costs are lower. It's critical that the quality of work produced is of an acceptable standard. It's also important to have several freelancers available, as one or two of them may not be available when you need them. To keep people focused on the quality of the job, pay for completing the job to the required standard rather than paying by the hour or the day. If the output is good and the deadline is met, it shouldn't concern you if it's taken an hour or a day if you've agreed a price for the job.

Appoint interns and apprentices

By their nature, interns are inexperienced and therefore your expectations have to be tempered and realistic. However, what interns may lack in experience they often make up for in attitude and enthusiasm. As well as keeping costs lower, one can view the period an intern works as an extended selection process. Both sides are hopefully looking at the relationship as a long term one.

Similar to interns, apprentices are another option. A little more costly and usually more of a commitment in terms of training. There can be short-term cost benefits, but these have to be weighed against reduced effectiveness and efficiency and the need for closer supervision. Many companies also complain that they find it difficult to find good apprentices. Select well and apprenticeship schemes can work well for all concerned. Select for great attitude, an aptitude for the work, and an eagerness to learn.

Whilst both are important, attitude is
more important than aptitude.

Rent out space

If you're not using all your office or production space, then consider subletting it. Go to the trouble of getting a simple but effective contract drawn up. Think about health & safety considerations, get proper insurance and, if needed, get your landlord or mortgage provider's permission. Also, think about when you may need the space back and at what notice period.

Move location

Do you have to be where you are? Having taken into account moving and disruption costs, are there cheaper alternatives? Consider what impact a move would have on your team, your suppliers and your customers.

Remote working & homeworking

The Covid-19 crisis has proved homeworking to be an effective and efficient option for many businesses. Whilst managers previously worried about how they'd monitor staff working at home and feared long coffee breaks and the distraction of household chores, the reality has been illuminating. During lockdown, managers were forced to trust staff. And in the majority of cases (not all), the results have been positive – more has been achieved in less time and without the hassles of commuting.

A blend of office and homeworking may increase effectiveness, productivity, staff well-being and reduce the need for costly office space. The use of video conferencing – or the good old phone – has also proved that communication in general and meetings in particular can also be enhanced.

Remote working from a local work hub can similarly prove a productivity boon and a cost saving strategy. Home may not be conducive to your best work, physically or psychologically, so a well-designed, well-equipped local work hub can be a good solution. Again, you don't need as much central office space, your team member saves their travel time (commuting can be energy-sapping, stressful and costly), work quality and output is maintained or improved, plus there's the benefit of social interaction too.

If homeworking proves to be effective for certain roles, it also widens the geographic catchment area for your next staff hire. It doesn't matter if they live in Eastbourne or Edinburgh, which may have competence and cost benefits. One point to bear in mind is that during lockdown, staff working from home all knew each other – ways of working, interacting, idiosyncrasies, and the general culture of the organisation was known and understood. Establishing a cohesive culture with newly recruited homeworkers would be harder – but surmountable.

Using Zoom, Microsoft Teams, Google Meet & tele-conferencing facilities

Embracing technology can make us more effective and efficient. Moving around our roads seems to be getting harder and often isn't necessary. Phone or video meetings are usually shorter and often more productive. There's no travelling, no sitting around in reception, no waiting whilst people make cups of coffee. There are occasions when meeting face-to-face is important but there are many more occasions when you don't need to.

Regular, timely & detailed management accounts

Finalising your numbers 11 months after your year-end may satisfy your formal reporting requirements, but it serves no value in terms of understanding your business. Look at your numbers once per month, as soon after the month-end as possible. Certainly, no less than once per quarter. This gives you a chance to monitor performance, see the impact of different improvement initiatives, and take action on anything that may be drifting. It certainly helps keep overheads tight.

Even if you aren't large enough to require your accounts to be audited, an audit can pay dividends by revealing shortcomings, deficiencies and areas for potential improvement. Using third parties to periodically audit different areas of the business, especially high-cost areas, can quickly highlight areas of improvement and cost saving.

Change bank

People often stick with the bank they've always been with. As with every other provider, it is periodically worth looking at the cost and service provision of other banks. Banks have recently slipped into the marketing tactics employed by so many gyms, of offering the very best deals to new customers. (Existing customers should always get the best deals.) Ask your bank to give you the same deal that they're offering to new customers. If you don't ask, you don't get.

Check direct debits (DD) and standing orders (SO)

Don't assume that all your DDs and SOs are correct. It may be that you're not receiving a particular service, but your DD hasn't been cancelled. Or you may determine that you don't need a particular service or subscription that you're paying for every month.

If you're collecting regular payments from customers, then direct debit processing may make life far simpler and more cost effective. If you're already using a DD processing company, then periodically check other providers as rates vary greatly and are often being reduced as technology improves and competition increases. Check that all customers who should be paying by DD and SO are actually paying.

Stop any marketing that isn't working

Monitoring and measuring the effectiveness of your marketing and advertising is essential. If you can't set up some kind of monitoring for a particular marketing initiative, don't do it until you've established a monitoring mechanism. If a marketing campaign isn't being measured, many businesses claim that it's a 'brand-building exercise'. All marketing campaigns should be about generating enquiries. Cutting out ineffective marketing can reduce overheads and boost your net profits. Marketing should be an investment that generates a measurable return.

Reduce interest costs and bank charges

A focus on cash will help reduce interest charges on any outstanding loans and reduce the need for factoring services.

Reducing your payment terms for customers and increasing your payment terms to suppliers both serve to increase the cash in your business, which in turn reduces interest payments on any overdrafts.

Develop a robust invoicing and payment collection system to improve your cash position and reduce the time, aggravation, stress and cost associated with chasing overdue payments.

Other good cash generators include liquidating excess stock, dead stock, unused assets, and scrap. Have a look around and see what you can sell. You'll also be pleased to have less stuff hanging around and a tidier workspace.

If you've borrowed money – credit cards, overdrafts, loans – look at consolidating these into one loan at a favourable interest rate. It's also good to have just one loan that's visible and on the table, rather than several that are hidden away.

Go paperless

Going paperless can help speed up processes, improve accuracy and the retrieval of information, and reduce costs. There will be system, software and training costs, and integration and learning-curve implications to normal operations. The biggest factor impacting the success of initiatives like going paperless is probably the willingness of your team to embrace change. If people see that their lives will be easier and better, change is more likely to be embraced.

*People embrace change when they can envisage
their life getting easier or better.*

Buy your premises

Generally, land and property are a good investment over the long term. Buying your own building and renting it back to the business can be a good savings or pension strategy for a business owner. If the business is generating good levels of cash, this is something to discuss with your financial advisor.

Buying competitors

If you're a small business, you may think that it's not your place to buy another business. Perhaps you think mergers and acquisitions are the preserve of big business. Not so. You may well have competitors out there who are struggling to make ends meet. They may want to throw in the towel but don't know what else they'd do. Perhaps they feel they'd be unemployable. You might just want to suggest that you merge and that they come and work for you!

Businesses typically underestimate the value of their customer list. They think all the value is in their sales or their stock, but in truth their customer database and their trading relationships are often the most valuable assets they have. Perhaps look out for an owner-managed business where the owner looks as if they should be considering retirement or who seems to be working extremely long hours. You might just be their knight in shining armour. You might be pleasantly surprised at how little it costs to buy another business. If you've got sound systems and processes in place, you may be able to bring on a decent chunk of business without increasing your overhead costs.

Exercise: Reducing your overhead costs

- From the ideas shared in this section, which one or two capture your imagination?
- How could you get them going?
- Which team members could you get involved?

Summary

First and foremost, keep what you've got. Retain your profitable customers. This might be as simple as keeping in touch a little more often.

Ironically, the biggest hindrance to growth is opening up too many business development fronts. The danger is that you don't have the time or personnel to follow through and implement them all at the same time. Far better to start small, have some quick wins, gain confidence, and move forward from there. The best place to start is to identify what current initiatives are working well and which ones aren't. Stop doing the ones that aren't working. That will save you money and free up some time. For the ones that are working well, can you make them work even better or do more of them? Build on what's going well.

You don't have to work on something from all seven areas. Starting with just one is fine. The easiest and best places to start is gross margins and putting your prices up. Most companies underestimate the value their customers receive and can – should – move their prices up. As you improve and add more value to your customers, keep putting your prices up. And never discount. Well, only do it occasionally and strategically and always get something valuable in return.

The next best place to go is enquiry conversion. You're already getting enquiries coming in and a few simple improvements can make a big difference to your conversion rate. Remember, if your conversion rate goes from one in four to two in four, you've just doubled your gross profits and improved your net profits significantly. Just make sure you have the capacity to absorb twice as many customers.

Always ask for customer reviews. Always ask customers to refer you to other people who you may be able to help. Keep in touch with customers and potential customers on a regular basis. Show you care and don't fall victim to 'perceived indifference'.

In addition to the normal end-of-chapter checklist, there's also a table for capturing and prioritising your business development ideas.

Checklist Exercise: Business Development Strategies & Tactics

The following checklist exercise will be helpful in identifying the progress you've made and in selecting the areas you want to focus on next. It will be useful to review this checklist once a quarter as part of your quarterly planning process.

- Put a tick in the 'DONE' column for those items you already do or are happy with.
- Make a second pass through the checklist and highlight those things that you'd 'LIKE TO' work on next.
- For each 'LIKE TO' item that you've highlighted:

  » What benefits will come from completing it (or what consequences will be avoided)? Jot down the benefits (in your planning notebook).

  » How excited do you feel about cracking on with this activity? Score your level of excitement out of 10 and put your score in the third column of the checklist.

  » Prioritise your 'LIKE TO' activities based on their beneficial impact

and how excited you feel about taking action now.
  » Pick the one or two items from the top of your prioritised list and commit to making them a reality.
  » What's the simplest action you can take right now to get moving?
• Put this book down and make a start (or if impractical at the moment, schedule the activity in your calendar).

Some of the items on the list are relatively straightforward and self-explanatory. Others will need a plan behind them and assistance from other people. The purpose of this exercise is to identify which improvement initiatives you feel motivated to commit to, and to encourage you to find a first, small, simple action step to get you going.

	BUSINESS DEVELOPMENT STRATEGIES & TACTICS	DONE	LIKE TO	EXCITED
	INCREASING CUSTOMERS, SALES & PROFITS	✓	✓	Out of 10
1	We are tracking our 4 key result areas & each of the 7 profit improvement areas.			
2	We have improvement targets in each of the 7 profit improvement areas.			
3	We measure ALL marketing initiatives to know what's working & how well it's working.			
4	We have stopped marketing that doesn't make an acceptable return on investment.			
5	We have chosen 1 or 2 strategies to improve customer retention.			
6	We have chosen 1 or 2 strategies to increase the number of customer enquiries.			
7	We have chosen 1 or 2 strategies to improve our customer conversion rate.			
8	We have chosen 1 or 2 strategies to increase our average sales value.			
9	We have chosen 1 or 2 strategies to increase how frequency customers purchase.			
10	We have chosen 1 or 2 strategies to increase our gross profit margins.			
11	We have chosen 1 or 2 strategies to reduce our overheads.			
12	We have a system for regularly capturing online customer reviews.			
13	We have a system for asking customers to refer other customers who we can help.			
14	We have a system for keeping in touch with customers on a regular basis.			
15	Every quarter we determine if prices need to increase (as part of quarterly planning).			
16	We work on improving conversion rate before we work on generating more leads.			
17	We will put our prices up if our conversion rate is over 90%.			

When you've picked one or two strategies from seven different business development areas, that will give you a sizeable list that will need prioritising and scheduling. There's a danger that the excitement and enthusiasm of the checklist exercise will be closely followed by a feeling of overwhelm and paralysis when it comes to implementation. The following exercise will help you put your list of initiatives into a prioritised order. You can only work on one thing at once. Yes, if you have a team focused on these initiatives, you can work on a couple at the same time – but even then, it's often better to get one initiative implemented before moving onto the next one. In addition to the benefits of a specific initiative, you're also developing a continuous improvement mindset and culture. Developing the habit of small, continuous steps is better than an overlong stride and subsequent stumble.

Exercise: Capturing and prioritising your business development initiatives

	ACTIVITY AREA	INITIATIVE	Business Impact 1=High 2=Medium 3=Low	Ease to Implement 1=Very Easy 2=Medium 3=Hard	Cost 1=Free 2=Low 3=High	Excitement 1=can't wait! 2=very 3=okay	Resulting Priority 1 to 21	When?	Who?
1	Retention								
2	Retention								
3	Retention								
4	Enquiries								
5	Enquiries								
6	Enquiries								

7	Conversion								
8	Conversion								
9	Conversion								
10	Purchase value								
11	Purchase value								
12	Purchase value								
13	Purchase frequency								
14	Purchase frequency								
15	Purchase frequency								
16	Gross margins								
17	Gross margins								
18	Gross margins								
19	Overheads								
20	Overheads								
21	Overheads								

Closing Thoughts

Now is your time to shine.
Take action.
Today.
Towards something that's important.
Important to future you.
And the future of your business.

Take aim.
In everything.
Write down what you're aiming for.
Specifically.
Aiming for today.
And aiming for your tomorrows.
And take action.
Now.

Start small.
So small you can't fail.
Repeat on a daily basis.
Taking small, daily steps will get you further than striding.
You will stumble and fall.
That's inevitable and unimportant.
How you respond is important.
Get up, dust yourself down, take the lesson, and go again.
Take control.
By taking responsibility for everything that happens in your life.

Whatever's most important, schedule it.
First thing in the day.
When you're most energised.
At your best.
And your day hasn't yet imploded.
Stop all the clocks. Cut off the telephone.
Close the door. Turn off the notifications.
Concentrate and focus.
For 90 minutes.
On something that's important to your future.
Today.

Put up your prices.
You're worth more than you imagine.
You get better.
Your business gets better.
Your customers get more value.
Your prices need to keep going up.
Focus your clients on the value they receive, not the price they pay.

Keep score.
Make the score visible to all.
If it's important, monitor it.
If you want to improve it, measure it.

Notice.
Become aware.
Observe what's happening in the world.
In your business.
Especially with your people.
And with you.
Become self-aware.
It's the first step to self-improvement.

You have to do your own push-ups.
But you don't have to do them alone.
Surround yourself with good people.
Who care about you.
Assume you know nothing.
There's always a better way of doing everything.
Be humble.
Ask for help.

Keep learning.
Look for the lesson.
Keep applying the lessons.
If you're not occasionally falling over, you're not trying hard enough.
Security is an illusion.
Comfort is a thief.
Push the boundaries.
Step into the future.
Where there be dragons.

You're more resilient than you imagine.
You have more potential than you imagine.
Far more.
Keep imagining.
Keep growing.
Opportunities abound.
Everything you need is close at hand.
Very close.

Ten years is a long time.
Long enough to transform yourself.
Long enough to build at least one business.
Write down what your ideal future life will be like.
Who will you become?
Begin today.
Do something.
Today.
Aim.
Act.

Your business will be complete when it doesn't need you.
When will you appoint that General Manager?
When will you sell the business?
Diarise the date now.
Divide the intervening period into three-month chunks.
Define a specific aim and simple action plan for the next 90 days.
Take action each and every day towards your aim.

Systemise.
The routine.
It's the future – your future.
When you've got something working, turn it into a checklist.
A routine.
A process.
A system.
Systems will give you your life back.
And increase the sale value of your business.

Meetings are your business' rhythmic heartbeat.
Meetings are your job.
Give each one an aim.
Finish each one with committed actions.

Energy is more important than time.
Invest your highest energies into your most important work.
Manage your energy.
Restore your energy.
Get a good night's sleep.
Get up early.
Every week take a day off.
Restore your spirit and your soul.
You're spirit first, body second.

Remember your family.
They're more important than your business.
If you're blessed with children, they're your most important job.
Especially when they're young.
It doesn't last long.
You're their role model.
Not so much by what you say, but what you do.
Congruency between truthful words and deeds is a virtue.
Our job is not to be their friend.
Our job is to prepare them to survive and thrive in the world.
To slay dragons.
And live life to the full.
Children grow fast.
Very fast.

Ditto your team.
Spend 80% of your people-time with the 20% who contribute the 80%.
Give them clear expectations.
And high standards to aspire to.
And meaningful work.
And the hope of a bright future.
Only accept acceptable work and best efforts.
Say thank you.

Lead.
Set direction.
Become a strong leader.
Bring out the best in everyone.
Play to their strengths.
Be humble.

Be ambitious.
Be content.
Take time out.
To appreciate what you have.
On a daily basis.
Say thank you.
Smile.

What will be your challenge?
Who will you become?
Life is short.
Start now.
Today.
Aim.
Act.

Contact me and let's go do this.

Ten years is a long time. Definitely long enough to transform yourself. However, you can also achieve a lot in ten days. Now you have completed the book, it is time to act. Today. Select one or two things that are achievable and act on them. Today.

If you've adopted any of ideas I've shared, it's encouraging to hear about your progress and successes, so please let me know how you are getting on:

Email: mark@markdyble.com
LinkedIn: linkedin.com/in/markdyble

Also, perhaps I should practice what I preach, so I would be most grateful if you would leave a review on the platform from which you purchased this book.

About the Author

Mark Dyble is a published author. Now.

Mark is also a speaker. He loves a crowd. Sharing what he knows and what he's thinking – inspiring, challenging, encouraging.

SME Business Solutions was established in 2007. Since then, Mark has been a business coach, working alongside ambitious business owners and executives, helping them enhance their leadership skills and develop strong, sustainable and profitable businesses.

The 25 years Mark spent in commercial general management now feels like the perfect apprenticeship. The variety, the roles, the different companies, the different cultures, the highs and lows of commercial life, the lessons along the way.

Mark qualified as a mining engineer. His first taste of people management was as a coalface supervisor – a real baptism of fire. In the late 1980s he studied for an MBA at The Manchester Business School and McGill University.

In his early thirties, Mark tested his mettle in a different culture. Over three years he built a new business employing over 150 people in Malaysia.

Several years as a marketing controller allowed Mark to engage a true passion – practical, purposeful creativity. Effective ways of communicating and engaging with customers; launching new products and services; and brand building.

Crunching numbers as a financial analyst for a large PLC, Mark spent much time quizzing MDs and FDs about their capital expenditure, acquisition and expansion plans. He now brings that same challenging, questioning approach to his clients' ideas and ambitions.

As a management consultant, Mark enjoyed the strategic and intellectually challenge, but realised that consultants spend much time away from home and always have to be selling. Ironically, helping clients sell more effectively is now central to his coaching programme. But he rarely stays away from home.

Mark is a trustee of the Manchester charity, *Acting On Impulse*. He is also a part-time project supervisor on the MBA programme at the Manchester Business School.

Outside of work (which he doesn't really think of as work), he enjoys walking, cycling, skiing and photography. He recently cycled solo from Canterbury to Rome (the old Via Francigena pilgrimage route), raising funds for *Acting On Impulse*. Mark also enjoys reading, watching and listening to anything that's interesting, enlightening and thought-provoking. He also claims there's nothing better than sharing a simple meal with family and friends.

Acknowledgements

There are certain people who have had a profound impact on my thinking, my behaviour, my results, who I am today and therefore on this book.

First and foremost, is my father Michael, who built and sold multiple businesses. I once read in a magazine that he was the nicest workaholic you're ever likely to meet. An accurate description. He was always working, but somehow never missed a sports match, took us swimming every Sunday morning, to Goodison Park on a Saturday afternoon, and played rough and tumble with us every evening when we were small kids. Family first. A puritanical work ethic second.

Beyond the hard work, what stuck was the countercultural way in which he achieved commercial and business success. A propensity for breaking new ground and trying new things. A bias towards action. Being creative and innovative. Embracing change and a constant, forward momentum. Attention to detail. Knowing that things can always be improved. Probably the real differentiator was his people strategy – although I'm not sure it was a deliberate strategy, rather a natural approach to people in general. Attracting talented, enthusiastic and ambitious people – many of whom subsequently went on to set up their own (competing) businesses. Expecting high standards and high achievement from people. Caring for them and becoming good friends. Making work and business exciting. Little acts of kindness along the way. I wasn't conscious of any of this at the time. It came into view, often by way of contrast, as I made my way in the world as an adult. I thought everyone would be like my dad.

Unbelievably, a lifetime later, I still meet people who ask if I'm Mike Dyble's son, fondly sharing how he kick-started their careers. Years after he'd left his main business, one of the cleaning ladies was retiring and asked if my dad would go back and make her farewell speech. Even in his eighties, he continued to be involved in the leadership of local charities.

I hope you'll see my father's commercial astuteness and his focus on bringing out the best in people shining through the pages of this book.

At the other end of my career (so far), I'd acknowledge the impact of Brad Sugars, a serial entrepreneur who owns the Action Coach Business

Coaching franchise. Brad is a no-nonsense, action-orientated, highly successful business owner and coach. For me, more than anything, Brad is a constant, voracious learner – and someone who applies that learning in the real world. I thought I knew a lot before I met Brad. Oh, happy me, how wrong I was! My love of learning has been accelerated ever since. The fact that there's so much more to learn is life-enhancing.

Twenty plus years ago I attended a Scripture Union 'At Work Together' conference in Harrogate. A speaker that week who changed my life was the Managing Director of Gallup, Jill Garrett. In essence, Jill spoke about focusing on and developing strengths, rather than trying to fix weaknesses. She had all the evidence as to why that was a successful philosophy and strategy. It was a lightbulb moment for me. I become a leadership student of positive psychology. I have kept in touch with Jill over the years and I'm privileged that she's now my coach.

There are many authors who've impacted my thinking, my coaching and my life. (There is a list of recommended readings in Appendix B). These would include Don Clifton, Dale Carnegie, Earl Nightingale, Stephen Covey, Jim Rohn, Buckminster Fuller, David Sandler, Aubrey Daniels, Jordan Peterson, and James Clear.

I owe a debt of gratitude to my editor and writing mentor, Siân-Elin Flint-Freel, for guiding me through this book-writing process. Siân maintained a careful balance between encouraging me to keep writing, whilst holding me accountable to produce a level of quality of content and style that would result in a 'decent' book. The lesson of sacrificing work one had poured one's heart and soul into on the altar of relevance and readability was a tough one, as any first-time writer will know. I'm amazed at the impactful cover design and book layout created by Tanya Black. I only hope the contents of the book live up to the promise of the stunning cover, Tanya! I'm grateful to my dad for writing the brief for the cover and to my copywriting sister, Jackie Dyble, for coming up with the book title and subtitle. Again, I hope the contents live up to the expectation conjured up by the title.

Lastly, and most importantly, I also acknowledge a debt of gratitude to my faithful friend and wife, Hazel, for allowing me the space and time to write my first book. I appreciate your ever-tolerant, ever-forgiving nature – you have much to put up with!

Appendix A:

WORKING WITH MARK

Contact details
mark@markdyble.com or +44 (0)7931 882 555.

Coaching
Everybody benefits from a little coaching. Whether it's a one-off session to distil out your next priority and give you clarity and focus or an on-going programme to develop you and your business, you'll go further and faster and achieve better results with someone alongside you. Mark thinks of himself as a catalyst – an inspiring ingredient that will give you a better result in less time in a more enjoyable way.

Facilitating
An objective outsider, with a commercial head on their shoulders, and a knack for drawing a willing contribution out of people, will ensure a better outcome from your meeting. Good facilitation results in specific actions that participants fully committed to. If you wish, it also allows you to fully participate in the session without the burden and responsibility of leading and coordinating it.

Speaking
Mark is an inspiring speaker who can talk knowledgeably and convincingly on the subjects introduced in this book. He educates and entertains in the process, and causes people to think differently, but his aim is that people leave committed to make a positive change in their life.

Planning
Whether it's with an individual or a whole organisation, and whether it's for five years or the next 90 days, Mark has a proven process that generates a practical action plan for all types of organisation.

Team alignment sessions

When setting out to grow your business, it's vital that your whole team is included and involved, and that they're pulling in the same direction. Aligning people to ensure they understand and believe in the direction of travel, and that they are involved and contribute to the process, is a skill Mark enjoys using. There's nothing like seeing your team generating improvement ideas and picking up the responsibility for making things happen.

Team engagement surveys & workshops

Carrying out an anonymous engagement survey is relatively straight forward. With good positioning, Mark can ensure a high participation level. The real value comes in analysing the results and generating improvement initiatives and commitments with you and your team. And then ensuring that good intentions become a living reality. Any survey produces expectations that things will improve. It's important to recognise that aiming for a more engaged team is a far longer-term commitment than carrying out a relatively short, simple survey.

DISC behavioural profiling

Behavioural profiling is a powerful tool to aid better communication and cooperation within your organisation. It helps individuals raise their self-awareness and better understand their preferences. With that knowledge, they can manage their behaviour in different situations to be better understood and to achieve better results. Running the exercise with a full team is great fun and the interpersonal benefits are multiplied. Mark has facilitated DISC workshops for up to 30 people. DISC profiling is also useful as part of your recruitment process. It allows you to create a profile for the role and then to assess candidates against that ideal profile.

Strength assessments

Develop strengths, manage weaknesses. Mark is experienced at helping people discover their unique blend of innate talents, and how they might develop and manage those talents to become strengths in their work and their life. Mark is experienced at using Gallup's StrengthsFinder tool. StrengthsFinder can be used as part of a recruitment campaign and as an important tool in a team member's personal development.

Appendix B:

RECOMMENDED READING LIST

I'm an avid reader and recommend any person in business to read as much as possible. It is a fabulous short-cut to a concentration of good ideas. I thought it'd be useful to share some of my favourite books, should you want to investigate any of the areas further.

Developing a Business
- *Start With Why* by Simon Sinek
- *Think and Grow Rich* by Napoleon Hill
- *Billionaire in Training* by Brad Sugars
- *Building the Happiness Centred Business* by Dr. Paddi Lund
- *Built to Sell* by John Warrillow

Leadership
- *The One Minute Manager* by Spencer Johnson & Kenneth Blanchard
- *First, Break All The Rules* by Don Clifton & Marcus Buckingham
- *Drive* by Daniel H. Pink
- *The 21 Irrefutable Laws of Leadership* by John C. Maxwell
- *Bringing Out the Best in People* by Aubrey Daniels
- *The Jelly Effect: How to Make Your Communication Stick* by Andy Bounds
- *Positive Psychology at Work* by Sarah Lewis
- *Influence: The Psychology of Persuasion* by Robert B. Cialdini
- *How to Win Friends and Influence People* by Dale Carnegie
- *Never Split The Difference* by Chris Voss

Sales & Marketing
- *The Ultimate Sales Machine* by Chet Holmes
- *You Can't Teach a Kid to Ride a Bike in a Seminar* by David Sandler
- *The Sales Bible* by Jeffrey Gitomer
- *Go For No* by Richard Fenton & Andrew Waltz
- *Guerrilla Marketing Remix* by Jay Conrad Levinson
- *Common Sense Direct* Marking by Drayton Bird

Systems
- *The E-Myth Revisited* by Michael E. Gerber
- *The Checklist Manifesto* by Atul Gawande
- *Traction* by Gino Wickman

Personal Development
- *Personal Development for Smart People* by Steve Pavlina
- *Soar With Your Strengths* by Don Clifton
- *Now, Discover Your Strengths* by Curt Coffman & Marcus Buckingham
- *Strengths Finder* (including online strengths assessment code) by Tom Rath
- *12 Rules for Life* by Jordan Peterson
- *7 Habits of Highly Effective People* by Steven Covey
- *Mastery* by George Leonard
- *The Inner Game of Work* by W. Timothy Gallwey
- *Man's Search for Meaning* by Victor Frankl
- *Change Your Thoughts Change Your Life* by Dr. Wayne Dyer
- *The Ruthless Elimination of Hurry* by John Mark Comer
- *Willpower* by Kelly McGonigal
- *How to Stop Worrying and Start Living* by Dale Carnegie
- *Don't Sweat the Small Stuff* by Richard Carlson
- *The Relaxation Response* by Dr. Herbert Benson

Time & Self-Management
- *The One Thing* by Gary Keller
- *Deep Work* by Cal Newport
- *Atomic Habits* by James Clear
- *Busy* by Tony Crabbe
- *Time and How to Spend It* by James Wallman
- *The Compound Effect* by Darren Hardy

Getting the most out of your reading, listening and watching

Before buying and reading any of these books, check out TED Talks or YouTube for any talks these authors have given. You'll also find short written and animated summaries of these books online, which is a useful starting point. It is useful to read the customer reviews before purchasing. Some readers leave excellent book summaries. Bear in mind that given your different situation, you may well glean different learnings to someone else.

Have an aim in mind when you read. Look for ideas that you can immediately implement in your business or personal life. It can be good to read for a short period, say twenty minutes, and then spend ten minutes thinking about and making notes on what you've read.

Set yourself the challenge of capturing what you've just read in a sentence or a couple of bullet points. Aim to share what you've read and learnt with someone else as soon as possible. This will help you read with greater focus and concentration. Try to summarise the book on one side of A4 or in three to five sentences. A great challenge is to commit to leaving a review of the book online, summarising the elements of the book that proved most useful for you.

To engender a learning culture in your organisation, it's a great idea to all read the same books. You can then share and discuss the things you've learnt and what you've applied – or are going to apply. This in-house business and personal development book club could be a game changer. To have a physical library in a communal area sends out a powerful message about the sort of organisation you're growing. Encouraging anyone in the organisation to borrow and read those books could spark an educational transformation for them and for the organisation.

As with other important tasks, ensure you're reading in a conducive environment. Remove distractions such as email, phones, notifications, television and screaming children. Remember that whilst the book may have cost £15, your time is probably worth £100 per hour (based on the high-value tasks you do in your business). Get the most out of the time and energy you invest in reading (or listening or watching).

Lightning Source UK Ltd.
Milton Keynes UK
UKHW021319170921
390742UK00008B/1589

9 781838 451301